CULTURE AND THE PUBLIC SPHERE

Culture and the Public Sphere addresses cultural policy from a critical and multidimensional perspective. It is informed by some of the most advanced ideas in contemporary social theory, drawing particularly upon the work of Pierre Bourdieu, Michel Foucault and Jürgen Habermas.

The book challenges an instrumentalist agenda for 'cultural policy studies' and proposes an alternative view of cultural policy as a matter for the widest possible critical and public debate. Illustrating his case with examples from recent cultural policy initiatives in Britain, the United States and Australia, Jim McGuigan considers a range of topics which include: the American 'culture wars'; the flattening of cultural hierarchies and the blurring of cultural boundaries according to a postmodernist and petit-bourgeois imaginary; the rise of managerialist and market reasoning in public arts administration and broadcasting; the 'post-Fordist' restructuring of the cultural industries; urban regeneration strategies under conditions of de-industrialisation and worsening social exclusion; national culture, museums, theme parks and the global phenomenon of heritage tourism; problems of 'race', identity and cultural citizenship; panopticism, market censorship and moral regulation, especially with regard to children's media consumption; and the role of computer-mediated communications in democratic discourse.

Throughout, McGuigan argues that even in a postmodern world there is a place for value judgements in the arts and media, and seeks to map out a new terrain for policy-oriented cultural studies in education, research and professional practice.

Jim McGuigan is Principal Lecturer in Communication, Culture and Media at Coventry University.

CULTURE AND THE PUBLIC SPHERE

Jim McGuigan

London and New York

First published 1996
by Routledge
11 New Fetter Lane, London EC4P 4EE

Simultaneously published in the USA and Canada
by Routledge
29 West 35th Street, New York, NY 10001

© 1996 Jim McGuigan

Phototypeset in Garamond by Intype London Ltd
Printed and bound in Great Britain by Clays Ltd, St Ives PLC

British Library Cataloguing in Publication Data
A catalogue record for this book is available from the British Library

Library of Congress Cataloguing in Publication Data
McGuigan, Jim.
Culture and the public sphere / Jim McGuigan.
Includes bibliographical references and index.
1. Cultural policy. 2. Politics and culture. I. Title.
CB430.M392 1996
306 – dc20 96–12701
CIP

ISBN 0–415–11262–1 (hbk)
ISBN 0–415–11263–X (pbk)

To Christopher and Jenny, who I hope will be both practical and critical

CONTENTS

ACKNOWLEDGEMENTS

In writing a book such as this one you become indebted to various people for reasons large and small, not all of which are easily remembered at the point of public acknowledgement. I am sure, for instance, that I have learnt all sorts of interesting things from my day-to-day colleagues. It is politic to thank every one of them for whatever nuggets of wisdom I have culled from their company since it would be invidious to name names, that is, except for Martyn Lee, with whom I have worked closely in recent years and who has influenced my thinking on a number of questions. My initial interest in cultural policy was almost accidental. I found myself working as a researcher at the Arts Council of Great Britain several years ago, a temporary appointment which resulted in the publication of my *Writers and the Arts Council*. I am still grateful to Paul Filmer, Robert Hutchison and Kate Manton for the help they gave me with the Arts Council project. And I recall how that strangely controversial report would not have seen the light of day without the intervention of Eva Figes, Robert Hewison, Richard Hoggart and Blake Morrison. I should also like to thank both Graham Murdock and Janet Wolff for their advice at the time on how to be both practical as well as critical in research and for their continuing support over the years.

Recalling past debts, I am also keenly aware of how much I learnt in collaboration with my old pal in Leeds, Derek McKiernan. More recently, I have benefited greatly from the intellectual example and generosity of Franco Bianchini, Doug Kellner, Mike Peters and Chris Rojek. Some of the material in this book was tried out in seminars that I was invited to address by Ken Gelder, Tim O'Sullivan, Sabina Sharkey, John Storey, Helen Thomas, Jeff Wallace and Derek Wynne. I always find that teaching helps me clarify my ideas and, for this reason, I am especially indebted to students. During the writing of this book, I found discussion with the following students particularly helpful: Kirsty Allan, Abish Eftekari, Eriko Fujii, Suzanne Perry, Jim Power,

ACKNOWLEDGEMENTS

Jerry Rothwell and Mike Walford. Finally, and by no means least, I thank my family for their forbearance: Christopher, Jenny, Lesley and Madge.

January 1996

INTRODUCTION

What would be the point of critical reason if it bore no direct relation to practical politics? The point is to keep open the possibility of another way of thinking and doing. In theory, critical reason is not obliged to be immediately useful. In practice, though, its purpose may seem obscure. Lack of dialogue between thinkers and doers is annoying for those who put practice before theory: it is also frustrating for those who put theory before practice.

In the field of cultural studies, the silence between theoretical critique and practical policy has been tentatively broken. Voices with different accents have begun to speak to each other and occasionally with each other, albeit in rather muted tones. Cultural studies has finally come around to addressing cultural policy. But what is cultural policy? There is more than one answer to this question. The narrowest answer is to say that it is about the administration of 'the arts', which should, of course, be of interest to cultural studies. The broader answer which frames the argument of this book, however, is that cultural policy is about the politics of culture in the most general sense: it is about the clash of ideas, institutional struggles and power relations in the production and circulation of symbolic meanings. Such a perspective on cultural policy is inclusive, not exclusive: in fact, so inclusive that all the nooks and crannies that could be delved into cannot possibly be covered exhaustively in a single book.

The main argument of this book is that issues of cultural policy may usefully be considered from the point of view of a critical and communicative rationality, that these issues are not merely practical matters of instrumental reason. It applies a number of theories to a series of difficult questions. In the first instance, the book was provoked by an agenda mapped out for 'cultural policy studies' in Australia, an agenda that takes its starting point from a dissection of the practical deficiencies of cultural studies and draws upon the work of Michel Foucault in order to theorise its potential practice in the 'real world' of culture. The first chapter criticises that particular agenda and seeks to outline an alternative, in some ways complementary, and more critical approach to the study and practice

1

of cultural policy, which is inspired by the work of Jürgen Habermas. Cultural policy is a matter of urgent public debate, according to the view propounded here, and not only a technical problem of administration.

Any public debate implies a dispute over values. In the cultural field, value has become increasingly hard to determine due to the erosion of generally agreed standards of judgement, and, in consequence, the grounds for policy are difficult to formulate. However intractable they may appear, none the less, questions of value remain unavoidable. To historicise value or, in Pierre Bourdieu's terms, to treat taste as a social construct and not derived from essential qualities is a necessary move. Yet, in the end, such a move is insufficient since aesthetics and ethics are not simply reducible to sociological variables. Chapter 2 explores some of the aesthetic, ethical and social coordinates of the contemporary cultural field in 'Western' society, now characterised, especially for 'middle-class' strata, by a post-modernism which appears to know the price of everything and perhaps the value of nothing, to borrow from Oscar Wilde.

I do not believe that cultural policy can be treated satisfactorily in isolation from the wider economic and political determinations operating upon culture and society during a period of epochal change, associated with the crisis of modernity and the rise of 'postmodernity'. Two key developments concern me here: the shift from a Fordist regime of accumulation in the older industrial states towards a more 'flexible' post-Fordist regime; allied to which is the attempt to dismantle the welfare state and dispense with nation-state regulation generally, hastened by the 'globalisation' of market forces. Of particular significance, with specific reference to cultural policy as well as social policy, has been the New Right attack on social democracy and its so-called 'dependency culture'. This resulted in various forms of 'de-regulation' and 'privatisation' with varied and widespread ramifications. In chapter 3, instead of discussing these issues in general, I am primarily interested in tracing a discursive shift actually *within* public sector institutions of culture, for instance with regard to the systems of public arts patronage and public service broadcasting in Britain. My aim is to track the emergence and dissemination of a pervasive managerialist and market reasoning in the public sector itself, a development which I view as profound and highly questionable from the point of view of public need and responsibility.

In chapter 4 the industrial aspects of culture are discussed. This involves reconsidering the original Frankfurt School formulations on the 'culture industry', recalling the policies of the Labour-controlled Greater London Council in the 1980s, and examining 'vertical disintegration' in the music, film and television businesses. I am also interested here in a peculiar coalescence of left-wing and right-wing perspectives on the economics of culture and the role of cultural industries in urban regeneration, which is the topic of chapter 5. Over the past few years there has been a growing awareness of the spatial dynamics of cultural and social life on a global scale. In particular, with the collapse of heavy industry and manufacturing in many North American and European cities, strategies for economic renewal have deployed aspects of communications and cultural policy, frequently with dubious success. Transformations of the urban fabric have been so dramatic, including the dereliction of inner cities left untouched by gentrification and flight to the burgeoning 'Edge Cities' in the USA, that it is difficult, in any case, to turn some places around. Moreover, the civic boosterism often associated with flagship projects aimed at tourists and incoming professional and managerial groups rings especially hollow where social exclusion is stark and civil unrest is likely to occur.

The issues are international but there are local and national specificities that require close attention. Nation-states are probably indeed becoming less important now than in an earlier phase of modernity and 'global culture' may already be a reality, yet there is little sign of diminishing national sentiment in vast tracts of popular culture. The national imagination is closely attached to representations of the past, the mythical histories of nation-building. Nostalgia for past glories is heavily pronounced in 'an old country' that has seen more powerful days: here I speak of Britain, 'the first heritage state'. Chapter 6 examines the decline of Britain and its fixation on a supposedly glorious past. England and the British Isles are not, however, exceptional, comparatively, in turning 'heritage' into a tourist industry. In this chapter, I also consider debates over the political valency of heritage and changes in museum culture.

Valorising the past is especially problematical with regard to citizens from the erstwhile colonies in Britain or, taking other examples, Native Americans in the USA or Aboriginals in Australia. Migration is disruptive of fixed ideas of identity, resulting in complex and varied forms of cultural interaction and segregation. Chapter 7 considers problems of identity and citizenship in relation to 'race', drawing particularly upon the work of Paul Gilroy, Stuart Hall, Bhikhu Parekh and Cornel West. The aim is to try to make sense of what might possibly be meant by a recently emergent notion of 'cultural citizenship' under changing national and global conditions.

Citizens of democratic states have all sorts of rights, some of which are protected and some of which are not, for instance the rights to know what is being done on our behalf and what is known of us. In liberal democracies, censorship is generally seen as an evil except, controversially, for reasons of state or, perhaps less controversially, in order to protect the innocent from adverse influences. The problem with much discussion of censorship is that it too easily falls into either-orism and concentrates too much on the role of the state. For libertarians, all censorship is oppressive, yet censorship has never been and probably never will be entirely abolished. The issues here are very complex indeed and chapter 8 seeks to chart a way through them by discussing modern panoptic and market mechanisms of communicational control and moral regulation. Conservative and communitarian arguments concerning 'moral crisis' are also assessed. Substantively, the chapter focuses in upon the question of children's media consumption and aims to move the argument on from the repetitive and futile debate concerning manifestly harmful effects to discussion of the diffuse role of media conglomerates in children's culture and moral education.

It should be evident from this brief outline of chapter content that I am mainly concerned with the terms of debate and the larger issues of cultural policy. The very concept of a 'public sphere' is to do with rational-critical discussion. There is no single public sphere to which we all have access and in which we all participate equally. The public sphere is fragmented and, at best, multiple and diverse in its manifestations. No doubt the experience of many people, however, is of no say in any recognisable public sphere at all: the big decisions are made at the higher reaches of public and business administration, behind closed doors. Even intellectuals who debate these matters in public are not necessarily where the real power lies. This raises a number of matters concerning the role of intellectuals and the forms of critical and administrative work in the contemporary cultural field. To accept a situation of apparent closure in public debate unquestioningly is too fatalistic and, from the point of view of critical reason, irresponsible. The surest means of destroying what there is of a public sphere is not to engage in critical debate, not to ask awkward questions or not to dream of 'unrealistic' solutions to the problems of life and art. There are, of course, periodic eruptions of optimism, such as those surrounding 'the Net' as a new reality and democratic means of communication, which is discussed in the final chapter of this book. I am personally less optimistic about the magical powers of computer-mediated communications but I do believe every opportunity to communicate our hopes and plans should be seized if we want a more democratic culture and polity.

1

CULTURAL POLICY STUDIES

> Speak truth to power.
> Seventeenth-century Quaker epithet

How does cultural studies relate to policy-oriented theorising and research? As an interdisciplinary field of inquiry, cultural studies has shown considerable interest in *cultural politics*, in the sense of aesthetic practices that challenge the mainstream. Practical engagement with a *politics of culture*, including policy analysis and policy formulation, however, has been restrained by comparison, due perhaps to an excessive critical purity and a suspicion of becoming involved with regulatory processes.[1] The hybrid of 'cultural policy studies', proposed by a school of thought inspired by Michel Foucault, is a bid to forge a much stronger relationship between critical analysis and policy orientation in cultural studies. This prospective agenda requires a careful consideration of the actual and potential meanings of cultural policy from the perspectives of social and cultural theory, two leading strands of which are discussed in this chapter. There is, on the one hand, Foucauldian theory, with its close connections to 'the epistemic shift' associated with post-structuralism and postmodernism; and there is, on the other hand, Habermasian theory, with its persistent commitment to 'the unfinished project of modernity', a perspective which has been influential in the critical analysis of communications policy. These rather different yet not necessarily incommensurate theoretical frameworks may be seen to illuminate urgent matters of culture and politics. Such theory also offers a means of clarifying how those most directly involved with formulating, implementing and contesting cultural policies understand what they are doing. Cultural policy studies, then, in both of the contrasting theorisations under discussion, presents new possibilities, not only to theorists and analysts of culture but also to agents of cultural policy.

This book is concerned with cultural policy in a sense much broader than is normally meant by the term within the professional discourses of arts management. The words 'culture' and 'policy' are not restricted to the arts and public administration respectively, although they certainly include those meanings. 'Culture', it is often remarked, has two general fields of referent: first, the arts and higher learning; and, second, ways

5

of life. The second of these referential fields, the traditional object of anthropology, has tended increasingly to subsume and transform the first referential field, thereby, in effect, democratising how we think and talk about culture. However, this expanded notion of culture, in spite of its positive qualities, is not wholly satisfactory since it is too expansive for certain analytical and practical purposes. The anthropological concept of culture encompasses literally everything and, in so doing, obscures important and useful distinctions between that which is principally cultural and that which is not first and foremost about meaning and signification. For example, economic arrangements are cultural: they are human constructs and they are historically and geographically variable in form and operation. They are not, though, primarily to do with the production and circulation of meaning. Economic arrangements are fundamentally about the production and circulation of wealth, whatever is being produced, which is not to say they are without meaning.

Raymond Williams (1981: 207) sought to overcome this dual problem of scope and delimitation with 'the concept of culture as a *realized signifying system*'. From this point of view, 'culture' refers specifically to the practices and institutions that make meaning, practices and institutions where symbolic communication is usually, by definition, the main purpose and even an end in itself, like going to the cinema to see a feature film. Film-making and cinema-going are socio-economic activities but they are, none the less, distinguishable from the production and consumption of commodities specifically to sustain life, such as food, or products that function routinely as means rather than ends in themselves, such as transport systems. Food and transport are meaningful but, unlike cinema, that is not their main *raison d'être*. Of course, one can always bring to mind particular exceptions to a general rule of this kind, for example wolfing down a hamburger just before going on a roller-coaster ride, which may not be rational but is indeed cultural.

Because culture is so difficult to pin down, so hard to fix in a precise definition or unambiguous mode, the very idea of cultural policy, which seems to imply that something so fragile and indeterminate as a 'realized signifying system' can be consciously regulated, is, to say the very least, problematical. The problem is related to the etymological connection between 'policy' and 'policing'. 'Cultural policy' has deeply entrenched connotations of 'policing culture', of treating culture as though it were a dangerous lawbreaker or, perhaps, a lost child.

POLICING CULTURE

The Old French word 'police' came into English usage during the sixteenth century to refer to government in general and eventually to policy. In 1732, Jonathan Swift could say, 'Nothing is held more commendable in all great cities ... than what the French call *police*; by which word is meant the government thereof' (*OED*). By the end of the eighteenth century, the word was acquiring its modern and much narrower meaning: 'The police of the town is managed by two constables' (Aitkin, 1795, *OED*). Yet still it was possible for Young, following Adam Smith's essay of 1776 on 'The Police of Grain', to advocate in 1792 'a good police of corn ... a police that shall, by securing a high price to the farmer, encourage his culture enough to secure the people at the same time from famine' (*OED*). Writing to her sister Cassanda in 1813, Jane Austen mentioned an essay she was reading on the 'Military Police and Institutions of the British Empire' in a way that blurred the modern distinction between governmental administration in general and the particular duties of a police force. In 1830, however, Lord Wellington was able to congratulate Robert Peel on his successful setting up of the Metropolitan Police in London, at which point the definitive specialisation of the term in English had occurred.

While English-speaking Britons forged 'policy' out of 'police', the French themselves came to use the word 'politique' to refer to both politics and policy (the word 'Politik' is similarly used in German). Incidentally, in French, the masculine form, 'le politique', refers to institutionalised politics, whereas the feminine form, 'la politique', refers to the science of politics and policy. It is significant that this later French alternative to policy as policing returns to the ancient Greek root of 'polis', the city state. The view of policy presented in this book emphasises the relationship of policy to politics as a field of contestation between rival discourses, ideologies and interests rather than confining it to the more technical, though hardly unpolitical, connotation of policy as policing. Cultural policy raises questions of regulation and control but its meaning should not be restricted to an ostensibly apolitical set of practical operations that are merely administered and policed by governmental officials.

Although there are still those who would prefer to keep politics out of culture entirely, to treat culture exclusively as, say, the polishing of personal sensibilities (another semantically available version of cultural policy), culture has always been political and shows no sign of escaping the ruses of power and public controversy. The political heat around culture has generally been greatest in societies where the state has played a manifest role in its regulation, often a manifestly oppressive role, most notably, under conditions of modernity, in communist states. Where culture is left to the market a cooler politics is usually displayed. It is curious, however, that just at the moment when European communism was disintegrating in the late 1980s, having failed amongst other things to 'culturally enlighten' its subjects (White, 1990), 'culture wars' broke out spectacularly in the land of free speech and of the free market, the United States of America. These culture wars, albeit generated by sheer ethnic diversity resulting from a complex history of immigration, were focused particularly upon two key issues: public subsidy of the arts and the university humanities curriculum.[2]

The trouble started with Andres Serrano's *Piss Christ*, his photograph of a cheap plastic crucifix immersed in a jar of the artist's own urine. In May 1989, Republican Senator Alphonse D'Amato dramatically tore up a reproduction of the offending work and scattered its pieces on the floor of the US Senate. Serrano had been the recipient of a $15,000 prize from the South East Center for Contemporary Art in Winston-Salem. The money came originally from the National Endowment for the Arts (NEA), the American equivalent of the British Arts Council, founded by a Democratic presidency during the 1960s. Although the NEA had not directly rewarded Serrano for his ambivalent commentary on the status of Jesus Christ in a commercial culture, D'Amato drew the all-too-obvious conservative inference from the relationship, in his eyes, between such blasphemous obscenity and public funding of the arts.

During the following month, an anxious Corcoran Gallery administration in Washington cancelled its presentation of 'Robert Mapplethorpe: The Perfect Moment', a retrospective exhibition for the photographer, who had died of AIDs in spring that year. The exhibition, containing the notorious 'X Portfolio' from the late 1970s, had already been seen at other publicly subsidised galleries across the country. Mapplethorpe's 'X Portfolio' consisted of photographs representing a series of homo-erotic images of male genitalia and the remarkable receptivity of human orifices. Amongst these photographs was Mapplethorpe's self-portrait depicting him in devilish guise with a bull whip for a tail hanging from his rectum. In the circumstances it was bold and perhaps deliberately provocative of the Washington Project for the Arts to immediately put on the exhibition that had been dropped by the Corcoran.

Fast on the heels of the journalistic debate over public funding for the arts that followed these events, in July, Jesse Helms, the Republican Senator for North Carolina, proposed an amendment to the procurement bill for voting money to the NEA:

> None of the funds authorized to be appropriated pursuant to this Act may be used to promote, disseminate, or produce –
> (1) obscene or indecent materials, including but not limited to depictions of sadomasochism, homo-eroticism, the exploitation of children, or individuals engaged in sex acts; or
> (2) material which denigrates the objects or beliefs of the adherents of a particular religion or non-religion; or
> (3) material which denigrates, debases, or reviles a person, group or class of citizens on the basis of race, creed, sex, handicap, age, or national origin.
>
> (Bolton, 1992: 73–74)

Although much modified when eventually legislated into existence in October 1989 by the inclusion of the standard artistic merit defence, Helms's proposal epitomised, in the judgement of First Amendment liberals and cultural radicals on the Left, the conservative backlash against anything remotely offensive to virtually anyone. Moreover, as Robert Hughes (1993: 162) has observed shrewdly, it encapsulated the growing penchant for cultural policing and what he calls a 'culture of complaint' that was spreading across the entire political spectrum of American intellectual life: 'The most obvious and curious feature of the Helms amendment was that, if it had not issued from a famously right-wing Republican senator, you could have mistaken it – especially in the last two clauses – for any ruling on campus speech limitations recently proposed by the nominally left-wing agitators for political correctness.' The apparent convergence of sections of the Left with the moralising Right in 'the culture of complaint' is not to be taken, however, as an erasure of the actual differences in source and implication between 'progressive' and 'conservative' positions on 'political correctness' and 'multiculturalism'.

In spite of what appeared to Hughes as a striking consensus on the control of speech and representation, the right-wing political context for the attack on public funding of the arts in the USA must not be underestimated. There were at least three sometimes separate yet more often than not interconnected ideological discourses in play on the Right: cultural elitism, market populism and ethico-political reaction. The cultural elitist strand, which was also most prominent in the attack on 'political correctness' in academia, was enunciated particularly by the writers of the *New Criterion* magazine, such as Hilton Kramer and Samuel Lipman, who wished to defend the established canons of American and European art. The public attribution of artistic status to a piss-artist photographer like Andres Serrano was in itself offensive to their highly-refined sensibilities. To an extent, however, that merely repeated the historical contest between cultural establishments and various self-styled *avant gardes*.

For populists it was also difficult to see quite how certain kinds of work could be deemed art. Their case rested rather more substantially on the issue of 'tax dollars', a key ideological figure in the debate. When accused of censorship, Helms and his allies denied the accusation by arguing the work from which they wanted to withdraw public subsidy should suffer the test of market forces. As Helms himself put it: 'Artists who seek to shock and offend can still do so – but at their own expense' (Bolton, 1992: 101). Why should the hard-pressed American taxpayer be expected to shield these enemies of the American Dream from the laws of supply and demand? But, again bringing sanity back into the debate, Robert Hughes (1993: 200) has pointed out: 'The American taxpayer contributes $0.68 to the support of the arts every year, compared to $27 in Germany and $32 in France.' In effect, public subsidy for the arts in the USA functions as modest seedcorn to attract private patronage and corporate sponsorship to concert halls, galleries and theatres. The NEA annual budget was always much less than that of the British Arts Council, which has since the 1940s covered a population one-fifth the size of the USA.

The debate was not really about money at all, as the more sophisticated critics of the conservative backlash have argued. Richard Bolton (1992) and Carole Vance (1992) placed the attack on public arts subsidy within a much broader right-wing ethico-political agenda fostered by groups such as the American Family Association, an agenda which had hardly been marginalised by the Reagan and Bush administrations through the 1980s and into the 1990s. To quote Vance:

> In the past ten years, conservative and fundamentalist groups have deployed and perfected techniques of grass-roots and mass mobilization around social issues, usually centred on sexuality, gender and religion. In these campaigns, symbols figure prominently, both as highly condensed statements of moral concern and as powerful spurs to emotion and action. In moral campaigns, fundamentalists select a negative symbol which is highly arousing to their own constituency and which is difficult or problematic for their opponents to defend. The symbol, often taken literally, out of context and always denying the possibility of irony or multiple interpretations, is waved like a red flag before their constituents. The arousing stimulus could be an 'un-Christian' passage from an evolution textbook, explicit information from a high school sex-education curriculum or 'degrading' pornography said to be available in the local adult bookshop. In the antiabortion campaign, activists favor images of late-term fetuses or better yet, dead babies, displayed in jars. Primed with names and addresses of relevant elected and appointed officials, fundamentalist troops fire off volleys of letters, which cowed politicians take to be the expression of popular sentiment. Right-wing politicians opportunistically ride the ground swell of outrage, while centrists feel anxious and disempowered to stop it – now a familar sight in the political landscape.
>
> (1992: 108)

This is a very astute account of how authoritarian embers are fanned into the flames of draconian cultural policing in a liberal democracy, detailing the manouevres that frequently catch libertarians by surprise and often too late in the process to respond effectively. Ethico-political reaction puts enlightened sections of the community on the defensive in such a way that the only realistic tactic in response is to try to reduce the full force of the backlash. Vance, in addition, identifies two comparatively novel aspects of this ethico-politically motivated reaction with regard to the campaign against the NEA. First, there is the assault on high culture as a valid experimental space and, second, there is the claim that the actual policies proposed do not constitute censorship, which involves 'an artfully crafted distinction between absolute censorship and the denial of public funding' (Vance, 1992: 109) that is derived from a coalescence of authoritarianism and populism with free market ideology.

The way in which the issue of 'political correctness' in the academy burst into widespread public debate during the early 1990s was another feature of the conservative backlash against cultural leftism. Dinesh D'Souza's 1991 book *Illiberal Education* was written with a grant from the American Enterprise Institute and promoted with a grant from the Olin Foundation, both right-wing organizations explicitly committed to reversing the gains of 'multiculturalism' in American society (Graff, 1992: 166–167). D'Souza's inaccurate claim that Shakespeare and other members of the pantheon of 'dead white male' cultural superstars were being expelled from the American university curriculum reiterated similarly ill-founded claims that had already been made during the 1980s, such as, for example, Christopher Clausen's much quoted and thoroughly unsubstantiated observation that Alice Walker's *The Color Purple* was being taught more widely than all of Shakespeare's plays put together. Inspired by Allan Bloom's 1987 book *The Closing of the American Mind*, a defence of absolute value enshrined in the great works of Western culture and an attack on its relativistic enemies were thus mounted. This was not only an assault on the study of popular culture, Afrocentrism, Marxist, feminist and gay writing and criticism, but a challenge to an apparently new kind of linguistic policing that put a premium on minding one's 'p's and 'q's and which is based upon a set of assumptions concerning the relationship between ordinary language and various forms of social and cultural oppression.

Although at bottom deadly and even deadeningly earnest, there was a good deal of humour in the debate, initiated it must be said from the Right, which may be illustrated by the American Hyphen Society's tongue-in-cheek definitions of both the 'correct' term, 'multiculturalism', and the 'incorrect' term, 'politically correct':

> **multiculturalism.** A broad, pluralistic social movement that, through the celebration of 'difference', champions a more tolerant, diverse, inclusive and realistic view of America and (in the memorable words of the New York State Social Studies Review and Development Committee) 'the peoples who person it'. Indeed, 'multiculturalism' encompasses virtually the entire spectrum of views that have come to be known, not always without irony, as 'politically correct'. Unfortunately, since reactionary critics have co-opted the term in a none-too-subtle attempt to silence the **multiculti**, it is no longer 'politically correct' to say 'politically correct' . . .

11

politically correct. Culturally sensitive; multiculturally unexception-
able; appropriately inclusive. The term 'politically correct' co-opted
by the white power elite as a tool for attacking multiculturalism is
no longer 'politically correct'.

(Beard and Cerf, 1992: 40, 87)

Whereas trivialisation of important matters undoubtedly occurred on
both sides of the debate, Edward Said (1993: 389) is right (or is it 'correct'?)
to have observed that the issue, as it emerged in the wider arena of public
discussion, was rather more the product of 'a new conservative dogmatism
claiming "political correctness" as its enemy' than resulting directly from
the excesses of the cultural Left. It is also necessary, though, to appreciate
that there was no smoke without fire. A certain humourless and evangelical
radicalism was indeed evident on many campuses. Of much deeper significance than this, however, is the tendency to transform and displace politics
in general onto an exclusively academic and cultural terrain, a phenomenon
that is probably symptomatic of the comparative powerlessness of oppositional forces in the USA, instead of manifesting their decisive incursions
into the power structures. Gerald Graff (1992) remarks that, in North
American universities, 'cultural studies', which was instrumental in
heightening the politicisation of culture and has done much to theorise the
intellectual opposition, has become something of a euphemism for 'leftist
studies' and, no doubt, it has been marginalised as such. In his sardonic
yet even-handed commentary on the American 'culture wars', Hughes
(1993: 76) also makes an acute observation regarding political displacement:
'in the universities, what matters is the politics of culture, not the politics
of the distribution of wealth and real events in the social sphere, like
poverty, drug addiction and the rise of crime'.

BECOMING USEFUL

Cultural studies is vulnerable to both hostile and sympathetic questioning
on several counts.[3] From the sympathetic but policy-oriented points of
view discussed in this chapter, the most serious deficiency is a gulf between
the political pretensions of cultural studies and its practical effects. Connections between cultural critique in the academy and a larger universe of power,
the so-called 'real world' of politics, are somewhat tenuous. Ironically,
however, hostile attacks on cultural studies from outside the field itself
only serve to amplify an already exaggerated sense of political importance.

The desire within cultural studies to become useful in a more practical
sense than in the past has clearly motivated the Australian development of
'cultural policy studies', associated particularly with the Key Centre for
Cultural and Media Policy in Brisbane, directed by Tony Bennett. In fact,
there are a number of different positions on the relationship between

cultural studies and policy-oriented theorising and research in Australia that may be located, for shorthand purposes, on a Left/Right continuum, which does not, however, stretch all the way over to the Right of the wider political spectrum.[4] Bennett's 'rightist' position derives from a dissatisfaction with the politics of neo-Gramscian cultural studies and is inspired by the later work of the French historian of discursive formations, Michel Foucault. The key idea is Foucault's much extended concept of 'governmentality':

> By this word I mean three things:
> 1. The ensemble formed by the institutions, procedures, analyses and reflections, the calculations and tactics that allow the exercise of this very specific albeit complex form of power, which has as its target population, as its principal form of knowledge political economy, and as its essential technical means apparatuses of security.
> 2. The tendency which, over a long period and throughout the West, has steadily led towards the pre-eminence over all other forms (sovereignty, discipline, etc.) of this type of power which may be termed government, resulting, on the one hand, in the formation of a whole series of specific governmental apparatuses, and, on the other, in the development of a whole complex of *savoirs*.
> 3. The process, or rather the result of the process, through which the state of justice of the Middle Ages, transformed into the administrative state during the fifteenth and sixteenth centuries, gradually becomes 'governmentalized'.
>
> (Foucault, 1991: 102–103)

Embedded in this definition of governmentality are a number of Foucault's major themes: the discursively formed operations of administrative procedure, the complex imbrications of power and knowledge, the always at least implied critique of modern 'Reason' and scepticism of historical progress. The impact of such themes on how cultural studies constructs its own history is particularly evident in Ian Hunter's (1988a) 'genealogy' of cultural criticism and the disciplinary formation of English as a curriculum subject, *Culture and Government*. Hunter's main adversary, in this revisionist account, is Raymond Williams (1958), whose tracing of the 'culture and society' tradition drew the cultural debate towards his own materialist attempt to radicalise Matthew Arnold's idealist 'criticism of life'. Hunter (1988b) argues that the critical and anthropological notion of culture promoted by Williams's cultural materialism misses the historical point of cultural education. According to him, modern schooling practices in Britain were introduced by state functionaries such as Kay-Shuttleworth in order to operate as 'a governmental pedagogy organised by the technology of moral supervision' (Hunter, 1988a: 21) rather than to disseminate the critical ideals of nineteenth-century men of letters. In practice, the idea of culture as criticism of life remained forever a minority pedagogic value aimed, adopting another Foucauldian and indeed Nietzschean theme, at the cultivation of an ethical self (Foucault, 1987 and 1988), that of the sensuous and self-conscious intellectual, and of precious little relevance to majority populations whether for good or evil. Consequently, for Hunter and similarly minded 'Right' Foucauldians, the 'cultural struggle', as understood and propounded by cultural materialists and neo-Gramscians, is fundamentally ill-conceived and misplaced because it fails to grasp the finely tuned operations of particular technologies and objects of discourse, whether they are applied to the classification and regulation of 'populations' or to the cultivated 'care of the self'.

Tony Bennett (1992a), in his programmatic statement 'Putting Policy into Cultural Studies', stresses the preoccupation of cultural studies with questions of culture and power. This preoccupation, however, places certain practical obligations on cultural studies for which it is badly equipped. The first obligation is to conceptualise 'culture' as constituting 'a particular field of government', 'government' meant not only in the narrow sense of governing the state but much more encompassing than that, including all power/knowledge relations; in effect, the mechanisms of social management. Second, the different 'regions' of culture need to be identified and their managerial operations studied. For instance, to give a straightforward example, this involves an appreciation of how the news is regulated differently from, say, painting: both are regulated, but differently. Third, there are specific forms of politics pertaining to each region of culture that must be understood if the cultural policy analyst is serious about engaging with them. For instance, pursuing the same example already used, this would require knowledge of how the flow of news is managed and how legislation on governmental secrecy and freedom of the press works. In the region of fine art, the roles of funding bodies, public and private galleries, and academic standards of taste would be pertinent objects of study. Fourth, research is needed that engages in genuine dialogue with the organizations of cultural governmentality. Dialogue is unlikely to occur if research in cultural policy studies merely displays implacable hostility to such organizations.

Bennett (1992a) does not, however, discuss how a proper balance is to be struck between 'useful' knowledge and 'critical' knowledge in the field of cultural policy studies. For obvious reasons, knowledge that is produced solely for official use and funded accordingly rarely questions the fundamental aims and objectives of the client organization. Under such conditions, it is very difficult for a policy-oriented research programme to observe the critical aims and responsibilities that have characterised a 'disinterested' cultural studies. In any event, cultural studies as normally practised is in no fit condition to play the policy game, according to Bennett, not because of its critical independence but, instead, because of practical weaknesses to do with the neo-Gramscian theorising of 'culture' and 'hegemony' which Bennett, at one time, himself espoused.[5]

To understand what is at stake here, it is necessary to be clear, however schematically, about the complaints against cultural studies that are made by Tony Bennett. The politics and critical practice of cultural studies focus heavily upon textual analysis with the aim, in Bennett's (1992a: 24) words, of 'modifying the relationship between persons'. Texts, mainly drawn from mass-popular culture, are read from perspectives that seek to reveal how textual processes construct meaning, position reading subjects, and how these positionings are adopted, negotiated and resisted. Such practice is routinely concerned with, for instance, issues of gender, sexuality, 'race' and identity. Written, visual, aural and audio-visual texts are studied with these matters in mind and with the implicit purpose of producing critical readers and consumers alert to the operations of dominant and subversive discourses. In its most optimistic neo-Gramscian inflection, in particular, the desire of cultural studies was to cultivate oppositional intellectuals capable of contesting prevailing power relations: radical readers who might somehow organically activate radical collectivities. The trouble with this cultural politics, in Bennett's view, is its more or less exclusive concern with significatory processes and the struggle over meaning at the level of the text. For that reason, cultural studies is 'liable to the criticism', says Bennett (1992a: 25), of paying 'insufficient attention to the institutional conditions that regulate different fields of culture'.

Like Hunter, Bennett is also concerned with challenging the legacy of Raymond Williams, whose explication of the meanings of the word 'culture' stands at the fountain-head of what came to be known as 'cultural studies'. Bennett criticises Williams for failing to follow through the full implications of the 'culture' and 'government' couplet in seventeenth-century English Republican discourse and for providing cultural studies with a very loose, anthropological definition of 'culture' in contrast to the aesthetically narrower one. In *Keywords* (1983c) Williams had, in fact, quoted the Puritan poet John Milton's tract of 1660, *The Ready and Easie Way to Establish a Free Commonwealth* ('the natural heat of Culture and Government'), yet he missed the eventually Foucauldian import of the connection to 'governmentality', the very connection which had been uppermost for critics of monarchical absolutism in the period of the English bourgeois revolution. For them, culture was the means and purpose of government, the medium of social regulation. Picking up this lost thread in the culture and society tradition, Bennett (1992a: 26) now finds it preferable to treat culture 'as a historically specific set of institutionally embedded relations of government in which forms of thought and conduct of extended populations are targeted for transformation – partly via the extension through the social body of forms, techniques, and regimens

15

of aesthetic and intellectual culture' in relation to discourses of moral regulation.

Bennett cites Foucault's use of the early-modern meaning of 'police' and its role in the French theorist's concept of 'micro-power' to further elaborate upon the culture and governmentality couplet. 'Police' once had a wider frame of reference than now, stretching beyond simple nomination of the agents of law and order to signify, roughly, governmental regulation in general. The expansive Foucauldian use of 'police' is warranted etymologically and also linked to Foucault's rejection of the conventional zero-sum conception of power, which confines it to a fixed quantum emanating from a central point over which struggle is waged, as in hegemony theory, restricted to the vertical dimension of social control from above, ultimately directed by the state, and resistance by popular forces from below. Foucault's concept of power (Gordon, 1980) is much more diffuse, proliferating horizontally from a multitude of social sites and not, therefore, limited to a finite amount, the sharing out of which is routinely held to be at issue in politics whether conceived in the terms of hegemony theory or otherwise. This Foucauldian idea of politics as extending beyond its official forms has proven especially attractive to cultural studies since it allows power to be conceived of as produced and not only sought from below, bottom-up power, thus giving theoretical force to the ubiquitous notion of 'empowerment' that ranges in colloquial usage from feminism through community politics to management training. The associated idea of 'capillary power' suggests a sense of power flowing endlessly around the veins and arteries of the body politic, regulating social and cultural relations at innumerable minute points and with specific regional properties. To convey the distinctiveness of this Foucauldian conception of power adequately, it is necessary to quote at some length from the definition that Foucault himself gave in the first volume of *The History of Sexuality*:

> [P]ower must be understood in the first instance as the multiplicity of force relations immanent in the sphere in which they operate and which constitute their own organization; as the process which, through ceaseless struggles and confrontations, transforms, strengthens, or reverses them; as the support which these force relations find in one another, thus forming a chain or a system, or on the contrary, the disjunctions and contradictions which isolate them from one another; and lastly, as the strategies in which they take effect, whose general design or institutional crystallization is embodied in the state apparatus, in the formulation of the law, in the various social hegemonies. Power's condition of possibility, or in any case the viewpoint which permits one to understand its exercise, even in its more 'peripheral' effects, and which also makes it possible to use its mechanisms as a grid of intelligibility of the social order, must not

be sought in the primary existence of a central point, in a unique source of sovereignty from which secondary and descendent forms would emanate; it is the moving substrate of force relations which, by virtue of their inequality, constantly engender states of power, but the latter are always local and unstable.

(1981a: 92–93)

Another relevant and characteristically Foucauldian idea is that of 'cultural technology', which is, again, a concept with a much broader referential field than it would normally have in common-sense usage, going beyond, say, the hardware of communications, in general, or information-processing and transmission systems, in particular. It may be taken to reference the 'machinery' of institutional and organisational structures and processes that produce particular configurations of knowledge and power. Bennett's main example of a cultural technology, in 'Putting Policy into Cultural Studies', is the public museum, a machine for making art and history socially intelligible. The public museum arose as an institution of the modern civilizing process, a means of shaping popular dispositions towards culture through exhibitionary display and thus contributing to the regulation of social conduct.

On the tasks of studying museums as technologies of culture and formulating a practical politics in relation to them, Bennett (1992a) seeks to illustrate the instrumental value of Foucauldian cultural policy studies and he elaborates upon the comparative deficiencies of neo-Gramscian cultural studies. Neo-Gramscianism would tend to conceptualise the public museum as an hegemonic apparatus, yet another instance of vertical and top-down power over which to struggle, a device for inculcating dominant ideologies in a subject population, functioning to misrepresent the past and reproducing culturally mediated social relations of domination and subordination. Bennett acknowledges the validity up to a point of such an analysis of the public museum's mode of address historically. However, of greater pertinence is that the public museum has been and continues to be, in practice and no doubt in comparison with commercial representations of the past, more an institution for social differentiation and exclusion in the Bourdieuan sense (Bourdieu and Darbel, 1969, 1991) than for the reflection of cities and nations, as officially claimed, or for providing the ideological education of majority populations, as neo-Gramscian hegemony theory might suggest. Should, it be the case, for example, that the public museum has misrepresented and/or excluded the working class, this is hardly an offence that working-class people are up in arms about. Insofar as the working class persists as an identifiable collectivity with shared interests, its members are not dashing *en masse* to revolutionise the museum: far from it. The basic weakness of a neo-Gramscian perspective, now for Bennett, is that it is unable to deal adequately with the micro-political

17

level, that is with the specific 'regional' properties of the museum, and so, does not really address the social agents who are actually in a position to do something about museum policies. These agents are 'museum critics, sectional pressure groups like WHAM, committees of management, teams of designers, curators, sometimes even boards of trustees' (1992a: 31). If cultural studies has something to say about museums, then, it must be saying it to them.

Bennett quotes Bertolt Brecht's maxim concerning 'truth': that it is of no use unless communicated to someone who can do something with it. Like Brecht for his own reasons and Foucault for other reasons, Bennett's conception of truth is exceptionally pragmatic. In effect, 'truth', it would seem, is what the social agents engaged in specific institutional practices, such as museum curators, are prepared to believe: in Foucauldian parlance, there are, after all, only 'regimes of truth'. The consequential logic of such a concept of truth is that a piece of relevant and potentially valid knowledge might just as well be untrue, for practical purposes, when it happens to be disbelieved by those agents who possess the discursive power to put it to use were they, instead, to believe it. Bennett does not explain how this excessively pragmatic conception of truth could be reconciled with a critical conception of truth that does not depend upon ready and willing accept-ance by the present agents of power in order to claim validity. Political acceptability in contingent and, therefore, changeable circumstances is a questionable criterion of truthful knowledge. One only has to recall Gal-ileo's dilemma concerning politically unpalatable truth, which also interested Brecht, to appreciate the dubious relationship of knowledge to that which is currently politic according to spiritual and temporal authority.

Tom O'Regan (1992: 420) describes the position enunciated by Bennett as 'a "pragmatic" politics as the horizon of the thinkable'. Clearly, this relates to the issue raised here concerning pragmatism and truth, which has enormous implications for how critical intellectual work is conducted and what its policy worth is to be or not to be. There are two main grounds of O'Regan's 'Left' critique. First, he disputes what appears to be an attempt to revise cultural studies as a whole, to move it lock-stock-and-barrel from 'criticism' to 'policy'. According to O'Regan, such a com-prehensive transformation of the field of study is both undesirable and unnecessary. 'Cultural studies' is a broad rubric for a wide range of inquiry, not all of which is or need be directly policy-related. Besides, a great deal of cultural studies is of policy relevance, but from the point of view of 'the recipient, the victim and the marginal' (1992: 409), that is seen from the 'bottom-up', not the 'top-down'. This leads on to O'Regan's second main objection to Bennett's version of 'cultural policy studies', its apparently close alignment with the perspectives of administrative and bureaucratic power, which must inevitably set limits on its critical capacities. O'Regan sets out his own alternative and critical agenda for policy-oriented cultural studies that admits a series of different and conflicting purposes:

- *state purposes* – efficiency, equity, excellence, etc.,
- *reformist purposes* – which involve working 'within' administrative knowledge but with the aim of effecting changes;
- *antagonistic purposes* – which involve critique and opposition, both general and policy-specific;
- *diagnostic purposes* – in which policy emerges as a politics of discourse in a descriptive enterprise.

(1992: 418)

Although Bennett (1992b) defends himself strenuously against the accusation that he is polarising critical theory and policy orientation in cultural studies, he still refuses to 'pull the punch' on policy. Cultural critique may continue, according to Bennett, but he insists that 'all such work is indirectly affected by policy issues and horizons' (p. 395). It would be mistaken to read him as merely saying that in the end cultural analysis is unavoidably political. Bennett (1992b: 406) is quite unambiguous and very precise indeed about his instrumentalist agenda for policing the horizons of cultural studies: 'cultural studies might envisage its role as consisting in the training of cultural technicians: that is, intellectual workers less committed to cultural critique as an instrument for changing consciousness than to modifying the functioning of culture by means of technical adjustments to its governmental deployment'.[6]

REMAINING CRITICAL

The 'Right' Foucauldian wish to relinquish disengaged criticism and turn cultural studies as a whole over to governmental usefulness, an improbable outcome in any event, leads directly on to what is in fact a very familiar terrain, that of administrative research. Such research is, by definition, subject to the pre-existing agendas of policy-making and policy-implementing bodies. In their original distinction, both Paul Lazarsfeld (1941) and Theodor Adorno (1945) contrasted 'administrative' research with its opposite, 'critical' research, the kind of research that pipes to no paymaster but at the same time runs the risk of political marginalisation. The desire to bridge the gulf between critique and practicality in cultural policy studies is not so novel as it imagines itself to be. Jay Blumler (1978) once postulated a form of communications research that combined the disinterestedness of criticism with the usefulness of administration and dubbed it 'meliorative'. Tony Bennett's intentions may be similar but one cannot be sure since there are no normative principles other than administrative usefulness made explicit in the 'Right' Foucauldian framework for cultural policy studies.

19

Stuart Cunningham's (1992a and 1993) 'Centrist' position has the virtue, in comparison, of situating itself explicitly and unambiguously within a 'real world' ideological and political context, that of Australian social democracy. The Labour Party held office in Australia throughout the 1980s and into the 1990s, at a time when the New Right was busy dismantling ameliorative social and cultural policies in Britain and the USA. The very idea of governmental intervention in the field of culture under modern liberal-democratic conditions has been associated historically with social democracy in Western European nation-states and was a distinctive feature of the post-Second World War political settlement in Britain. The growth of public arts subsidy and the keen preservation of public service principles of broadcasting, in effect, represented the cultural branch of the welfare state.

Bennett (1992b) concurs with Cunningham's (1992a and 1993: 137–138) call for a shift in the 'command metaphors' of cultural studies: 'a policy orientation in cultural studies would shift its "command metaphors" away from rhetorics of resistance, oppositionalism and anti-commercialism on the one hand, and populism on the other, towards those of access, equity, empowerment and the divination of opportunities to exercise appropriate cultural leadership'. Yet, on endorsing the aims of this passage from Cunningham, Bennett (1992b: 396) turns immediately to a repeat attack on Williams's 'misreading' of the 'culture and society' tradition instead of addressing himself to the implications of Cunningham's avowedly social-democratic politics of cultural policy. Cunningham (1993: 134) could be speaking directly to Bennett's position when he says: 'The missing link is a social-democratic view of citizenship and the trainings necessary to activate and motivate it ... Replacing shop-worn revolutionary rhetoric with the new command metaphor of citizenship commits cultural studies to a reformist strategy within the terms of a social-democratic politics, and thus can connect it to the wellsprings of engagement with policy.'

To advocate social-democratic citizenship in such a direct manner inevitably raises questions concerning the social rights that were established by the post-Second World War welfare state and, furthermore, suggests a possible category of 'cultural citizenship'. T. H. Marshall (1950/1992) theorised the development of citizenship historically beyond the civil rights necessary to enable a market economy and the political rights of democratic participation onwards into the field of social rights as a matter of distributive justice. To argue, as Peter Townsend (1979) did before the New Right assault on social democracy became hegemonic, that to be without a television set in a modern society is to be poor indicated how social entitlement was already blurring into cultural entitlement. Marshall (1950/1992: 48) himself had said, 'Common enjoyment is a common right.'

Cunningham argues his social-democratic case in very different circumstances from those of its post-Second World War heyday and, also, in recognition that national policies are increasingly constrained by economic and cultural globalisation. Many an old-fashioned social democrat would gag, for instance, on his recommendations for ensuring Australian content in the 'unworthy discourse' of advertising (Cunningham, 1992a: 71). Cunningham, in effect, refuses to hive off questions of *cultural* policy from those of *communications* policy, and he particularly stresses the centrality of television for a policy-oriented cultural studies.

The linking of policy issues around communications and culture has also been of prime concern to the political economy perspective in British media sociology, best exemplified by the writings of Nicholas Garnham (1990), Peter Golding and Graham Murdock (for instance, 1986 and 1989). The political economy approach analyses major institutional transformations and is especially concerned with the relations between capital and technology. It has often been criticised for lacking a discursive form of analysis which is properly sensitive to the complexity of symbolic process and the meaning and use of cultural products in specific contexts, which has been the great strength, in comparison, of cultural studies. There is no necessary incompatibility, however, between political-economic analysis, on the one hand, and textual and contextual interpretation, on the other hand (McGuigan, 1996). Moreover, one of the great strengths of the political economy perspective is to emphasise citizenship rights and the conditions of public debate, in addition to economic analysis, matters which have tended to be neglected in mainstream cultural studies.

For a critical social theory of communications and culture, 'the public sphere' and the operations of rational-critical debate, conceptualised and analysed most famously by the German social philosopher Jürgen Habermas, are of focal concern. Whether one agrees or not with Tony Bennett's version of a Foucauldian framework for cultural policy studies, there is more to be said than it has to say for and about the formation of cultural and governmental relations according to modern principles of democracy. In the spirit of dialectics, then, I shall in the rest of this chapter counterpose the elements of a Habermasian framework to the particular Foucauldian perspective already outlined. Throughout the book as a whole, however, I will be making liberal use of the insights of both Foucault and Habermas where appropriate in order to illuminate particular issues of cultural policy.[7]

The cardinal theme of Habermas's work generally concerns how we make sense in public, especially how we negotiate our differences with one another and decide upon common purposes (Holub, 1991). This runs from his *Habilitationshrift*, published in 1962 as *Strukturwandel der Öffentlichkeit*, translated into English in 1989 as *The Structural Transformation of the Public Sphere*,[8] and through his two-volume *magnum opus* of 1981, *Theorie des Kommunikativen Handelns*, *The Theory of Communicative Action* (English translation, 1984 and 1987a). Initially, Habermas was interested in accounting for the emergence of liberal-democratic conversation with the rise of the bourgeoisie in the late eighteenth and early nineteenth centuries and how, according to him, such conversation degenerated into manipulative communications with the expansion of modern commercial media and the advent of what he calls 'the social-welfare state'. Habermas's later work, after his 'linguistic turn' of the 1970s, moved towards an abstract and rigorously procedural model of language performance and away from the historically grounded theory of communications and culture represented by his first major book. There is, however, a definite continuity between Habermas's early and later work in spite of the various theoretical revisions he has made to his position over the years.

Public conversation may be considered culturally in two main senses for present purposes. First, it is in itself cultural, enabled by the languages, knowledges, beliefs, and so on, that circulate socially. In a liberal democracy, participation in public conversation, whether it is conducted honestly or dishonestly, with conscious intent or unconscious effect, is a citizenship right, which is the second sense of public conversation germane to the current argument. In principle, as citizens, we are permitted to speak openly about culture and society. Such a right is the rationale for the specialist activities of cultural criticism, and in the general sense that Terry Eagleton (1984) has sought to revive by arguing that literary criticism and theory, in particular, have to a significant extent lost sight of their larger responsibilities for social and political critique even when they seem most radical in the academy.

From a policy-oriented perspective in cultural studies, the angle of vision is shifted partially from attention to the cultural text and its meaningfulness in order to open up questions concerning the *conditions of culture*; and, in this, yet a more general sense, it has a close affinity with the political economy perspective on communications and culture. That is what cultural policy is principally about, the conditions of culture, the material and, also, the discursive determinations in time and space of cultural production and consumption. The study of cultural policy and the practical intent of contributing to the framing of policies does not deny the importance of criticism and textual interpretation but rather puts issues concerning how texts are made and circulated socially into the foreground. Fundamental to the position on cultural policy stated in this book, then, is the normative view that, in a democratic society, 'the public will', however that is understood and constructed, should decisively influence the conditions of culture, their persistence and their potential for change. This is where a Habermasian view parts company most sharply from an exclusively Foucauldian view. The Foucauldian might typically regard such thinking as touchingly idealistic, as rooted in a long-redundant Enlightenment rationality and humanism. Although the Habermasian might be just as suspicious as the Foucauldian of official claims concerning democracy and public

22

accountability, nevertheless, he or she chooses to wager upon the possibility of turning formal claims into substantive truths and acts accordingly.

In Britain, the use of the term 'public sphere' became caught up in the academic debate over public service broadcasting. Nicholas Garnham (1983 and 1990) used it in his defence of the ideal of public service broadcasting, not to uncritically endorse the actual history of public service broadcasting, nor simply to protect the BBC as a venerable institution. Without a significant measure of regulation in the interests of the public good in communications, the democratic function of broadcasting, limited though it was in practice, might be lost, he argued. As Richard Collins (1993) has observed, this seemed to equate the public sphere with the public sector and left no space for the market as a stimulus to and provider of broadcast culture. That was not, in fact, the actual position held either by Garnham or by John Keane (1991), whose thinking on these matters is rather similar. Theirs is much more a critique of the problems inherent in an exclusively market-driven media system. Without provision for public accountability and control, and without some attempt to foster alternatives to an overbearing state and untrammelled market forces, the prospects for democratic debate and cultural experiment would be curtailed and, indeed, imperilled. Raymond Williams (1962) put forward a similar argument long ago and, coincidentally, in the same year that Jürgen Habermas's *Strukturwandel der Öffentlichkeit* was originally published in Germany. Such arguments, of necessity, draw on liberal-democratic principles of political thought as much as they do, if not more than, upon socialism. This line of argument assumes that liberal principles of democratic freedoms and rights are influential at least residually and open to further development and radicalisation. Moreover, the assumption is that, under late-modern conditions, the earlier modern principles of political democracy remain of critical relevance and are increasingly in contradiction with the liberal economics that they originally facilitated and which have in the closing decades of the twentieth century threatened to eclipse their legitimacy.

The finest study of the historical embodiment of liberal-democratic thought in public communications and culture is Habermas's *The Structural Transformation of the Public Sphere*. Habermas (1962/1989) identified the emergence of distinctly new forms of public debate in the advanced European nation-states of Britain, France and Germany during the eighteenth and nineteenth centuries, particularly in the period of the British Industrial Revolution, following the earlier mercantile revolution, and the French Revolution, which articulated the modern political ideals of liberty, egalitarianism and solidarity. The ancient Greek city state of Athens had also produced a discourse of democratic citizenship and a meeting place for its articulation, the famous *Agora*, but without the ostensible universalism of the bourgeois public sphere. An absolute distinction was made by the ancient Greeks between the men who exercised their citizenship rights by speaking in the city square and women and the slave population who were denied participation. In comparison, the bourgeois public sphere assumed, in theory, boundless equality. That was a formal claim made for reasons of philosophical consistency and not, in fact, borne out by the actual functioning of public culture and politics in Britain, France and Germany two centuries ago. Only property owners, on strictly capitalistic grounds, were really admitted to the public sphere. Women were excluded, in any case, on patriarchal grounds and confined to what Habermas calls 'the intimate sphere' of home and family, which was integrally related, however, to the public sphere insofar as it was the domestic institution, the inviolable personal base, that legitimated the bourgeois gentleman's individual presence in the outside world of politics in addition to the *raison d'être* of his economic interests in 'the private sphere' of business and trade. So, right at the heart of the bourgeois public sphere was a social contradiction, between the formally universal claims of equal citizenship and the substantive exclusions according to class, gender and, indeed, race, with few exceptions. Although Habermas is often criticised for idealising the bourgeois public sphere, he, none the less, always stressed its contradictory and partial make-up, which he contrasts, in both his early and later work, with the ideal of a genuinely democratic public sphere where no such exclusions would be permitted.

The eventual decline of the bourgeois public sphere was connected to its founding contradictions as well as resulting from the commercialisation and bureaucratisation of public communications from the late nineteenth century. However, this should not, according to Habermas, prevent us from appreciating the progressive historical role of the bourgeois public sphere and the principles of rational and critical debate amongst acknowledged equals that it represented. As Terry Eagleton (1984: 17) has commented: 'What is at stake in the public sphere, according to its own ideological self-image, is not power but reason. Truth, not authority, is its ground, and rationality, not domination, its daily currency. It is on this radical dissociation of politics and knowledge that its entire discourse is founded; and it is when this dissociation becomes less plausible that the public sphere will begin to crumble.'

The bourgeois public sphere was the medium through which the middling classes wrested power from absolute rulers and the feudal aristocracy. Its discourse of power and knowledge, which, as Eagleton notes acutely, involved the formal suspension of extraneous force under the proper conditions of debate in order to privilege 'Reason', was enunciated informally by the literary culture of the eighteenth century, which expressed values of individual freedom and rational critique. The political public sphere was thus *culturally prefigured*. One need only think of the writings of Voltaire and the other *philosophes*, like the *Encyclopaedists* D'Alembert and Diderot, of pre-revolutionary France to appreciate the political outcomes of such intellectual ferment. In Britain, the London coffee houses were the equivalent of the Parisian *salons* and became the gentlemanly settings for 'rational-critical debate'. Addison and Steele's *Spectator*, meanwhile, was the leading journal for circulating the cultural principles of liberal-bourgeois politics.

For the rising bourgeoisie, then, the public sphere which they created came to mediate the relationship of civil society to the state. In fact, it actually produced the conditions for an independent civil society of private persons with demanding public rights. The private spheres of civil society, business (trade and capital accumulation) and the family (the sphere of intimacy and cultural consumption) increasingly achieved representation or protection against arbitrary state power, securing the various liberal freedoms of public expression and personal conscience that a member of a modern liberal democracy might be expected, mistakenly, to take for granted. To quote Habermas's catalogue of liberal-bourgeois rights:

> A set of basic rights concerned the sphere of the public engaged in rational-critical debate (freedom of opinion and speech, freedom of press, freedom of assembly and association, etc.) and the political function of private people in this public sphere (rights of petition, equality of vote, etc.). A second set of basic rights concerned the individual's status as a free human being, grounded in the intimate sphere of the patriarchal conjugal family (personal freedom, inviolability of the home, etc.). The third set of basic rights concerned the transactions of the private owners of property in the sphere of civil society (equality before the law, protection of private property, etc.). The basic rights guaranteed: the *spheres* of the public realm and of the private (with the intimate sphere at its core); the *institutions* and *instruments* of the public sphere, on the one hand (press, parties), and the foundation of private autonomy (family and property), on the other; finally, the *functions* of the private people, both their political ones as citizens and their economic ones as owners of commodities (and, as 'human beings', those of individual communication, e.g. through inviolability of letters).
>
> (1962/1989: 83).

Habermas remarks that Karl Marx, writing from the 1840s and 1850s, 'treated the political public sphere ironically' (1962/1989: 123). He saw it as an ideological construct masking the real foundations and interests of bourgeois democracy under the rhetorical cover of 'freedom' and 'equality'; yet it was not merely to be denounced as a sham. Marx himself operated in both the official public sphere, as a journalist, and also in what Habermas calls 'the plebeian public sphere' of radical politics. Habermas is frequently criticised for neglecting the plebeian public sphere, though he did register and name it. More recently he has acknowledged the importance of E.P. Thompson's (1963) historical research for *The Making of the English*

Working Class, which was published the year after Habermas's book on the public sphere.[9] Thompson traced a radical intellectual tradition and culture in Britain, inspired by the American and French Revolutions, and functioning through reading groups, corresponding societies and publications that were harried and criminalised by the early nineteenth-century British state. This radical, alternative public sphere, represented by popular newspapers such as *The Poor Man's Guardian*, had a powerful impact upon the bourgeois public sphere, not only in opposition but also as a source of progressive ideas that were, to a considerable extent, incorporated and subsequently realised after much bitter struggle in the nineteenth century, for instance resulting in suffrage reform and legal recognition of trade union rights. Marx, like the protagonists of the plebeian public sphere in Britain, took the official claims of the bourgeois public sphere very seriously indeed. Such principles and claims had to be viewed as though they were realisable in practice, not only in order to expose the contradictions of liberal democracy but because they would be essential in a socialist democracy (see Williams, 1983a). The irony, of course, eventually rebounded fatally upon Marx and Marxism with the illusory claims of social equality and cultural democracy that were made by the twentieth-century communist states established in his name. According to Habermas, the radical-democratic aspirations of nineteenth-century socialist politics, which sought to hitch onto the bourgeois public sphere and change it into the forum for a democratic culture, failed to realise their anti-capitalist potential in the twentieth century. These aspirations were frustrated in spite or, rather, partly because of the growth of communications media organised for profit and, also, in spite of the real popular gains represented by the foundation of the social-welfare state.

In the second half of *Structural Transformation*, which most commentators regard as the least satisfactory half, Habermas describes a grim view of modern mass-popular culture in the pessimistic terms of his Frankfurt School precursors, Theodor Adorno and Max Horkheimer (1944/1979), and constituting what he calls 'the re-feudalization of the public sphere'. The pleasures of leisure-time consumption and popular entertainment are depicted as essentially alienated and alienating in a society where, to quote Habermas (1962/1989: 164), 'the conversation itself is administered'. The public sphere was hijacked by sophisticated communicational techniques of advertising and public relations, and rational-critical debate became distorted. Power was not sufficiently devolved with universal suffrage: instead, the partnership between state and capital came to organise the conditions of everyday life and the processes of representation in both the political and cultural senses. Habermas's variant of the mass-culture critique was a good deal more fashionable and widely accepted by critics in the early 1960s than it is in the 1990s. Nevertheless, the claim that the distance between ordinary social and cultural experience, on the one hand,

and the processes of public decision-making, on the other hand, has widened rather than narrowed during the twentieth century is not negligible, nor is it without support amongst 'postmodernist' commentators. It is similar, for instance, to Jean Baudrillard's (1988) cool argument that the mass of people just do not care about politics and, in effect, to use Habermasian terminology, do not participate significantly in the public sphere of rational-critical debate. Such debate is for the most part simulated by media personalities and image-conscious politicians who appear on the television day in and day out. The reality is, to be sure, much more complex and contradictory than this vision of an entirely depoliticised mass-popular culture and a public sphere that has degenerated into completely manipulative communications.

John B. Thompson (1993) has usefully clustered into four categories the range of criticisms that are made of Habermas's original thesis on the public sphere. First, it is criticised on historiographical grounds for neglecting the role of popular movements in particular, as we have seen with regard to 'the plebeian public sphere'. Second, it is criticised for failing to properly address the masculinity of the bourgeois public sphere, not only in the physical exclusion of women but in terms of its ideological constitution as a gentleman's club. Third, it is criticised for misunderstanding the active powers of popular cultural consumption and reception as well as the opportunities that the modern and especially electronic media actually do and potentially afford informed public debate on serious issues. Fourth, the theory of the public sphere is criticised for the vagueness of Habermas's proposals concerning a renewal of rational-critical debate and the conditions for democratisation: 'the objectively possible minimizing of bureaucratic decisions and a relativizing of structural conflicts of interest according to the standard of a universal interest everyone can acknowledge' (Habermas, 1962/1989: 235). Thompson (1993: 186) goes a step further by mentioning his own criticism of the 'essentially *dialogical* conception' of the public sphere, which he takes to be founded in a model of exclusively face-to-face interaction. For this reason, Thompson contends, Habermas's theory of the public sphere cannot adequately account for the temporal and spatial displacements of technologically mediated communications. However, like other sympathetic commentators, Thompson believes that the public sphere remains a vital conceptual tool of analysis and, moreover, a normative guide to democratic practice.

An example of the inspiration that is still drawn from Habermas's original idea is James Curran's (1991) model of a radical-democratic public sphere adapted to late modern conditions and contrasted with liberal, critical Marxist and communist conceptions. Curran's radical-democratic model is based upon the assumption that 'a central role for the media should be defined as *assisting the equitable negotiation or arbitration of competing interests through democratic processes*' (p. 30). Left to its own

27

devices, the market will not bring this about, nor have democratic communications ever been achieved under exclusively state-controlled systems, although public intervention and regulation, in Curran's view, are still necessary requirements. Such arguments are commonly made with regard to democratic entitlement to the culture and information necessary for exercising citizenship rights knowledgeably: debate on the communicative properties of the public sphere, institutional and technological change, from the broad perspective of the political economy of communications and culture, usually stresses these considerations. However, Curran (p. 28) goes further by including 'entertainment' in his model with the idea of 'society communing with itself', inspired by Raymond Williams's hopeful anticipation of the cultural relations and mutual understanding that would be fostered by democratic systems of communication.[10]

During the course of the following chapters, I aim to contribute to the radical-democratic perspective on rational-critical debate concerning communications and culture through discussion of a series of linked and substantive issues of cultural policy. My chosen strategy is to deploy the critical ideal of the public sphere as a normative reference point in its plural and context-specific forms, rather than as a single and abstracted entity, and in relation to a conception of culture and the cultural field which includes art, popular media, everyday forms of pleasure and identity. This approach represents a departure from the usual treatment of the public sphere in communications policy research where the politics of information tends to be privileged over the more affective aspects of culture. Having said this, however, I do not believe nor intend that discussion of 'culture' should be conducted in artificial separation from the social and technological development of information and media systems.

The broadly Habermasian perspective outlined here is a corrective to a certain kind of instrumentalism which is implicit in the economic reductionisms and technological determinisms that frame much policy debate in the cultural field and from which a critical political economy of the media is not always immune. While 'communications' are treated in this instrumentalist manner, 'culture' has been hived off, in the past, and equated simply with 'the arts', a marginal yet worthy area of public policy. It has now become common, however, for 'culture' to be resituated within the economistic and technicist discourses of public policy and in this way is tied into the governmentality of communications media on industrial and economic grounds. In many respects, this is a major advance for cultural policy and potentially for affective communications, placing them much closer to the centre of politics. What tends to get lost, though, is the specifically cultural, culture as communication and meaning, practices and experiences that are too complex and *a*ffective to be treated adequately in the *e*ffective terms of economic and bureaucratic models of policy.

The Habermasian perspective focuses upon the operations of discursivity

in a fashion that is not entirely dissimilar to Foucauldian discursive formation analysis, whilst stressing in contrast, however, the normative conditions for democratic communication. None of these theories and
perspectives, Habermasian, Foucauldian, neo-Gramscian, political economy, and so forth, are in themselves sufficient for all analytical and practical
purposes. Steven Best and Douglas Kellner (1991) are right to call for a
multiperspectival approach in order to address the sheer complexity of
a multidimensional social and cultural reality. This book does not purport
to provide such a comprehensive and catholic approach but it does seek to
look at cultural policy from a number of points of view. At the heart of
consideration, though, is the function of public debate. In consequence, it
is necessary to look beyond the purely academic and to engage critical
reasoning with the issues that are generated routinely in the practical
discourses of culture and society.

2

QUESTIONS OF VALUE

Beauty is truth, truth beauty,' that is all
Ye know on earth, and all ye need to know.
John Keats, 'Ode on a Grecian Urn'

It is frequently remarked, in our ironic times, that there is a crisis of value. This has several variants, including a disruption of stable criteria for cultural judgement. At one time, so the story goes, there was a fixed hierarchy of culture, stretching from the ignoble base to the apex of excellence. Clearly distinguishable forms and practices were allocated to their appropriate levels on the hierarchical shelving, each with its aesthetic valuation firmly attached. Now, in the postmodern vernacular, whereby recently innovative philosophical ideas enter into educated common sense, the situation is characterised by a collapsing or flattening of hierarchies, not only the cultural but also the organisational and the social; and, furthermore, by a blurring of boundaries. These collapsing hierarchies and blurring boundaries are held to obliterate older distinctions between, say, art and popular culture. If this really is so, then it follows that the foundational assumptions and functional rationales of much of what passes for public policy in the cultural field, particularly reasons for state subsidy and regulation, are called into question and perhaps rendered redundant. What is the point, it may well be asked, of making 'good' culture more widely available or protecting it from the cold winds of the market when it cannot be distinguished satisfactorily from 'bad' culture?

Although we are concerned here specifically with *cultural value*, it should be noted that 'value' has a range of different connotations, all of which may be relevant to policy issues in the contemporary cultural field. 'Value' immediately connotes 'money', financial measurement, as in 'value for money' and 'exchange value'. Problematising this economic market definition of value, there is the still illuminating distinction between 'exchange value' and 'use value', which weighs human creativity and need much heavier on the scales of value than the going price for labour and commodities. Other connotations come to mind as well, such as 'principles' and 'standards'. Value can thus be located on a number of discursive sites.

In addition to economic value, we may speak of aesthetic, ethical, political and religious values.

The notion that a cultural product is as valuable as its price in the marketplace, determined by the choices of 'the sovereign consumer' and by the laws of supply and demand, is currently a prevalent notion of cultural value and maybe the most prevalent one, albeit deeply flawed. Its fundamental flaw is the reduction of all value, which is so manifestly various and contestable, to a one-dimensional and economistic logic, the logic of 'the free market'. Should we wish, alternatively, to hold on to a conception of value over and above that of monetary calculation, the distinction between use value and exchange value is still important. Some would say that such a distinction is no longer tenable because of the semiotic erasure of lived and material reality in a 'media society'. Postmodernists of the Baudrillardian school are thus inclined, mistakenly in my view, to reduce everything to 'sign value'. Others prefer to retain an idea of aesthetic value, an idea that has played a significant but not always noble role in the determination of cultural policies, whereas yet others emphasise the ethical dimensions of culture.

The calls that are made periodically for a recovery of cultural value from the reductive forces of the market are usually grounded in arguments concerning aesthetic or ethical value, occasionally with a political inflection. Neither satisfactorily account, however, nor could they, for the social crisis or, at least, apparent undecidability of value, although ethical positions may provide some better answers to the questions that are posed concerning value than do purely aesthetic positions. For that reason, in this chapter, I shall begin by considering the sociological move in the value debate through a discussion of the work of Pierre Bourdieu, which suspends the tasks of cultural evaluation and formulation of evaluative criteria in order to make sense of how cultural values or, rather, 'tastes' and 'dispositions', in his terminology, are produced and circulated. I shall then proceed to consider the strengths and weaknesses of the sociological move in relation to the aesthetic and ethical moves in the endless play of cultural value.

COLLAPSING HIERARCHIES

Compared with Foucault and Habermas, Bourdieu has been much more directly involved with cultural policy.[1] Interestingly, as well, Craig Calhoun (1993) has argued that Bourdieu's theorising, in general, offers a third way between the attack of postmodernist particularism associated with Foucault and the defence of modernist universalism for which Habermas (1981) is well known. According to Scott Lash's (1993a: 193) exaggerated estimation, 'Bourdieu's general sociology of culture is not only the best, but it is the only game in town.' He compares the French sociologist's work favourably and quite justifiably with a cultural studies that deals exclusively with textual analysis and reception but does not study the institutional matrix of culture.[2]

Bourdieu's sociology of taste is an exercise in collapsing cultural hierarchies by showing how they are socially constructed and reproduced, and not the result of absolute standards of value. His major study, *Distinction* (1984), originally published in France in 1979, and subtitled 'A Social Critique of the Judgement of Taste', seeks to dethrone Kantian aesthetics once and for all. There is, according to Bourdieu, no pure judgement of art that can be sustained on 'disinterested' philosophical grounds. Art and culture only exist socially and they are caught up in struggles for 'distinction'. In effect, Bourdieu replaces aesthetics, the philosophical judgement of art, with the sociological categories of distinction and taste. For Bourdieu, taste is a marker of class, mediated through a dispositionary 'habitus', deriving from differential socialisation in the family and schooling: it is deployed partly consciously and partly unconsciously for socially strategic purposes. People are disposed by their class position, which is not only an economic position but also a cultural position, to understand, appreciate and enjoy works of art, media products and also, for instance, types of cuisine in the approved ways for consuming such fare.

Introduced in the 1960s (Bourdieu, 1971 and 1973) and developed with greater sophistication in the 1980s (Bourdieu, 1993), Bourdieu has produced an economic analogy for the operations of the cultural field in which competition operates asymmetrically according to the unequal possession of various kinds of capital by participants. In addition to economic capital, there is cultural and symbolic capital. 'Symbolic capital', for example 'correct' speech such as Oxford English, facilitates power struggle and may be augmented and, indeed, triggered by economic capital, but, in Bourdieu's theory, is also supported by reserves of culturally acquired competency, including art appreciation. Of particular relevance to the appreciation of art, 'cultural capital' refers to cultivated competence, knowledge of the classificatory schemes, codes and conventions of cultural forms and the ability to display such knowledge to social advantage with game-playing confidence. This was originally formulated in the 1968 essay 'Outline of a Sociological Theory of Art Perception' (reprinted in Bourdieu, 1993), and is nicely illustrated in the following passage of commentary by Graham Murdock:

> Take Van Gogh's celebrated painting of sunflowers. An incompetent person in Bourdieu's terms would classify it simply as a picture of flowers. A slightly more competent person would be able to specify that it was by Van Gogh and provide some minimal contextual background – that he also painted a pair of old boots, that he cut off his ear and sent it to his girl friend, and that he eventually committed suicide. A truly competent person, however, would be able to place

the picture in relation to Van Gogh's total oeuvre, to compare his subject matter and technique to other artists of the period, to say that it was expressionist rather than impressionist and so on. Competence in this sense means mastering the dominant vocabulary of classification and criticism; it means knowing what's in the catalogue and programme notes without having to look it up. But full competence consists not only of knowing about the works themselves, but also of knowing how to respond to them. This is particularly crucial in situations like theatres and concerts where responses are subject to public scrutiny.

(1980: 11.4–5)

To be impressed by the prestigious reputation of official culture, traditionally the classical arts and whatever other forms were consecrated by tasteful judgement, but to lack the necessary competences to consume such culture 'properly' can be anxiety producing for both adults and children. Confronted by ₁prestigious culture and the aura surrounding it, many people, particularly from lower-class backgrounds, in Bourdieu's account, are made to feel personally inadequate and, in consequence, tend to avoid it, settling for being 'uncultured'. According to Bourdieu, class-differentiated cultural competences are reproduced across the generations by family and schooling. Children learn early on what kind of culture is for them and what is not. Exclusion from prestigious culture has both material and symbolic dimensions. The cultural possibilities of poorer people are constrained by money and time, sheer financial incapacity and, consequently, they may be unable to dedicate their limited leisure time to consuming prestigious culture. Yet material disadvantage is not necessarily the most important constraint and, for the unemployed, lack of time on their hands is not the problem.

Bourdieu's early studies of attendance at public art museums (Bourdieu and Darbel, 1969/1991), where entrance is free or reduced by subsidy, indicated that the vast majority of visitors came from non-manual work stratas of society. Visiting art museums, in this comparative European research that Bourdieu directed in the 1960s, is closely correlated with level of educational attainment. He remarks, 'nothing would be more naive than to expect that simply reducing admission charges would lead to an increase in visiting amongst the working class' (Bourdieu and Darbel, 1969/ 1991: 19). At first sight such an observation might be construed as opposed to the culturally ameliorative policies of 1960s social democracy, and consistent with a 1990s market realism. However, Bourdieu's thinking on these matters, certainly in L'Amour d'art, was quite evidently framed by a social-democratic problematic. He insisted that cultural 'disadvantage' was so deeply embedded that it could not be assuaged by easier access to museums. The solution, instead, was compensatory education:

33

The specific function of the school is to develop or create the dispositions which make for the cultivated individual and which are at the same time qualitatively and quantitatively the medium of intense and lasting practice. As such, it could compensate (partially at least) for the initial disadvantage of those who do not receive in their family environment any encouragement of cultural practice or of the development of the familiarity with works of art which is presupposed by any educational discourse on them, only provided that it uses all available methods to break the circle of cumulative processes to which all cultural education is condemned.

(Bourdieu and Darbel, 1969/1991: 67)

Although Bourdieu's sociology of taste is famous for anthropologising Culture with a capital C, he uses that notoriously difficult term here in the narrower arts-and-learning sense rather than in the broader anthropological sense, which is also true mainly of his usage in *Distinction*. He began his disquisition on taste, then, by deploring the exclusion of the working class from 'Culture' with a capital C. There was a shift in Bourdieu's thinking subsequently whereby he problematised the value of art and high culture that was taken for granted in his earlier work. That became evident by the time the social survey and ethnographic research findings on cultural consumption, begun in the 1960s, were gathered together and codified theoretically for the publication of *La Distinction* in 1979.

Immanuel Kant may have believed that aesthetic judgement was 'disinterested', situated somewhere above the barbarism of everyday life. The cultivated members of the mid to late twentieth-century French bourgeoisie, studied by Bourdieu and his colleagues, displayed their interest, however, in its very disavowal. Their 'charismatic' ideology of true art and culture, which was a bourgeois adaptation of an aristocratic sensibility, created a serviceable misrecognition. In an article published in 1983 (reprinted in Bourdieu, 1993), Bourdieu described this ideology as 'the economic world reversed'. Aesthetic value was judged autonomous in spite of the fact that, for rich art-lovers, *avant-garde* and ideally obscure works of visual art, in particular, constitute a store of economic wealth. The judgement of aesthetic value, from the perspective of the charismatic ideology of art, of course, is said to be unsullied by such pecuniary considerations.

In *Distinction*, unremarkably, Bourdieu identifies three levels of 'taste': 'legitimate', 'middle-brow' and 'popular'. In the next section of this chapter I shall concentrate on 'middle-brow' taste. It is important, however, to register how Bourdieu sets up the opposition between 'pure' taste and 'popular' taste. To quote Bourdieu on:

THE POPULAR 'AESTHETIC'. Everything takes place as if the 'popular aesthetic' was based on the affirmation of continuity between art and life, which implies the subordination of form to function, or, one might say, as a refusal of the refusal which is the starting point of the high aesthetic, i.e., the clear-cut separation of ordinary disposition from the specifically aesthetic disposition.

(1984: 32)

Working-class and peasant taste, the 'popular aesthetic', cannot be doing with a refined appreciation of form, detached from the immediacy of experience and displaying a mode of consumption so restrained that it is difficult to recognise as something resembling pleasure. This is represented in the body, dress and deportment in addition to a preference for, say, Hollywood movies over conceptual painting. Bourdieu's originary sympathy with the popular aesthetic is evident in the following passage in which he describes a working-class meal in folksy and, no doubt, politically incorrect terms:

The art of eating and drinking remains one of the few areas in which the working classes explicitly challenge the legitimate art of living. In the face of the new ethic of sobriety for the sake of slimness, which is most recognized at the highest levels of the social hierarchy, peasants and especially industrial workers maintain an ethic of convivial indulgence. A bon vivant is not just someone who enjoys eating and drinking; he is someone capable of entering into the generous and familiar – that is, both simple and free – relationship that is encouraged and symbolized by eating and drinking together, in a conviviality that sweeps away restraints and reticence.

(1984: 179)

Bourdieu's possibly nostalgic evocation of working-class eating and drinking was written in the 1970s and much of the research for *La Distinction* was done in the 1960s, though the example scarcely depends upon it, and specifically in France where the 'art of living' has been a keen preoccupation. Time has passed and the social organisation of taste and class-differentiated habitus is no longer so hierarchised and tightly bounded, according to the postmodern culture that is supposed to have swept us all up since then. Discussing the apparently sudden popular commercialisation of classical music in the early 1990s, Luciano Pavarotti, Nigel Kennedy, and so forth, Frank Mort has said of the changing social and cultural landscape:

There was a time when culture came clearly labelled. If there was no consensus about cultural values, then at least it was clear what we were getting. Highbrow or mass culture, avant-garde or middlebrow, modernist or popular – these were the signposts guiding specific publics through the maze of styles and genres. Of course, hierarchies of taste and distinction came along as part of the package – the system was by no means value-free – but you knew where you were. These certainties are fast disappearing. Late 20th-century culture scrambles styles, publics and patterns of taste to an unprecedented degree. Popular forms collide with high art genres and postmodernism celebrates the clash, while the leisure industries re-think their markets for everything from concert-going to cycling.

(1990: 32)

What we have to consider now is whether Bourdieu's seminal work on taste, lifestyle and class is outdated by these developments, the possibly actual collapsing of hierarchies and blurring of boundaries, or whether he was onto such developments more or less at their outset and, therefore, enables us to put them into sharper sociological focus than the usual postmodernist reading would allow.

BLURRING BOUNDARIES

Postmodern culture, in the most elementary sense, is about the flattening of hierarchies, such as 'the collapse of the distinction between high art and mass/popular culture' (Featherstone, 1991), and the blurring of boundaries between, say, classical and popular music, which is not only to do with formal interactions but also to do with modes of consumption. So, for example, Nigel Kennedy turned a violin recital into something like a rock concert and Pink Floyd demanded a reverence from their audience comparable to that of a classical music concert. Newer technologies and the refinements of target-marketing contribute to these crossovers, as in the increased sales of the classics on CD. The proliferation of 'pick 'n' mix' hybrid forms further accentuates the postmodernisation of culture: Hollywood films, for instance, appropriate 'modernist' devices without losing the popular audience, and the levels of meaning are multiplied in such a manner that a new breed of populist intellectual is kept busy deconstructing and teaching mass-mediated entertainment.

The blurring of boundaries does not stop with culture as narrowly conceived or as expanded by populist intermediaries. It is also claimed that we are entering a new epoch of 'postmodernity'.[3] A key idea in this respect is the 'de-differentiation' of social relations and conceptual discourse, outlined in the following passage from Chris Rojek's *Ways of Escape*:

De-differentiation may be formally defined as a condition in which former social, economic and political distinctions cease to obtain. For example, the private sphere can no longer be analytically or symbolically separated from the public sphere; the Cartesian separation of body and mind ceases to hold good; the categorical distinctions between male and female roles seem insupportable; the division between work and leisure is no longer clear-cut; in short, the divisions which gave stability to the modernist order of things seem to be untenable – they do not correspond with people's actual experience of things.

(1993: 4–5)

If de-differentiation is such an all-pervasive phenomenon, it must also have implications for social class, the main explanatory variable in Bourdieu's sociology of taste. What, then, are the consequences of a blurring and an apparent erosion of class differences? On the question of de-differentiation, a digression into the sociological problem of 'the middle class' and the perennial issue of *embourgeoisement* is necessary. The divisions between 'upper' and 'lower', 'bourgeois' and 'proletarian', were always complicated by the existence of intermediary groupings, the betwixt and between, 'middle class' and 'petit-bourgeois'. Still, whatever the complications, as Eric Olin Wright (1993: 27) says, 'Class is a powerful causal factor because of the way in which class determines access to material resources and thus affects the use of one's time, the resources available to pursue one's interests and the character of one's life experiences within work and consumption.' Which is not to say that the category of class explains everything: it never did.

Class distinctions represent material and cultural boundaries between social groups that are situated in the flux of time and the phantasmagoria of space. As means of distinguishing between people, their categorial fixity is a convenient aid for making sense of social relations, but at the inevitable risk of over-simplification. Such distinctions, whether to do with class or any salient phenomenon, tend to form into binary oppositions. This was so in the classical Marxist theory of class with its two socio-economic categories, one of positivity, 'the proletariat', and one of negativity, 'the bourgeoisie'. It is unnecessary to hold a strictly structuralist view of cognition to apprehend the ambiguity and sociological problem of a 'boundary zone' where two different and contrasting conditions overlap (Leach, 1976); for instance, the grey area of the middle class of petite bourgeoisie.

Eric Olin Wright (1978 and 1985) sought to solve the problem theoretically with his original idea of 'contradictory class locations', attempting to account for the complexities of the in-between in class terms. This led him to examine different forms of 'domination' amongst groups that were both dominant and dominated. In his later work, Wright (1993) has revised this formulation by recovering the classical Marxist concept of 'exploitation'. It is quite possible, he believes, to classify different intermediary groupings according to their particular relations of exploitation: for example, managers. Managers may be exploited for their skill in organising subordinates who deliver surplus value to the managers' bosses. That also puts them in an exploitative role. They are both exploited and exploiting, which is the general fate of the middle class and which makes its politics so indeterminate and malleable. Wright quite deliberately developed his theory of 'contradictory class locations' to counter theories of the emergence of a distinctly 'new class' (for instance, Galbraith, 1958). However, this has not stopped others of a similar theoretical persuasion coming up with exactly that, such as the Ehrenreichs' (1979) conceptualisation of the 'Professional-Managerial Class (PMC)'. Barbara and John Ehrenreich (1979: 12) define 'the Professional-Managerial Class as consisting of salaried mental workers who do not own the means of production and whose main function in the social division of labour may be described as the reproduction of capitalist culture and capitalist class relations'.

Towards the end of the 1970s, the Ehrenreichs estimated the membership of the PMC in the USA as somewhere between 20 and 25 per cent of the population. The 'old middle class' of self-employed professionals, small traders and farmers was, according to them, about 10 per cent and the 'ruling class', the owners of the major means of production, was around 2 per cent of the population. In fact, the Ehrenreichs give an unusually high estimate for the 'working class' at 65 to 70 per cent; of necessity, including white-collar employees who normally regard themselves as 'middle class'. Theirs is not, then, one of the most extravagant notions of a mushrooming 'new class'. The Ehrenreichs do say, however, that the PMC is a nodal group, in effect, the managers of the working class. This new class grew into significant existence from the early twentieth century in order, first and foremost, to fulfil functions of social control, not only in business management but also in the various 'caring professions' such as social work and teaching. Although many of them may be bearers of 'progressive' ideologies, their 'objective' relation with the working class is tragically 'antagonistic'. They exercise authority and, for this, they are resented by a working class only too willing to accept the right-wing populist depiction of the PMC as full of 'pinko intellectuals' and 'effete snobs'.

The Ehrenreichs' conception of the PMC is crucial to Fred Pfeil's (1991) bold thesis concerning the American 'baby-boom' generation and post-modernism. Inspired by Raymond Williams (1961), he conceives of postmodernism as a generational 'structure of feeling' rooted in a huge PMC. Pfeil claims that, in 1980, 59 per cent of the 25 to 35-year-old age group in the USA were PMC and 82 per cent of this age group in paid employment were in PMC occupations. These estimates give an incredible force to Pfeil's (1991: 3) claim that ' "postmodernism" is the distinctive cultural expression or "structure of feeling" of a largely white professional-managerial class produced by the social formations ... of the developed world'. His startling claim is made deliberately against Fredric Jameson's (1984) celebrated but excessively 'totalising' thesis of postmodernism as 'the cultural logic of late capitalism'. Pfeil seeks to provide a much more precise sociological location for postmodern sensibility, albeit, at least for the USA, of a majoritarian generational grouping.

During the 1960s and 1970s the trajectories of working-class and of middle-class youth converged sharply, particularly in terms of access to higher education, where they participated in a 'counter-culture' which loosened established social attitudes and values. Concurrently, however, there was also a further erosion of the public sphere, in Pfeil's estimation, signified by the growth of privatised living in suburbia and the ubiquity of televisual mediation of the world. Passing from university into management and the professions, for this generation, a distinctive 'class ethos' gelled, characterised by bureaucratic professionalism and 'an almost guild-like sense of individual autonomy and ability within the more-or-less horizontally perceived company of one's own peers with whom one not only works but "networks"' (Pfeil, 1991: 105).

Pfeil (p. 107) goes on to ask, 'for whom is the "breakdown" of the mass/ high culture distinction more real, the American working class or the PMC?'. The everyday ethos is individualistic yet, according to Pfeil, the postmodernist cultural forms favoured by the PMC, from 'mass' to 'high', are characterised by 'de-individualization', by which he means the play with stereotypes on, for instance, 'satire' shows and the intertextuality displayed by 'serious' work. Postmodern pleasure in cultural consumption is, for the PMC, the pleasure of recognition, of knowing the references. All this adds up (or does not add up, as the case may be) to a kind of Sartrean 'serialised logic' in a 'lifestyle' where a sense of collectivity is weak, to say the least. A second major feature of postmodern culture, identified by Pfeil (p. 114), is *kenosis* – evacuation of content, numbing-out of feeling and sense'.

It may be objected, of course, that Pfeil's treatment of postmodernism is too slight to sustain his case, for instance in comparison with Jameson's (1984) much more sustained account of its philosophical and aesthetic aspects. Moreover, Pfeil is vulnerable to the criticism of class reductionism. The problem here is specifically to do with the distinction that must be drawn between the professional-managerial class in general and those particular sections of it that are directly employed in practices of cultural mediation and consumer management (see, for instance, Featherstone, 1989). A refinement of Pfeil's thesis with regard to the role of 'cultural intermediaries' is, incidentally, quite consistent with Bourdieu's own position on these matters, originally stated in *La Distinction*, as we shall see. Finally, resistance to postmodernism is not at all uncommon amongst 'babyboomers', especially within the academy. Enthusiasm for postmodern culture may, in fact, be much more commonplace amongst the younger 'generation X', who have been denied many of the opportunities of the older generation and have less to find defensible in modernist and rationalising sensibility.

At which point we may return to Pierre Bourdieu. Because Bourdieu refuses to treat cultural products as containing essential and fixed values in order to 'explore the economy of symbolic goods' (Lee, 1993), how values are generated, circulated and accumulated, his work is particularly germane to a consideration of uncertainty at the boundaries of social and cultural difference. In an early study (Bourdieu, 1965/1990), he and his colleagues examined the problematical status of photography as *un art moyen*, and how certain groups of photographers strive to give it and themselves status. This 'middle-brow art' was of particular interest to clerical workers with upwardly mobile aspirations. The issue becomes much more generalised in *Distinction*:

> '[M]iddle-ground' arts such as cinema, jazz, and, even more, strip cartoons, science fiction or detective stories are predisposed to attract the investments either of those who have entirely succeeded in converting their cultural capital into educational capital or those who, not having acquired legitimate culture in the legitimate manner (i.e. through early familiarization), maintain an uneasy relationship with it, subjectively or objectively, or both.
>
> (1984: 87)

Although Bourdieu has paid scant attention to the literal economics of culture and its role in postmodern capitalism, in terms of class analysis his sense of the politics of culture is particularly acute with regard to the 'new bourgeoisie' as well as the 'new petite bourgeoisie'. The rapid growth of an information economy has brought with it a new fraction of the dominant class – to give some latter-day examples, the Silvio Berlusconis, the Bill Gateses, the Calvin Kleins, the Rupert Murdochs and the Saatchis – who play and have played a directive cultural role:

> The new bourgeoisie is the initiator of the ethical retooling required by the new economy from which it draws its power and profits, whose functioning depends as much on the production of needs and consumers as on the production of goods. The new logic of the economy rejects the ascetic ethic of production and accumulation, based on abstinence, sobriety, saving and calculation, in favour of an hedonistic morality of consumption, based on credit, spending and enjoyment. This economy demands a social world which judges people by their capacity for consumption, their 'standard of living', their life-style, as much as their capacity for production. It finds ardent spokesmen in the new bourgeoisie of the vendors of symbolic goods and services, the directors and executives of firms in tourism and journalism, publishing and the cinema, fashion and advertising, decoration and property development.
>
> (1984: 310–311)

It would be a shame if attention to the cultural strategies of the new petite bourgeoisie were to blur our perception of this masterful fraction of the bourgeoisie. As Bourdieu (1984: 111–112) says, 'blurring is particularly visible in the middle classes and especially in the new fractions of these classes, which are grey areas, ambiguously located in the social structure, inhabited by individuals whose trajectories are extremely scattered'. Insightful and percipient though it is, there is a peculiar venom in Bourdieu's analysis of the rise of this new petite bourgeoisie, which is so similar to the Ehrenreichs' PMC.

He pokes fun at their lack of comfort with themselves, the way in which they are ill at ease with their bodies in comparison with both the bourgeoisie and the proletariat, which anxiety, according to Bourdieu, is generative of the new 'body culture'. This is related, more broadly, to issues of 'presentation and representation'. Again, Bourdieu (1984: 359): 'The new petite bourgeoisie comes into its own in all the occupations involving presentation and representation (sales, marketing, advertising, public relations, fashion, decoration and so forth) and in all the institutions providing symbolic goods and services.' Most of what Bourdieu seems to regard as the pseudo-radicalism of 'Sixties' culture still flows through the social veins of this fraction. Clearly, Bourdieu's remarks are framed by his cynical view of the aftermath of May '68, particularly concerning how French intellectual workers, especially cultural intermediaries, came to terms with the 'counter-revolution' and reinvested their energies in 'life-style'. Yet another lengthy quote is necessary to demonstrate quite how harsh his judgement is:

> Obliged to live out the contradictions of their messianic aspirations and the reality of their practice, to cultivate uncertainty as to their social identity in order to be able to accept it, and therefore condemned to a questioning of the world which masks an anxious self-questioning, these 'intellectual lackeys' are predisposed to experience with particular intensity the existential mood of a whole generation, which, weary of desperately hoping for a collective hope, seeks in narcissistic self-absorption the substitute for the hope of changing the social world or even of understanding it.
>
> (1984: 366)

I should imagine that this kind of writing might make many and perhaps most of the readers of *Distinction* and of *this* book feel uncomfortable or angry. He is talking about *us* or, at least, people like us. What is not clear is whether or not Bourdieu excuses himself, as a sociologist, from the new petite bourgeoisie's 'dream of social flying, a desperate effort to defy the gravity of the social field' (1984: 370). What is quite clear, however, is that Bourdieu has a much grimmer view of the politics of this class fraction than do Marxist writers such as Lash and Urry (1987), Lee (1993), Pfeil (1991) and, indeed, the Ehrenreichs (1979), who were writing in the same year as the publication of *La Distinction* and also the same year, 1979, that

41

Margaret Thatcher came to power in Britain. In spite of their sense of tragedy, Barbara and John Ehrenreich actually saw real potential for the persistence and renewal of oppositional cultural politics in the PMC. Not so Bourdieu (1984: 371): 'the new ethic espoused by the vanguard of the bourgeoisie and petite bourgeoisie is perfectly compatible with a form of enlightened conservatism'.[4]

REVALUING VALUES

Bourdieu's sociology of culture may not be 'the only game in town' but it is, undoubtedly, a game worth playing because of its demystifying force and powerful capacity to pose unsettling questions. However hard Bourdieu tries, though, he cannot finally close off questions of 'what', in his words, 'some would mistakenly call values' (1984: 466), not least of which concern his own value position. John Corner (1993: 6) has, for instance, posed 'the big question' regarding Bourdieu's work on distinction and taste: 'how far is the real problem for him the unequal social distribution of cultural dispositions and competencies or how far is it the power of those with cultural capital to impose a system of cultural value which fits in with their own tastes?' The foregoing account, in this chapter, would suggest a shift from the former to the latter position. If that is so, then the politics and the policy inferences that might be drawn from Bourdieu's sociology have changed over the years. He is no longer the champion of the 'culturally disadvantaged' but, instead, the satirist of the postmodernist petite bourgeoisie. Yet, as Corner insists, the question of inequality remains paramount and is linked to issues of cultural 'quality'.

Another commentator who is dissatisfied with the policy relevance of Bourdieu's work is Nicholas Garnham (1993a). He fixes upon the emptiness of Bourdieu's treatment of culture, the evacuation of content and, in effect, value. For example, on the question of 'news values', a Bourdieuan style of analysis, similarly perhaps to many a 'postmodern reading', might simply deconstruct the values of 'responsible' journalism, showing them to be mere 'professional' self-justification in a game of symbolic power. However, this should not necessarily be construed as Bourdieu's own personal view concerning journalistic responsibilities and the ethics of cultural practice in general, judging by his conversations on the American 'culture wars' with the German artist Hans Haacke (Bourdieu and Haacke, 1995). To return to Garnham's point: for many journalists, seeking a measure of autonomy from and resistance to the powers exerted upon them particularly by their proprietors, the appeal to 'news value' can have important critical force, enabling a 'truthfulness' of reporting that might otherwise be entirely absent.

Must sociological analysis necessarily eliminate formal and substantive questions of value? Janet Wolff (1983/1993), in arguing the case for a sociology of art, thinks not. She says that 'the central theme' of her book *Aesthetics and the Sociology of Art* is 'the irreducibility of "aesthetic value" to social, political, or ideological co-ordinates' (p. 11). Although art and aesthetic judgement are always socially and historically located, within any particular social and historical location questions of value and what is peculiarly artistic value are bound to arise. The attempt to ascertain value through a process of argumentation cannot be reduced to something other than what it is about, although the answers to the questions posed are not for all times and all places. This is rather more fundamental than a sudden rediscovery of value in the 1990s in reaction to a period of wholesale relativism during the 1980s (see Squires, 1993).

Wolff (1983/1993) identifies three main attitudes towards the sociology of art and culture: first, a conservative defence of aesthetics against any socio-historical explanation; second, a total denial of aesthetic value; and, third, a general acceptance of the sociological case while simultaneously claiming that truly great art transcends its social conditions of production. The second view would seem to be shared by both the Bourdieu of *La Distinction* and postmodernists influenced by Jean Baudrillard. The third view was most strongly associated with the Hegelian strand of Marxist aesthetics. The first view represents a very familar and resilient position yet a theoretically discredited one. To give a much publicised example, the English playwright David Hare's assertion: 'finally, Keats is a better poet than Bob Dylan'.[5]

Hare's assertion was made in response to the way in which the radical project of the 1960s and 1970s to 'broaden culture', no longer to confine it to an established aesthetic canon, had, during the 1980s, turned into a market and marketing phenomenon in which everything meaningful appeared culturally 'interesting', in the much over-used word of the former *Late Show* presenter Michael Ignatieff, under the equivalence of exchange value. For this kind of reason, Patrick Wright (1991), normally an astute critic of culture and cultural policy, defended Hare's attack on a postmodern populism that is closely aligned with commercial promotion. Hare himself had been one of the 'Sixties' generation of cultural radicals yet, by the 1990s, he wanted a reassertion of 'a more demanding idea of cultural value'. However, Hare's own 'soundbite' produced a peculiarly inapt comparison between similarly canonised poets, Keats and Dylan, that displayed only a lack of historical sense and which missed the more obvious targets of anything-goes culture, for instance some of the cheaper academic disquisitions on the latest fads and fashions of popular leisure. The comparison also inscribed within it certain characteristic features of 'traditional' aesthetic judgement: authorship, textual objectivism and finality. In effect, it evinced an absolutism of cultural value that was quite unusual even by the standards of contemporary 'conservative' criticism.

As Steven Connor (1992) has argued, the tension and, indeed, oscillation between absolutism and relativism constitute a recurrent and perhaps unavoidable dialectic of value and of cultural value debates. Politically distinguished forms of relativism have tended to argue their case against the oppressiveness of cultural absolutisms which function as means of denigrating and marginalising subordinate cultures of class, ethnicity, gender, race and sexuality. Yet, there is a persistent yearning, on the other side of critique, for judgements that are not only deconstructive but also reconstructive. There is, according to Connor (p. 2), a 'necessity of value ... the irreducible orientation towards the better'. John Fekete (1987: i) has made a similar observation, somewhat less elegantly: 'we live, breathe and excrete values'. Connor deals with questions of value largely via an aesthetically mediated excursus through contemporary theory, taking in poststructuralism and deconstruction, discourse ethics and Marxism along the way, to no particularly useful conclusion. In the end, he remarks that 'the quickening predicament of value' escapes theorising (1992: 255).

There are a couple of fairly obvious reasons for this failure of theory. First, it is in the nature of the beast, especially *aesthetic* value, to remain comparatively undecidable, to which point I shall return. Second, a purely theoretical discourse on the sociality of value, for that is what is at stake, compares unfavourably, in practice, with the concretely sociological approach of a Bourdieu. To a great extent, questions of value in social circulation are best treated as empirical questions, as matters of research, not just abstract theorising. It is my own feeling that the field of global *popular* culture itself, quite apart from its still problematical relations with 'legitimate' culture, albeit much less hierarchical and demarcated than in the past, operates a complex range of distinction strategies to do with the construction of identities in which class is only one of a number of determinations and, also, in which evaluative judgement as to quality is routine and unexceptional. Paul Willis's (1990a) concepts of 'symbolic creativity' and 'grounded aesthetics', as common features of everyday life, already capture something of this process.

John Frow (1995) has sought to clarify and resolve some of the issues at stake with his concept of 'regimes of value', on the model of Foucault's 'regimes of truth'. For Frow, value has been irrevocably relativised: no longer can, for instance, 'high culture' be held superior to 'popular culture' and no longer can, say, European culture present itself as 'universal'. In Lyotard's (1984) influential and simplifying use of Wittgenstein, 'forms of life' are utterly incommensurate with one another and the 'language games' we play are radically different from those of others. Following such relativistic reasoning, Frow (1995: 144) formulates the concept of 'the *regime of value*, a semiotic institution generating evaluative regularities under certain conditions of use, and in which particular empirical audiences or communities may be more or less fully imbricated'. Such regimes of value may clash with one another in relations of unequal power, as in the public reappropriation of privatised space signified by graffiti-writing which is viewed from above by public officials as criminal 'defilement' and, then, perhaps fetishised by an *avant-garde* art establishment as yet another commodifiable aesthetic. Uncertainty regarding value, moreover, poses enormous problems of cultural policy:

> Given the fact (if this is conceded) of incommensurability between different regimes of value, and given the intense social interests that play around these fractures and asymmetries, how is it possible for judgements of value to be applied in the routine and everyday manner required by school and university curricula, by editorial decision-making, by decisions about arts funding and research funding, and about the exhibition of artefacts?
>
> (Frow, 1995: 154)

A real danger, certainly from a critical perspective, is to fall silent about questions of value as a result of extreme relativism, typically in negation of conservative and absolutist positions, because such questions are thus thought to be somehow tainted. There are two initial ways out of this trap, both of which are consistent with Frow's discussion of 'regimes of value'. The first is really rather common-sensical and none the worse for it. This is that a cultural performance may be deemed 'good' or 'bad' of its kind, that is, within its own discursive field. Such an assumption dispenses finally with the dogma that different kinds of culture, say, Literature with a capital L and television, are inherently superior or inferior media forms. It also opens up the possibility of value debate and discussion as to quality across the whole spectrum of the cultural field. The second point, and closely connected to the first, is the assumption that value and quality are also multiple and variable in relation to specific media, forms and socio-cultural contexts. There is no gold standard that applies to all cultural currency: value is various and variously contestable across different positions, though there may be more scope for communicating across different positions than is imagined by extreme relativism.

That an 'illegitimate' medium, in Bourdieu's terminology, might be viewed according to a number of different ways of conceiving value can be illustrated with reference to Geoff Mulgan's (1994) discussion of the qualities of television. According to Mulgan (p. 88), the question of quality is exceptionally complex and, '[l]ike all modern social issues it is reflexive – bound up with social self-understanding and misunderstanding'. He identifies no less than seven conceptions of quality in policy discourses around television. First, there is 'producer quality and professionalism'. This is tied up with a professional craft idea that there are general skills in making good television programmes irrespective of the genre. It also, especially under public service arrangements, marks the space of 'creative freedom' for producers, directors, camera personnel, recording engineers, writers and designers. Second, there is 'consumer quality and the market'. It is, in many respects, opposed to producer quality and is founded upon the notion of 'consumer sovereignty', which may be evinced by audience members or, more likely, by new production entrants to the television market, particularly in conditions where the old public service ethos is under attack. Third, there is 'quality of the medium – television's aesthetic'. There is a tradition of seeing television as solely a mediator of other cultural forms. This is challenged by the view that television has developed distinctive modes of representation in its own right that require medium-specific appreciation. Mulgan (pp. 101–102), however, notes Bourdieu's argument that the 'popular aesthetic', normally associated with mass media like television, is inimical to the formulation of evaluative criteria, thereby eliminating the possibility of a specifically televisual aesthetic. It is not feasible, on strictly Bourdieuan grounds, to bring television within the 'pure gaze' of 'disinterested' aesthetics. None the less, the claim that the specificity of the medium has to be accounted for, in my opinion, is a strong one. Fourth, there is 'television as ritual and communion'. This plays on the semantic relationship between 'communication' and 'community'. The near universality of television-viewing provides good reason for seeing it as a distinctly democratising medium. Fifth, there is 'television and the person'. This has close connections with 'ritual and communion' but begins from the point of view of the individual conceived of as a citizen with rights of access to the cultural goods that television distributes. Sixth, there is the 'television ecology', often invoked during periods of institutional change when it is likely that an 'imbalance' in the system might be brought about by, for example, commercial entertainment eliminating public service information and education. Mulgan is unhappy with the metaphors of 'pathology' that are sometimes deployed by this discourse but he sees value in its idea that 'truth needs to be protected from falsehood and that television, like all the media, must play its part in sustaining truth and bearing witness' (p. 110). Seventh, there is 'quality as diversity'. This recognises that there are 'minority' as well as 'majority' tastes and interests; and it is right that these should be provided for, which must be a matter of deliberate policy and not only of market forces. This final idea also inscribes within it a sense of multiplicity and 'many different levels' essential to any serious consideration of such an important medium as television.

Mulgan's discussion of the 'qualities' of television indicates how ethical questions, which are also political questions, are integrally related to cultural value. Questions of cultural value are not only confined to the aesthetic. This is similar to the conclusion that Terry Eagleton arrives at in his history of (Western bourgeois) aesthetics, *The Ideology of the Aesthetic* (1990). Eagleton radically historicises the aesthetic as a philosophical category and locates it on the bodily expressive as opposed to the economically instrumentalist side of capitalism's ideological coin. For him, it is a contradictory category, at once 'a vision of human energies as radical ends in themselves which is the implacable enemy of all dominative or instrumentalist thought' and possessing a powerful sense of 'concrete particularity' whilst, at the same time, representing 'a specious form of universalism' (p. 9). Eagleton has no greater sympathy for the mystificatory claims of 'disinterested' purity that have traditionally been made on behalf of bourgeois aesthetic sensibility than does Bourdieu. Yet, differently from Bourdieu, he finds values worth retrieving from this tradition that are consonant with Habermas's discourse ethics:

> The aesthetic began with Baumgarten as a modest assertion of the claims of the *Lebenswelt* upon an abstract reason; and it is just this project, now inflected as a radical critique of capitalist society, which Jürgen Habermas takes up in our own time. What has come about in the later development of capitalist society, so Habermas argues, is a progressive conflict between 'system' and 'life-world', as the former penetrates more and more deeply into the latter, reorganizing its practices in accordance with its own rationalizing, bureaucratizing logic. As these anonymous political and economic structures invade and colonize the life-world, they begin to instrumentalize forms of human activity which require for their effective operation a rationality of a quite different kind: a 'communicative rationality' which involves practical and moral agencies, democratic and participatory processes, and the resources of cultural tradition. Such a rationality, bound up as it is with subjectivity, cultural know-how and the sphere of the affective, will never submit without a struggle to such remorseless systematization; and in imposing its own alien logic upon it, late capitalism risks eroding some of the very cultural resources essential to its own legitimation.
>
> (1990: 401)

Habermas's own work, often criticised for being ultra-rational and detached from the actual flow of everyday life, depends upon a conception of ordinary human resource that underpins, if not necessarily founds, in the sense of philosophical foundationalism, the possibility of a 'communicative rationality' that has a distinctively aesthetic dimension. As he says with crystal clarity in *Moral Consciousness and Communicative Action*, 'Everyday communication makes possible a kind of understanding that is based on claims to validity and thus furnishes the only real alternative to exerting influence on one another in more or less coercive ways' (Habermas, 1990: 19). Built into mundane conversation and social interaction is the taken-for-granted assumption that we can make sense with one another and that we are sincere in what we communicate. Claims are made routinely concerning 'truth', 'rightness' and 'truthfulness' that facilitate sense-making. Truth claims are to do with statements of 'objective' value and are related to cognitive knowledge and, at a certain level, scientificity. Claims to 'rightness' are moral claims; and, 'truthfulness' claims sincerity. Validity claims of the three different orders, objective, intersubjective and subjective, are each supportable by reasons and, in principle, open to critical interrogation. Such communicative rationality at least enables mutual understanding though not necessarily agreement. How does all this relate to cultural value? To quote Habermas:

> [C]ultural values . . . transcend de facto behaviour. They congeal into historical and biographical syndromes of value orientations through which subjects can distinguish the good life from the reproduction of mere life. But ideas of the good life are not something we hold before us as an abstract 'ought'. Rather, they shape the identity of groups and individuals in such a way that they form an intrinsic part of culture or personality. Thus the development of the moral point of view goes hand in hand with a differentiation within the practical into *moral questions* and *evaluative questions*. Moral questions can in principle be decided rationally, i.e., in terms of *justice* or the generalizability of interests. Evaluative questions present themselves at the most general level as issues of the *good life* (or of self-realization); they are accessible to rational discussion only *within* the unproblematic horizon of a concrete historical form of life or the conduct of an individual life.
>
> (1990: 108)

What Habermas is saying here, amongst other things, is that value judgements are historically and culturally specific, related to particular forms of life; and, in a general sense, dependent upon social agreement, consensus, if they are to have more than eccentric meaning. But, even then, especially in the field of aesthetics, it is difficult and unnecessary to apply the most rigorous criteria of argumentation, perhaps more than anything because it causes greater harm to make people all agree, for example, that a work of art is good or bad than it does to permit differences of opinion to exist and be debated. One can readily think of a number of historical circumstances and atrocious incidents that would provide evidential support for such a view. There is still a huge and mistaken temptation, however, to claim that artistic 'truth' is a demonstrable phenomenon in the Kantian sense, as in Albrecht Wellmer's (1991) version of this continuing pursuit of the philosopher's aesthetic stone, influenced rather more by Adorno than by Habermas, who has tended to dodge detailed questions of aesthetic judgement. Wellmer says:

> [I]t is reasonable to suppose that the truth of art will have more to do with a *potential* for truth in works of art than with truth in the

literal sense . . . . There is something about art which leads us to view works of art themselves – or at least many of them – as vehicles of truth-*claims*; and these claims to truth that are made by works of art are connected with their *aesthetic* claim to validity.

(1991: 24)

However residually tempting, albeit questionable, is the idea of aesthetic *truth*, *truthfulness* is another and, arguably, much more serious matter. John Mepham's (1991) 'rules' of 'quality' in television, covering social diversity and cultural usability, emphasise the normative framework of an 'ethic of truth-telling': *'It is precisely because there is no Truth, no guaranteed foundation of true principles which could act as a criterion of truth, no certainty derived from access to reality independently from our research and its instruments, that an ethic of truth-telling is essential'* (p. 26). Such an ethic of truthfulness is formulated in historical conditions where there is serious doubt concerning the good intentions of those in power over the most popular medium of information and entertainment in the world. It is perhaps too limited for dealing with aspects of pleasurable television-viewing that may not have much if anything at all to do with truthfulness, never mind truth. However, one can see readily how an ethic of truthfulness might function as a professional ethic and a standard of criticism, obviously in the case of news and 'factual' television, but not irrelevant to other forms, especially representations of 'otherness' in fiction and entertainment. Moreover, it is consistent with a critical and questioning attitude to culture and politics that always has policy value under conditions of genuinely open debate and which is neatly summed up in Simon Frith and Jon Savage's distinction between cultures of 'self-satisfaction' and 'dissatisfaction' with prevailing ways of art and life that do not seem to have been all that much affected by collapsing hierarchies and blurring boundaries:

> Current arguments about popular culture rely on a series of dichotomies: the ordinary versus the elite, the journalist/media worker versus the academic, the conservative versus the progressive. We would summarize all such dichotomies under a more general heading: the culture of self-satisfaction versus the culture of the dissatisfied. From the dissatisfaction position the argument always has to be that life could be different, could be better, could be changed – both art and education rest on such premises; they are meant to make us see things differently. They are designed to show us through the imagination, through reason, the limitations of our perspectives, to doubt our common sense.

(1993: 115)

The culture of dissatisfaction is the perpetual bugbear of any official cultural policy: the very officialness of governmental policy, in effect, makes it conservative, the upholder of the status quo, from the point of view of a restless dissatisfaction with the way things are presently constituted. However, there is a considerable difference between open and closed forms of cultural policy-making. The new ideas and most important issues are always engendered by a sense of dissatisfaction coming from outside the currently official system. Official institutions and practices of cultural policy are like authoritarian states ultimately doomed when they are closed to the constant pressures exerted by cultural dissatisfaction. At the very least, it can be said, they are insufficiently reflexive about what they do. Scott Lash (1993b) argues that a feature of late- or post-modernity is a ubiquitous aesthetic *reflexivity*, which is most commonly understood as the aestheticisation of everyday life and is characterised by a popular awareness of social and semiotic contingency. Furthermore, one can add, reflexivity, and, especially, a critical reflexivity, refuses to take prevailing social and cultural conditions for granted as somehow naturally given: they are perpetually being put into question.

3

FROM STATE TO MARKET

The times they are a-changin'.

Bob Dylan

Since the 1970s there has been a general shift rhetorically and in organisational practice from state to market regulation of social and cultural life. This is evident not only in the rejection of command economics in the former communist states but also in the move away from demand-management economics in liberal-democratic societies where, in the middle decades of the twentieth century, governments had sought to plan production, distribution, exchange and consumption in a more or less comprehensive fashion, through either measures of public ownership and provision or extensive rules and regulations pertaining to the private sector of industry and finance. The political claim was made that by freeing market forces a more satisfactory means of general regulation which met the needs of the citizen as customer with greater effectiveness would be achieved, although normally the word 'de-regulation' has been used to refer to such withdrawal of direct state intervention from various parts of civil society. The accelerated globalisation of an already highly internationalised economy seemed, in addition, to substantiate the view that the role of the nation-state should be limited as a matter of elementary realism. These familiar trends tell us little enough in themselves without some comprehension of why they have come about. Undoubtedly, the crisis of the world economy in the 1970s and what became known as 'the fiscal crisis of the state' created favourable conditions for a switch to the market-oriented politics of the New Right, offering old-new solutions to a number of chronic problems. The precipitate decline of a still historically quite novel Fordist system of mass production and consumption in the advanced industrial nation-states and response strategies for accomplishing a much more flexible 'post-Fordist' regime of accumulation, particularly with the aid of micro-electronic and computing technologies, further accentuated the dramatic changes of recent decades.

In the 1970s, Jürgen Habermas (1976) was quick to identify an emerging 'legitimation crisis' of 'the social-welfare state', partly associated with issues of economic management and public administration but also exacerbated

51

by a 'motivational crisis' whereby the system was producing people with attitudes and values, in effect, inimical to the system. While 'the system' of consumer capitalism and welfare protection had, up to a point, produced a politically apathetic 'civic privatism' in everyday life which was pacific, it had simultaneously generated a crisis of rising expectations and a counter-culture, especially amongst the young, that challenged privatised existence and labour discipline. Resuming his discussion of these issues at a later date, Habermas made an interesting observation concerning the cultural policy implications of the New Right solutions to problems of social organization:

> [C]ultural policy is assigned the task of operating on two fronts. On the one hand, it is to discredit intellectuals as the standard bearers of modernism, at once obsessed with power and unproductive; for postmaterialist values, especially expressive needs for self-realization and the critical judgements of a universalist Enlightenment morality, are seen as a threat to the motivational bases of a functioning society of social labour and a depoliticized public sphere. On the other hand, traditional culture and the stabilizing forces of conventional morality, patriotism, bourgeois religion, and folk culture are to be cultivated. Their function is to compensate the private lifeworld for personal burdens and to cushion it against the pressures of a competitive society and accelerated modernization.
>
> (1989: 61)

Habermas's observation is percipient but it does not register the para-mount role of 'the market' in cultural policy discourse for the New Right. To identify the attack on modernist intellectuals who display the wrong kind of motivational structures is accurate and the return, in certain respects, to cultural traditionalism is evidently so. Moreover, this latter point enables us to make sense of the persistence of state intervention in the cultural field and public subsidy for 'the arts' in spite of pressures towards privatisation and the free play of market forces that might have been expected to result in the total abolition of state-sponsored culture had the economic extremists of the New Right had their way entirely. What Habermas fails to register, though, is the power of 'the market' as an idea and also, particularly in broadcasting, its material representation of profitable interests. There is much to be said about the comparative diminution of the public sector in the communication and cultural industries generally. However, in this chapter, the emphasis is placed instead specifically upon a discursive shift from 'state' to 'market' *within* the public sector. This, in itself, is such a striking phenomenon that it merits close attention.

The construction of a new common sense is always a fascinating occurrence. That so many taken-for-granted assumptions of life in the post-Second World War 'social-welfare state' should have been so suddenly swept aside and replaced by a pervasive *market reasoning* is truly remarkable. In general and in many particular ways, there has been a shift from rhetorics of state intervention and public provision to rhetorics of market forces and consumer sovereignty. Explicating Michel Foucault's essay 'The Order of Discourse', Robert Young (1981: 48) has said that the effect of certain discourses is 'to make it virtually impossible to think outside of them'. Although Foucault (1981b) himself observed that 'societies of discourse' are ancient, represented by poets and storytellers in an oral culture, they also function under modern conditions of literacy and 'truth'. There are discourse control procedures for what can be legitimately thought and enunciated: exclusion procedures that mark the boundaries of a discourse, defining that which is permissible and impermissible to say; internal procedures that regulate the distinctive operations of a discourse; and access procedures that regulate entry to a discursive field. Where once was 'the state' there is now 'the market' in discussion of cultural policy. In order to make sense of this discursive shift and its practical consequences, the present chapter aims to reconstruct how the liberal-democratic state, in the case of Britain, became a modern patron of the arts and sponsor of culture before examining how the state was 'rolled back' discursively so that market reasoning became the prevailing discourse even in what was left of the public sector.

CULTIVATING THE MASSES

Although this chapter is principally concerned with the reversal of significatory value in a couplet of linked and frequently occluded binary oppositions, so that 'the market' negates 'the state' and 'the private' negates 'the public', it has to be said that in any reasonably long-term view of modernity the state has become increasingly expansive and has taken on the role of representing a public that was originally formed self-consciously to resist and wrest power from it. As Stuart Hall (1986: 26) notes acutely: 'The eighteenth-century state had no regular police, no standing army, and was based on a highly restrictive male franchise. The nineteenth-century state owned no industries, supervised no universal system of education, was not responsible for national economic policy or a network of welfare provisions.'

The powers of the nation-state, democratic and undemocratic, survive, if not necessarily intact, in spite of economic and culturally globalising, localising and privatising trends to the contrary; and individuals are still caught up in a web of state relations from 'the cradle to the grave', especially in the wealthier liberal democracies. However, as Hall says, it is mistaken to see the growth of the nation-state and its cultural interventions as a smoothly unfolding historical and teleological process prior to the late-twentieth-century project of reversing the modern trend. The role of the modern state has always been a massively contested one, not least regarding how boundaries are drawn and redrawn routinely between the public and private, where it is deemed the state should be and where it should not be at any particular time. During the nineteenth century, the alternative programmes of *étatist* and *laissez-faire* philosophies, in the form of political economy, clashed just as bitterly as the latter-day assault of Thatcherism upon social democracy.

The present system of state intervention and public subsidy of culture in Britain represents a complex mosaic of elements that have emerged and become sedimented together over the past century and a half.[1] It was as recently as 1992 that Britain eventually acquired for the first time a generic ministry of culture responsible for the whole field in some ill-defined sense, the Department of National Heritage. In comprehensiveness and scale of funding, the British system remains comparatively modest by Western European standards (Feist and Hutchison, 1990). It would probably be mistaken to exaggerate the greater coherence and rationality of, say, French national institutions or German regional institutions of cultural policy. Nevertheless, the intricacies of the British system defy simple summary and, besides, it would be pointless to merely describe the various elements in a book mainly concerned with the theoretical aspects of cultural policy. Rather more to the point is to identify the ways in which state intervention and cultural subsidy in Britain have been rationalised and revised historically, to be done through brief consideration of a series of discursive moments that may be labelled as follows: *social control* (from mid-nineteenth century to mid-twentieth century), *national prestige* (from 1940s to early 1960s), *social access* (mid-1960s to late 1970s), *value for money*, characterised by an increasingly pervasive *market reasoning* and *managerialist rhetoric* (late 1970s to the present and foreseeable future).

This chapter is not overly concerned with the tortuous distinctions that are made between 'art' and 'media' and between them and the more diffusely 'cultural'. I am interested here, principally, in clarifying the rationales and shifting discourses of 'public arts patronage' and, to a lesser extent, 'public service broadcasting', which needs also to be treated within the same context because of the institutional and ideological affinities that this 'odd couple' have had with one another. The most obvious difference, however, between public patronage of the arts and public service broadcasting is that the latter is only rationalised marginally on grounds of 'market failure', for culturally valued yet comparatively uncommercial genres of programming. A persistent feature of public arts patronage, through the various discourses under consideration, is the legitimating assumption that preservation and reproduction of classical art forms are not viable in a purely commercial market, that, for instance, grand opera or Shakespearian theatre depend upon subsidy for their very existence. Hard-line free marketeers dispute even this assumption. Yet, in actual fact, public subsidy for art and culture is not and never has been rationalised solely or even predominantly on grounds of market failure.

Nineteenth-century debates on state funding of museums, galleries, libraries and art education, all major public institutions that arose to prominence in the mid-century period, were framed largely by a discourse of *social control*, a discourse which was to an extent in contest with the generalised *laissez-faire* ideology of the time. These institutions were expected to cultivate the masses, to bring them up to a higher level of civilization. The political object, frequently stated with candour, was to contain class struggle and secure civil order. For example, at the height of agitation for parliamentary reform in 1832, Robert Peel, founder of the Metropolitan Police Force and future Tory Prime Minister, expressed this view during the House of Commons debate on whether a new building for the recently founded National Gallery should be sited in Trafalgar Square, a favourite place for public demonstrations of disaffection: 'In the present time of political excitement, the exacerbation of angry and unsocial feelings might be much softened by the effect which the fine arts have ever produced on the minds of men' (quoted by Minihan, 1977: 56).

The most sophisticated and far-reaching enunciation of the social control through culture discourse, in the mid-nineteenth century, was that of Matthew Arnold, critic, poet and schools inspector. Arnold was forever lecturing the Victorian bourgeoisie on the efficacy of social control through 'Culture' with a capital C in order to restrain 'Anarchy'. It is well known that his book *Culture and Anarchy*, originally published in 1869, was written in response to the Hyde Park Riot following the failure of the 1867 Reform Bill (Williams, 1980), but it is less well known that this was already a major preoccupation of Matthew Arnold. In 1861, Arnold's prefatory essay on 'Democracy' in *The Popular Education of France* stated the issue bluntly: 'Our society is probably destined to become much more democratic; who or what will give a high tone to the nation then? That is the grave question' (1970: 113). He went on to urge the businessmen whom he was addressing to 'seek the alliance of the State for their own elevation' and stop 'exaggerating their spirit of individualism' (p. 121). They should overcome their own Philistinism and assume the role of 'natural educators and initiators' of a soon-to-be emancipated working class (p. 122). Arnold, in spite of or perhaps because of his hard-nosed political attitude, became the cultural prophet of enlightened liberalism and nascent social democracy. He proposed a series of quite specific cultural policies that were subsequently implemented: for instance, the introduction of poetry into elementary schooling and the spread of English literary education generally, as well as initiating the lengthy campaign for a National Theatre. The public service precepts of the Reithian BBC can also be traced back to Arnold, although in this and other respects his voice was hardly an isolated one: it was, however, the most celebrated voice advocating state intervention in the cultural field against the free marketeers of nineteenth-century Britain.

By the time the British Broadcasting Corporation was established, the issue of enculturing the masses had become yet more urgent since they had then acquired the vote. It is unnecessary to recount in detail the story of how the BBC was incorporated into the state through Royal Charter in 1927, within five years of its original foundation as a private monopoly. The official version depends heavily on avoidance of the 'bad' example set by the USA's apparently chaotic system of commercial radio and the technical limitations of the airwaves. The BBC's equation of 'the national interest', represented by Baldwin's Conservative government, with 'the public interest' during the 1926 General Strike, and against the strikers, demonstrated its usefulness as an appendage to the state. This was not, however, dictated in a narrowly political sense, contrary to Home Secretary Winston Churchill's wishes. The first Director General, John Reith, sought to give substance to the BBC's much vaunted yet frequently abused independence from direct governmental control. Reith had an agenda for the BBC which he extolled successfully, as it turned out, in his book of 1924, *Broadcast Over Britain*. He saw the BBC as an institution for cultural enlightenment, a bulwark against the baleful influence of commercial entertainment, and for political education also, with the task of enabling a newly enfranchised general public to exercise their citizenship rights responsibly instead of allowing their hearts and minds to be captured by the evil forces of either Bolshevism or Fascism.

Paddy Scannell (1984) has shown how the Reithian BBC, in the pre-Second World War years, established itself as the leading institution of the Great British nation's culture. Localism and regionalism were neglected in order to construct a national audience. A sense of national identity was also fostered symbolically and ritually through the broadcasting of popular events such as, in sport, the Grand National and the FA Cup Final. The BBC aligned itself with the Royal Family, broadcasting the monarch's Christmas Day speech from the early 1930s onwards, with a mutually prestige-enhancing effect. The BBC addressed 'the family' and knitted together the public world of great events with the private circumstances of ordinary people in their daily lives. This British institution of public service broadcasting, then, wholly owned and regulated by the state for thirty years, until its modification in the 1950s with the advent of advertising-funded television, including the crucial wartime years when the BBC's reputation soared internationally, established routinely shared listening and viewing habits and the reality of a universally available diet of fairly diverse programmes, not all of them by any means 'serious' even under Reith in the 1930s (Frith, 1983; Scannell, 1989).

The BBC did, of course, actively promote 'serious culture' with broadcasts of classical music and drama in particular. This was an important contextualisation for the foundation of a permanent Arts Council of Great Britain at the end of the Second World War, succeeding the temporary wartime organisation, the Council for the Encouragement of Music and the Arts (CEMA), which had at first been funded privately by an American philanthropic millionaire in 1940. John Maynard Keynes, the economist, in his broadcast talk on the founding of the Arts Council in July 1945 (the text of which was printed in *The Times* on 12 July), remarked that during the war a wider audience for the arts had been discovered by CEMA through its touring operations, an audience that had already been cultivated by the BBC. No longer was state cultural intervention touted in terms of social control either explicitly or implicitly: the stress now was on *national prestige*. Nor was the state simply responding to a spontaneous need through agencies like the BBC and the Arts Council. Instead, the architects of the mid-century policies articulated a sense of constructive advance towards a more cultured nation with a set of state-sponsored alternatives to Hollywood and Tinpan Alley. No doubt, at some subterranean level, this was a compensation for Britain's declining economic and political power in the world.

The Keynesian legacy to public arts patronage in Britain, for Keynes died in 1946, is nicely exemplified by the pivotal task of retrieving the opera house in Covent Garden from its wartime function as a Mecca dance hall. As chair of the Covent Garden Trust as well as CEMA, Keynes secured a Treasury grant to renovate the auditorium; and, as it transpired, he effectively committed the new Arts Council to permanently heavy expenditure on this embryonic 'centre of excellence'. In her account of that, Janet Minihan (1977: 234) makes the wry observation that 'Keynes must have enjoyed negotiating with himself' since he was also chief economic adviser at the Treasury. Hugh Willatt (1980: 32), Secretary General of the Arts Council in the early 1970s, remarked that the Royal Opera House in Covent Garden was 'essentially a new creation, only possible under post-war conditions'. Considering the enduring significance of this expensive and controversial flagship of state-subsidised culture, it is apposite that Robert Hutchison (1982) should later describe the Arts Council as representative of 'the English Opera Class'.[2] The use of public money to build institutions of national and international prestige in London, serving the tastes not so much of a cultivated mass but of a metropolitan elite, went on virtually unchallenged, during a long period of Conservative government, throughout the 1950s and into the 1960s. Then, in the mid to late 1960s, consequent upon the new policy of Harold Wilson's Labour governments, the Arts Council's grant-in-aid was trebled over five years, during which period most of the Regional Arts Associations were founded, and many arts centres, public repertory theatres and concert halls were built in the English regions, Wales and Scotland, all with the general aim of increasing social and geographical 'access' to the arts.

By this time the BBC monopoly of public service broadcasting had ended with the advent of regional ITV companies in the 1950s. However, these companies, like the BBC itself, were required to observe principles of public service, which eventually they were disciplined into doing, alongside their populist aims: provision had to be universal and programming mixed, including editorially neutral news insulated from commercial pressures (sponsorship, again in response to the 'bad' example of the USA, was strictly forbidden) and a proportion of 'serious' programming had to be included in the schedule. Despite the would-be comprehensive state regulation of commercial broadcasting, an ITV franchise was, in a famous remark, a 'licence to print money' since it brought a monopoly of broadcast advertising revenue within a region. When profits were capped by the Wilson government of the mid-1960s, high production values in expensively made programmes became a hallmark of much British commercial television, as it was also of the BBC, now galvanised by competition from ITV and benefiting still from continuous growth of licence fee revenue with the spread of television set ownership and rental and the introduction of colour television.

In the 1970s, the twin institutions of public service broadcasting and public patronage of the arts were normalised and taken-for-granted features of the cultural landscape. Neither the 'cosy duopoly' of the BBC and ITV, nor the Arts Council and its associated organisations, however, were immune from critical attacks on particular operations and forms of representation. None the less, their general and institutionalised existence was not questioned fundamentally in the prevailing discourses of the time, including the radical ones. They also seemed to represent, even to critics, comparatively adequate solutions to the actual and potential problems of state intervention in an increasingly diverse cultural field. As Raymond Williams (1979) described the Arts Council, in an essentially critical article, it was an 'intermediary body' between the state and civil society, by and large avoiding the pitfalls, on the one side, of direct governmental control over day-to-day practice and, on the other, of the insidious pressures of commercial sponsorship.

Whole swathes of cultural activity were relatively neglected or for the problems of which no adequate policy solution was found, as seen from the perspectives of various interest group lobbies. Cinema in Britain, for instance, had since the 1930s and 1940s been treated primarily as a commercial industry rather than as an art form (Dickinson and Street, 1985). It was protected partially and largely unsuccessfully from American competition by quotas, although tax concessions were made to Hollywood companies during the 1960s to encourage production in Britain, which helped to sustain sophisticated technical capacity and specialist craft skills. Revenue from the Eady Levy on cinema receipts, abolished by the Thatcher government of the mid-1980s, had subsidised investment in production but, in general, the industry tottered repeatedly between recurrent false dawns and ever imminent collapse. The British Film Institute, founded in 1938, was still modestly funded to take a cultural view of cinema but mainly of a minority and specifically educational kind, with its limited remit for art film production and exhibition, film and, only latterly, television appreciation. In comparison with France, public policy for promoting a distinctly national film culture was slight and intermittent (Auty and Roddick, 1985).

The main challenges to the leading institutions of British cultural policy came at first, during the 1970s, from the Left, for instance over questions of 'access' in arts funding and the exclusionary 'consensus' ideology of public service broadcasting. Alternative and oppositional arts practitioners questioned the imbalance of the Arts Council's distribution of funds, which greatly privileged the national institutions in London that had been built up since the Second World War and kept community artists, political theatre groups, cooperative film-makers and the like, very much on the margins of public subsidy, picking up the crumbs (see, for instance, Braden, 1978; Itzin, 1980). For these currents of cultural politics, the discourse of *social access* was pushed to logical conclusions: for example, in the question that was posed frequently, why spend most of the public money on well-heeled audiences for Establishment arts when it would be better and more equitably spent on experimental and popular-participatory activities to the benefit of the less well off? The important point here is that the radical campaigns waged by the "68 generation' were articulated within the intelligible terms of the social-democratic discourse of access which had been forged during the 1960s and had sources going back to the 1930s. Even the case that was made by the Left of the Labour Party in the mid-1970s for elections to the Arts Council from appropriate constituencies instead of governmental appointment of 'the great and the good' to the council and panels had to be taken seriously, at least as debating issues, by the guardians of social-democratic cultural policy, such as Richard Hoggart and the then Arts Council Secretary General, Roy Shaw. Similar themes concerning radical plurality, participatory democracy and generalised cultural egalitarianism fed into the long-run campaign for the final piece in the public service broadcasting jigsaw, Channel Four, which finally came on air in 1982.

ROLLING BACK THE STATE

There has, since the 1970s, been a general turning away from large-scale planning in the capitalist world and, also, away from official legitimation of the whole panoply of entitlements associated with the 'social-welfare state', particularly in those countries that suffered most dramatically from de-industrialisation, such as the USA and Britain. These developments

59

were not just the result of abstract determinations, 'trends that cannot be bucked': there was, in fact, a good deal of political voluntarism involved, best exemplified by Ronald Reagan's two-term tenure of the White House and, in Britain, Margaret Thatcher's eleven years as Conservative Prime Minister, presiding over a series of governments that were committed with intensifying dogmatism, as time went by, to 'rolling back the state' in order to liberate market forces. Thatcherism presented itself as a crusade against socialism, which greatly impressed dissidents in Eastern Europe and encouraged *laissez-faire* conservatives everywhere. The Thatcherite project, inspired by a flood of New Right ideas from the USA and British 'think tanks' (Desai, 1994), was widely seen as the model of 'the capitalist revolution', as Peter Berger (1987) has put it, towards the end of the twentieth century. Much of what Thatcherism attacked was not inherently socialistic, however, although social-democratic politics had indeed played a major part in shaping the consensually agreed assumptions of the social-welfare state in general and its cultural interventions in particular. Governmental planning of economies and welfare measures had been introduced mainly to resolve crisis tendencies of an earlier phase of capitalism. And, quite specifically, it would be absurd to claim that state cultural institutions founded in the first half of the century, such as those already discussed here, the BBC and the Arts Council, were ever in any programmatic sense socialist, though they became, to an extent, rather more tolerant of oppositional forces and open to radical negotiation in the decades preceding the rise of Thatcherism. It is significant, moreover, that they survived the Thatcherite onslaught.

As Andrew Gamble points out, there was a paradox in the Thatcherite project in that it combined advocacy of 'a free economy' with 'a strong state':

The state is to be simultaneously rolled back and rolled forward. Non-interventionist and decentralised in some areas the state is to be highly interventionist and centralised in others. The New Right can appear by turns libertarian and authoritarian, populist and elitist. This ambiguity is not an accident. It derives in part from the fact that the New Right has two major strands: a liberal tendency, which argues the case for a freer, more open and more competitive economy, and a conservative tendency, which is more interested in restoring social and political authority throughout society.

(1994a: 36)

The paradox of Thatcherism and 1980s New Right government in Britain is underscored by the fact that public spending had actually risen in real terms by the early 1990s. Gamble (1994a: 228–229) further observes: 'Few [public-spending] programmes were terminated altogether and few radical solutions were applied.' There was, nevertheless, a certain reallocation of resources from the softer to the harder apparatuses of the state: policing, for instance, did rather better than education in per capita scale of funding. The costs of sustaining chronic levels of long-term unemployment, as the result of industrial 'restructuring' and deflationary fiscal policies, were high. 'Privatisation' or, rather, de-nationalisation measures were implemented, during the 1980s, with the selling off, usually at a knockdown price, of public utilities such as British Telecom, British Gas and British Airways. Further measures, including the privatisation of water supply, pushed the free market project ever onwards.

Margaret Thatcher's third and final term of office, from 1987 until she was so rudely deposed by her own followers in 1990, was characterised most visibly at first by a fickle economic boom, supposedly the fruit of the fierce economic policies of the early 1980s – a boom, however, which suddenly turned into a slump, the enduring consequences of which were inherited by the hapless John Major. That phase of Thatcherism was also characterised, however, by a more obscure, though far-reaching indeed, promotion of 'the new public management', exemplified by the Efficiency Unit's 1989 report on civil service reform, *The Next Steps*. Gamble (1994a: 135) describes this administrative philosophy as 'a set of ideas for managing all institutions in the public sector and involving devices such as internal markets, contracting out, tendering and financial incentives'. The proposal, for instance, that general medical practioners should become fundholders, playing the internal market of the National Health Service, also originally presented in 1989 in a white paper, further indicated the government's firm intention to drive business practices of managerial efficiency and market orientation ruthlessly through the public sector. All this coincided with the incessant promotion of a loud yet diffuse rhetoric of 'enterprise culture' (Keat and Abercrombie, 1991), which was not only about organizational change in both the private and public sectors but also about the cultivation of an 'enterprising self', a personal way of being contrasted with bureaucratic time-serving and vested professional interests in maintaining the status quo of public service.

The new discursive reality traversing the state and state-related institutions of British society can be described as a pervasive '*managerialization*', an ideological discourse, according to John Clarke and Janet Newman (1993: 428), 'which aims to make management the driving force of a competitively successful society'. It is clearly linked to the proliferation of managerial panaceas issuing from the USA during the 1980s (Huczynski, 1993), claiming to offer genuinely novel business solutions to the problems accumulating from the need to adapt organizationally to rapidly changing and confusing market conditions. Such managerial thought is often couched in a language of 'revolution' and, in a peculiarly postmodern reversal, sometimes echoes counter-cultural ideas of the 1960s and even Trotsky on 'permanent revolution', which is the particular stock-in-trade of one of the leading gurus, Tom Peters. His book of 1982, *In Search of Excellence*, written with Robert Waterman, said to be the best-selling management text of all time, famously advocated getting 'close to the customer' and 'loose-tight' structures.

The most profound accomplishment of New Right government in Britain may not be that it literally rolled back the state in order to release the full blast of market forces but, rather, that it inserted the *new managerialism* and *market reasoning* into the state and state-related agencies of the public sector, in effect calling upon organisations that are not themselves private businesses to think and function as though they were. So, for example, there is local management of state secondary schools that wind up competing with one another by marketing themselves enthusiastically to the parents of prospective students and vying for position on the league table like football teams. This is supposed to increase efficiency and serve 'customers' better, which it may do. On the other hand, it might force perfectly good schools out of business that do not market their wares effectively and it could even distract attention from some of the main purposes of universal education.

The sheer extent of this ideological revolution and discursive shift is indicated by how it came to frame the issues for social interests and political tendencies ostensibly opposed to New Right conservatism, manifested in both American Democratic Party and British Labour Party politics. That is the effect of powerful and normalising discourses, 'to make it virtually impossible to think outside of them'. This may be illustrated by a book which, in the early 1990s, became a major codification for new managerialist theory and practice in the public sector on both sides of the Atlantic, David Osborne and Ted Gaebler's *Reinventing Government* (1992). As Chris Painter (1994) has emphasised, *Reinventing Government* is by no means simply a New Right tract, despite the fact that British Conservative politicians took to quoting it liberally. However, Osborne and Gaebler certainly praised the governmental reforms initiated by Thatcherism, for instance putting out local government services for competitive tendering by private firms.

Although Osborne and Gaebler drew on the ideas of management gurus such as Peter Drucker and Tom Peters, their managerial principles, so they say and support with case studies, were inferred mainly from practical experiments conducted by US city governments in response to the 'tax revolts' of the late 1970s and, more broadly, the structural transformations brought about by the emergence of a 'post-industrial' society. Under tight budgetary constraints and faced with radically transformed economic circumstances, governments had to become much more 'enterprising' than they had been during the 'bureaucratic-industrial' era. The 'ten principles' thus adduced are as follows:

Most entrepreneurial governments promote *competition* between service providers. They *empower* citizens by pushing control out of the bureaucracy, into the community. They measure the performance of their agencies, focusing not on inputs but on *outcomes*. They are driven by their goals – their *missions* – not by their rules and regulations. They redefine their clients as *customers* and offer them choices – between schools, between training programs, between housing options. They *prevent* problems before they emerge, rather than simply offering services afterwards. They put their energies into *earning* money, not simply spending it. They *decentralize* authority, embracing participatory management. They prefer *market* mechanisms. And they focus not simply on providing public services, but on *catalyzing* all sectors – public, private, and voluntary – into action to solve their community's problems.

(Osborne and Gaebler, 1992: 19–20)

Although Osborne and Gaebler deny asking for government to be 'run like a business', their ideas undoubtedly originate from the practices of capitalist organisations that were being adopted by city governments. Osborne and Gaebler claim to be sceptical of and largely opposed to the wholesale privatisation of public agencies in order to achieve the political and what they believe are the ultimately non-profit-making aims of government and governance. That, however, further substantiates the main point of my argument here: the public sector has been required increasingly to function pseudo-capitalistically, which is not only an organisational phenomenon but a deeply imbibed ideological phenomenon and one which has had enormous impact on cultural agencies such as the BBC and the network of arts-subsidising bodies. This argument is meant not, necessarily, to detract from the positive effects, as well as the negative effects, that more business-like practices may have on public agencies but, instead, to raise issues of purpose that call into question, in the spirit of democratic debate, the ideological closures of currently prevailing managerial and market-oriented discourses.

During the 1980s, the role of the BBC and public service broadcasting generally became a hot issue in the new broadcasting market of multiplying channels, which was brought about partly by refinements to cable and satellite delivery systems and partly by the hitherto underexploited profit potential of television in Britain[3] and, to a lesser extent, radio. Against the original wishes of the second Thatcher government, the 1986 Peacock Committee decided not to recommend the replacement of the licence fee by advertising. Yet, it did extol the 'consumer sovereignty' virtues of pay-by-channel and pay-by-programme viewing, in addition to speculating about a possible role for the BBC as a kind of Arts Council of the air, funding only 'serious' programmes that might not otherwise be made under purely commercial market conditions. The tension between the mooted Arts Council model and retention of the BBC's universal reach and mixed programming continued to be an unresolved issue into the 1990s (Garnham, 1993b). By 1994, however, it was evident that nothing too transformative was going to happen to the BBC in the immediately foreseeable future that had not already been set in train. The BBC was more 'business-like', exploiting its huge library property of programmes, outsourcing in the independent sector, operating an internal market of producer choice and installing the new managerialism into its adminis-tration, personified by the Armani-suited Director General, John Birt.[4] As in other parts of the public sector, there was resistance or at least bitter complaint by standard-bearers of the pre-Thatcherite ethos. For example, John Tusa, former *Newsnight* presenter and Director of the BBC World Service, complained of what he called 'invasion of the outsiders', meaning the bearers of managerialist and market-oriented theory and practice derived from capitalist business (*Guardian*, 15.6.94).[5]

At the beginning of the 1980s, the mainstream social-democratic faction was coming to the end of its tutelage of public arts patronage, having recently succeeded in stemming the tide of the cultural Left. Arts Council grants to political theatre groups were ceasing to be renewed and com-munity arts were devolved to the Regional Arts Associations. The cultural Left, however, was not routed. Under Conservative central government, during the 1980s, the main site of oppositional activity in the public sector moved from national to local and regional levels, exemplified particularly by the 1981–6 Greater London Labour Council's policies for the arts, recreation and 'the cultural industries' (Bianchini, 1987). Most notably, the model of continental European-style civic culture became an ideal of the social-democratic Left during the long years of Thatcherism and beyond (see chapter 5).

Subsequent developments in the arts, as throughout the public sector, were very much marked by the discourse of *value for money* in response to the challenge of 'market forces' and threatened 'privatisation'. The 1976–7 Arts Council annual report was actually entitled 'Value for Money'. Labour Chancellor of the Exchequer Denis Healey had recently, in effect, introduced monetarism into Britain. In order to secure a loan from the IMF, so as to stem a sterling crisis, Healey had to agree to making public spending cutbacks. That was the context in which the Arts Council was starting to be defended with the argument that 'the arts provide an essential service to the community', similarly to the educational and health services. The cultural budget was a manifestly soft target for reducing public expen-diture.

Since the late 1970s, pundits on the Right like the novelist Kingsley Amis and the journalist Paul Johnson had been canvassing the idea of abolishing the Arts Council. Johnson complained that it was 'a mysterious and baroque institution' which did not serve popular tastes (*Evening Standard*, London, 26.6.79). Amis (1980) wrote a pamphlet for a Conservative think tank putting the 'consumer sovereignty' argument against public arts patronage more fulsomely and, in so doing, he echoed left-wing arguments that it only really subsidised the tastes of the well-off and highly educated in any case. Between them, Amis and Johnson were, in effect, fusing together populist criticism of the Arts Council for supporting obscure modernist and politically motivated work with an elitist disdain for the failed social-democratic attempt to disseminate 'serious' culture to the masses. However, successive Conservative governments, from 1979 to the 1990s, never endorsed the extremist line of privatising the publicly subsidised arts. Instead, of much greater significance was a series of measures to curtail local government and to impose capitalistic values across the public sector, with important consequences for the arts and culture as well as other areas of governmentality. In the mid-1980s, central government abolished a whole tier of regional government, the Metropolitan County Councils and the Greater London Council. The Arts Council's grant-in-aid was increased to make up for the shortfall resulting from the end of those authorities' funding of art and culture in the regions and especially in London. Non-elected bodies, 'quangos', were also formed to substitute for the strategic role of the abolished councils. In effect, the Arts Council's power under Thatcherism was, at first for a few years, enhanced rather than diminished, against many expectations. A major devolution, however, was subsequently to occur of much Arts Council funding and responsibility to the newly formed Regional Arts Boards, replacing the old Regional Arts Associations, at the beginning of the 1990s, on the recommendation of the Wilding Report (1989), followed in 1994 by the separation of the Arts Councils for Scotland and Wales from the Arts Council of England. The role of the Arts Council, no longer of 'Great Britain', and similar bodies, such as the Sports Council, had already been cast into doubt by the founding of the Department of National Heritage after John Major's 1992 general election victory. And when the National Lottery was introduced towards the end of 1994, becoming instantly very lucrative, public arts organisations were torn between optimism at the prospect of more money for infrastructural expenditure and a pessimistic anticipation that gambling loot rather than general taxation would eventually become the main source of their revenue funding as well.[6]

This was a period of considerable uncertainty and unevenness of change. No simple switch from one way of doing and rationalising cultural policy to a completely different one happened. Contrary principles vied with one another, frequently resulting in contradictory and sometimes thoroughly incoherent compromise solutions. That can be seen as late as 1993 in the Arts Council's *A Creative Future*, a policy prospectus which was meant to summarise the findings of a series of discussion papers, many of them incisive analyses of various strategic aspects of the arts and media, and organised debates around England. The outcome was, however, an anodyne combination of residually public-spirited good intentions and a normalised market 'realism'. To understand how this amalgam came about, it is necessary to recall the 1984 Arts Council policy document *The Glory of the Garden*, which simultaneously announced an expansion of activities in the regions, to finally ameliorate the scandal of metropolitan advantage, and evidenced a reluctance to seek any increase at all of public money in order to fund it. There was an underlying logic to this, the logic of achieving better 'value for money', what Osborne and Gaebler (1992: 35) call 'squeezing more bang out of every buck'. *The Glory of the Garden* announced the device of 'challenge funding', subsequently renamed in the rhetoric 'incentive funding' (Luce, 1987). Arts organisations were obliged to seek joint funding, augmenting Arts Council and local authority grants with business sponsorship, or else public subsidy would be denied them. The discourse of value for money really came into its own during the mid-1980s, functioning like earlier dominant discourses, particularly that of social-democratic 'access', to frame the terms of debate across the political spectrum of mainstream positions. In a speech at IBM's South Bank headquarters, the Arts Council's then chair, ex-editor of *The Times* and failed Tory politician William Rees-Mogg, outlined his syllogism concerning public arts patronage as a necessary form of economic investment:

> In 1984–85, the year just ending, the Arts Council grant of £100m was used to finance some £250m of arts turnover. The £250m includes some vital local authority support, some private funding and over £100m from the box office. Approximately £200m of the £250m was spent in salaries. That means that about 25,000 jobs were provided – the Arts Council gives the best value for money in job creation of any part of the state system – though of course many more than that were employed in the subsidised arts for part of the year. They paid some £60m in national insurance contributions and taxes. On the £100m of box office receipts £15m of VAT was paid, making a return of £75m in direct revenue to the Exchequer.
>
> The 25,000 jobs must be regarded as an addition to jobs that would otherwise have existed; unemployment in the arts is so high, and in general unemployment is so high, that it is probable that at least 20,000 would otherwise have been receiving unemployment and supplementary benefit, at a cost of some £50 million. Thus, with no resort to concepts such as the Keynesian multiplier, the actual cost to the Exchequer of not subsidising the arts by £100m would have been £75m of lost revenue and £50m of additional expenditure. The PSBR would have gone up by £25m if the Arts Council had not received a penny.
>
> (1985: 3)

On a television programme about arts funding that year, the then Director of the National Theatre, Peter Hall, who was representing himself at
the time as the implacable enemy of Conservative governmental meanness
and Rees-Mogg as its agent, demonstrated that he had also learnt to speak
the language of value for money: 'The word "subsidy" is wrong. It should
be called "investment"' (*Newsnight*, BBC2, 18.3.85). Economic arguments
for arts 'investment' were further supported by the researches of John
Myerscough (1988), particularly influencing Labour-controlled local
governments that were desperate to achieve urban regeneration in conditions of de-industrialisation. The debate continued, however, with the
right-wing think tanks over this latter-day cultural Keynesianism. The
Adam Smith Institute (1989) persisted with the claim that public subsidy
distorted what should be a competitive market and avoided taking seriously
the fundamental arbiter in matters of taste, as in all other things, namely
consumer choice. In November 1985, the Arts Council published *A Great
British Success Story*, subtitled 'An Invitation to the Nation to Invest in
the Arts'. The significance of this particular document is not so much to
do with any concrete proposals that were put forward but, instead, its
style of presentation, a style that was to become a normalised feature of
public sector discourse. *A Great British Success Story* presented the case
for public expenditure on the arts in the form of a glossy, multi-coloured
company prospectus, addressing a fictionalised investor seeking a good
return on share capital. As well as the business-like presentation, a pro-
miscuous array of arguments was marshalled for spending taxes on the
arts: increasing employment, regenerating inner cities, vitalising the entertainment industry, raising the nation's prestige, attracting tourist revenue,
giving pleasure – all of which was knitted together by the value for money
discourse. The extraordinary bottom-line argument of *A Great British
Success Story* was that arts investment could solve the problems of the
British economy: 'the government could do no better than put our money
into the arts' (p. 11).

MARKETISING ART AND KNOWLEDGE

The new managerialism in the public sector of art and culture sets great
store by markets and marketing. This was normalised to a remarkable
degree in a short space of time, having superseded the domain assumption
which preceded it that arts subsidy or library provision, for instance,
represent alternative modes to the supply of cultural goods through markets. State-funded cultural goods have become *marketised* to such an extent
that their circulation resembles that of the non-state sector, the 'private'
market of cultural commodities. Such a development constitutes a strand
in the larger process of commodification, whereby all value is ultimately
reduced to exchange value. However, 'marketisation', as it is used here, is

not strictly speaking to be subsumed under the concept of commodification since the important point is to do with *resemblance* rather than *identity*. Insofar as the state continues to hold some responsibility for cultural provision through the collection and disbursement of tax revenue, it is acting differently from the operations of a 'free market', however mythological an entity that itself may be. Whatever rhetoric is deployed, the rationales for state intervention in the cultural field, other than simply to facilitate the smooth functioning of the capitalist market, are not the same as those of a 'free market' where profitability is the fundamental and, when the chips are down, only goal. For anyone who believes that the democratic state has a function to perform in cultural provision, it would be mistaken to view its actual or potential mode of operation as indistinguishable from that of the market. Were these practices really indistinguishable from one another, then cultural policy would have passed entirely from politics to economics. A chronic problem of rationalisation for publicly subsidised art and culture has, nevertheless, arisen. The old rationales no longer work but, on the other hand, to embrace the market wholeheartedly is hardly the answer. Oliver Bennett poses the problem of rationalising public cultural policy in the form of an *aporia*:

> What of the future?
> There seem to be two alternatives: the first is to construct a new vision which can command widespread intellectual and political support. It is an extremely difficult task, complicated by the speed of contemporary cultural change. But it becomes even more urgent to dispense with out-dated rhetoric, and to build, in its place, sound theoretical foundations on which new cultural policies can be convincingly built.
> The second alternative is to abandon the notion of a cultural policy altogether, to submit to the *zeitgeist*, and to accept that there is no higher judge than the market. In so doing, we would be moving backwards and forwards at the same time – back to the old ideas of *laissez-faire*, but forwards to a new era of post-policy, finally liberated from the last traces of dependency culture.
>
> (1995: 215)

It is vitally important to appreciate that 'the market' is not so much a thing as an idea. As Fredric Jameson (1991: 260) observes, it is 'at one and the same time an ideology and a set of practical institutional problems'. We may have come to believe that the market rules our lives: but in what sense? Do we encounter the market as though it were a mountain to climb or a river to swim through, a natural barrier or facilitator? Or, do we encounter the market as an ideological framework, an enabling and exclusionary discourse, which shapes our sense of reality? I believe it is the latter, as do most critics of contemporary market reasoning. Jeremy

Seabrook (1990) talks of 'the myth of the market', being particularly concerned with concealments of suffering, and Alan Howarth (1994) of 'a market romance'. According to Howarth, 'The claim that wide-eyed trust in the free-market has more in common with fundamentalist religious faith than it does with any philosophically well-founded and defensible position is becoming increasingly commonplace' (p. 107). There is indeed considerable scepticism concerning the magical powers of the market and, yet, it still seems to confront us as a natural object.

The philosophical debate over the meaning of 'the market' is a wide-ranging and difficult one, the complexities of which need not detain us too much here. More germane to the present discussion is that the market may usefully be conceived of as a power/knowledge complex, in the Foucauldian sense. We need to consider how this operates in the public sector. Fundamental to market reasoning is the concept of consumer sovereignty, 'the customer is king'. It inscribes the idea of an all-rational and calculating subject, forever seeking to maximise marginal utility through 'choice'. That consumer knowledge as to 'opportunity costs' and 'quality' is always inherently limited and that some consumers are more sovereign than others because of the elementary facts of inequality (McGuigan, 1996) does not interrupt the rhetoric in general or prevent policies from being proposed on grounds of consumer sovereignty (Peacock, 1986; Adam Smith Institute, 1989). There has, for ideological reasons, been a 'spread of market or quasi-market forms of organization' (Keat et al., 1994: 3) throughout the public sector, including cultural institutions.

One of the reasons why Hayek's *The Road to Serfdom* (1944) had such appeal for the New Right is that it dispensed with the rationalist illusions of neo-classical economics, founded upon the fiction of the wholly rational consumer, and only called upon the eventual test of history to support political faith in the efficacy of market solutions to all problems (Wainwright, 1994). Blind faith is one thing; the actual process of selling another. What gives the lie to the inverted determinism of sovereign consumption is the sheer ideological and material effort that is put into selling goods to people. Andrew Wernick (1991: vii) has coined the term 'promotional culture' to refer to 'a rhetorical form diffused throughout our culture'. Although this encompasses advertising in the narrow sense, 'promotional culture' is meant to indicate how culture in general has become marketised, resulting in a 'pan-promotionalism of contemporary communications (private as well as public, political, academic, artistic, etc.)' (p. vii). We are all being sold something all the time: so, why should we not be sold the arts? And if the claim is that we are being sold what we really want, all the better. Since the 1980s, 'the arts', including its professional constituencies, which had romantically set themselves up against the market in the past, discovered that they could be sold forcefully too, that forms deemed uncommercial, such as classical music in Britain, could be marketed profitably and that, even where state subsidy was still needed, promotional activities could boost revenue.

Wernick's most striking example of the ubiquity of promotion is the promotionalism of university education. During the 1960s there had been a massive expansion of the universities as a deliberate state policy. In the years that followed this left a system vulnerable to constraints on public spending, especially when further expansion occurred, which happened acutely in Britain in the early 1990s. As public funding for universities was reduced per capita, the response was to be more market-oriented, to represent the corporate identity of the university promotionally and to get closer to 'the customer' with courses designed according to perceived market demand, involving cafeteria-style modularisation and focused increasingly upon immediate vocational outcomes. Revenue-earning pressures on research and academic careers meant that promotion and security of employment depended upon successful promotion. Perceived in a jaundiced way, this involved a harlotry of academia in constant tension with traditional humanist values and 'disinterested' scientific research and scholarship. Wernick (1991: 177) stresses 'the extent to which the pervasiveness of promotional language and activity leaves no discourse or project immune'.

This is not, of course, what your typical arts marketer would say of arts marketing. Marketing techniques, according to the professionals, are not just about advertising, publicity and selling things; they are, in the official discourse of the profession, about knowledge and communication. All professionals, especially during a professionalisation process, seek to accrue a certain dignity and mystique. After all, they also have something to sell. And arts marketers are especially keen to reassure the old romantics in the arts world that marketing is not just about filthy lucre in the sense of a vulgar scramble for profits. It is, instead, in the words of Keith Diggle (1984), about achieving 'the best financial outcome', using public money to the greater advantage of arts consumers. If you have a good product, why not sell it effectively? As Diggle points out, by public sector standards, there is a peculiar affinity of the arts with marketing:

> The arts are, from one point of view, no different from other vital but non-profit making concerns such as education, libraries, the National Health service and so on. They differ from such comparable activities because most arts bodies are in the business of selling something and thus, from a marketing viewpoint, have more in common with, say, a transport system.
>
> (1984: 22)

This similarity with transport, says Diggle, 'is not so much to do with their inefficiency as the extremely high cost of providing them set against their finite capacities' (p. 22). Hence, the basic aim of 'putting bums on seats', which Diggle himself would not articulate in quite the same way. In order to achieve that goal, Diggle distinguishes between 'attenders', 'intenders' and 'non-attenders'. Although he does not discount it, Diggle sees little point, albeit regretfully, in targeting 'non-attenders', many of whom may simply be hostile to the arts. From a practical viewpoint, he puts the emphasis on encouraging attenders to attend more frequently and intenders to attend. This makes sense in the terms of the particular arts marketing strategy that Diggle has advocated, subscription marketing, inspired by his own personal American guru, one Danny Newman. The purpose of such a widely used technique is multiple selling to achieve regular attendance, which is often supported with discounts. The pragmatic usefulness of this elementary marketing strategy and its successfulness are not in question. What needs to be appreciated, however, is that it is not ideologically neutral, especially from the point of view of a social-democratic discourse that was concerned at least rhetorically with 'non-attenders'. Because so many publicly subsidised arts venues are havens for a highly educated and overwhelmingly white middle class, any strategy that only targets 'attenders' and 'intenders' signifies a particularistic market realism that has evacuated an aspirational rhetoric of universal provision. Arts venues, in their policy statements, typically obscure this fact with a composite rhetoric of broadening the audience and managerial efficiency, but that is only a specific manifestation of the amalgam of frequently vacuous and residually good intentions, in the sense of social fairness, and market reasoning that characterise contemporary 'arts' policy in general.

Justin Lewis (1990) has sought to resolve the contradictoriness of an economistic rationale for public policy in 'the arts' by insisting upon *cultural purpose*, not only aspirationally but also in making sense of what actually happens. Lewis (1990: 130) argues that the economistic case put by the likes of Rees-Mogg (1985) and more substantially by John Myerscough (1988) is flawed when taken to its logical conclusion: 'If we wanted an arts funding strategy based upon economic benefit, we would *not* spend the money in the way we do now. The arts are funded according to particular aesthetic judgements, not on the basis of tourism and industrial strategy.' That is why questions of value and aesthetic judgement remain at the heart of cultural policy even where they have been strangely silenced by the relativising language of economics and markets. Still, Lewis sees marketing as essentially a neutral tool that can be put to alternative and conflicting purposes. The great strength of a marketing perspective is genuine concern with 'finding out about the needs, interests and desires of . . . [the] audience as consumers' (1990: 140). This would, in any event, be a feature of a cultural imperative and is not reducible to a commercial imperative aimed exclusively at achieving 'the best financial outcome'. Yet, in practice, such an approach is rare: a great deal of marketing is to do with 'manipulation'. The '*saturation* approach', based upon the prime economic motive of maximising audience revenue, which is the normal orientation of arts marketing, compares unfavourably, from Lewis's perspective, with an 'approach . . . based upon a cultural imperative' (Lewis, 1990: 148).

Although, in this chapter, I have stressed a profound shift into a discourse of managerialist and market reasoning within the public cultural sector, the closed character of which should not be underestimated, I do not mean to suggest that a total ideological closure has occurred. This, specifically in Britain, is related to the incompleteness of the Thatcherite project and the resilience of expectations cultivated under social democracy, perhaps best exemplified by the inviolable principle of public health care, if not necessarily its practice in straitened circumstances, that is still represented by the National Health Service, in popular consciousness. The tensions involved in not only discursive but organisational change can be illustrated further, with regard to the arts, over the issue of business sponsorship. In the early 1980s, the suspicion that the Thatcher government aimed eventually to replace public subsidy with business sponsorship was probably not pure paranoia in the arts world. Yet business sponsorship never grew much beyond a 10 per cent supplement to public subsidy in general. It has, to be sure, been a cheap device of promotional advertising for companies, usually bringing with it a leisure perk for managers. The effect of business sponsorship has been rather more ideological than material, forcing arts organisations to spend a great deal of time and energy obtaining temporary favours, and frequently giving the false impression that an arts event is subsidised solely by the extravagantly publicised company that has, in reality, contributed only modestly to its production (Shaw, 1993).

Another illustration of the tensions surrounding a marketising discourse that shouts down other discourses, on the one hand, and the persistence of a deeply rooted cultural realm that is associated with 'enlightened' state intervention, on the other, is the situation of the public library in Britain. As Liz Greenhalgh, Ken Worpole and Charles Landry (1995) have remarked, the public library in Britain is of 'high public esteem and low political visibility and concern'. The British public library system, developed since the mid-nineteenth century and greatly expanded in the twentieth century, is internationally renowned and has functioned as a genuinely popular and non-commercial public space for all strata of society, 'a living room in the city'; it owes nothing to the market and everything to the good intentions of local government routinely fulfilling long-established statutory obligations. It is the closest equivalent of the National Health Service in the cultural field and, for similar reasons, was difficult for marketising Conservative governments to tamper with, which is not to say that its future remained secure. In a thorough inquiry into the history, present condition and potential of the public library, Greenhalgh and her co-authors challenge a number of conventional wisdoms, not least of which is that it is already in decline. In fact, three hundred new libraries were built during the Thatcherite 1980s. Over half of the British population use public libraries, with about one-third of the population using them regularly. The service was adversely affected, however: because of budgetary constraints book buying was curtailed and opening hours were reduced. The Comedia study of public libraries (Greenhalgh *et al.*, 1995), in line with prevailing discourse, presents a kind of SWOT analysis, covering strengths, weaknesses, opportunities and threats. The strengths are to do with the non-commodified provision of culture and information by an accessible institution, with a physical presence in the places of everyday life, places that are otherwise increasingly dominated by commercial and promotional culture. Public libraries are vital to securing the citizen's 'right to know'. The sheer taken-for-grantedness of such an institution, an institution that might not be missed until it is gone, and the misleadingly nostalgic and out-dated image that is often constructed for the public library, are weaknesses. There are, however, enormous opportunities for the public library in an 'information society' where knowledge is closely associated with power, not only to do with lending books, audio, visual and audio-visual goods, but with accessing data banks and computer networks. The major threat, of course, is to do with the 'privatisation of information' and the further commodification and marketisation of the properties of the public sphere (Schiller, 1989).

4

CULTURAL INDUSTRIES

> [T]he 'Culture Industry' is not a theory of culture but the theory of an *industry*.
>
> Fredric Jameson, 1990: 144

It is commonplace to suggest that 'the arts' as traditionally conceived have become marginalised and increasingly irrelevant in the industrialised culture of the modern age with its proliferation of mass-mediated forms, messages and everyday experiences. In a book published in 1986, in hopeful and ultimately disappointed anticipation of a British general election victory for the Labour Party in 1987, Geoff Mulgan and Ken Worpole stated this now conventional wisdom in the form of a rhetorical question, the answer to which they gave instantly:

> Who is doing most to shape British culture in the late 1980s? Next Shops, Virgin, W.H.Smith's, the Notting Hill Carnival and Virago, or the Wigmore Hall, Arts Council, National Theatre, Tate Gallery and Royal Opera House? Most people know the answer, and live it every day in the clothes they wear, the newspapers they read, the music they listen to and the television they watch. The emergence (and disappearance) of new pursuits, technologies, techniques and styles – whether windsurfing, jogging, aerobics, Zen, compact discs, angling, wine-making, CB radio, rambling, hip-hop, home computing, photography or keeping diaries – represent changes that bear little relation to traditional notions of art and culture, and the subsidised institutions that embody them.
>
> (1986: 9).

Asserting the prevalence of mainly commercial culture over publicly subsidised culture was done here in the context of an attempt to generalise the practice of the 1981–6 Greater London Council to the level of potentially imminent central government. That this did not happen in Britain through the national agency of the Labour Party in 1987, nor did it in 1992, is a matter of 'what if?' history, though the impact of such thinking at Labour-controlled city government level was not negligible. What is particularly interesting, however, is the convergence of central government market reasoning under the tutelage of New Right conservatism with the newly found market realism of social-democratic politics. Mulgan and Worpole's position was not simply a leftist echo of a right-wing pro-gramme. They were troubled, as socialists, by the possibility of an unbridgeable chasm opening up between a public-subsidy system that merely served the well-off minority and a market system which captured the majority population, 'the popular classes', entirely:

> The worst result would be a two-tier culture: on the one hand a world of subsidised or sponsored arts and public service broadcasting for the elite, and on the other commercial, mass produced largely imported culture for the rest .... We argue for a shift away from the traditional, patronage-based models of funding towards new forms of investment and regulation more suited to the realities of culture as a modern industry, and geared to the independence of those who make culture.

> (1986: 10)

The social-democratic politics of 'investment' in the cultural industries that emerged in the 1980s represents a curious historical irony because the original formulation of an idea of 'culture industry' was, in fact, hostile to the industrialisation of culture. That, in itself, is not a weakness; yet the enthusiasm for a realistic politics of culture as industry needs careful probing since the rhetoric has tended to outrun and obscure the realities of power in the cultural field. In this chapter, then, I shall track back into the original formulation of 'the culture industry' by the critical theorists of the Frankfurt School of Social Research, Theodor Adorno and Max Horkheimer. It is useful to recall the mid-twentieth-century debate within the German tradition of theoretical response to the industrialisation of culture and the rise of highly technologised media, including Walter Benja-min's counter-position to that of Adorno and Horkheimer, in order to clarify recent issues concerning the relations between cultural policy and the cultural industries.

Beyond these debates of a Western Marxism that addressed culture and ideology more thoroughly than political economy (P. Anderson, 1976), it is necessary to outline some specifically economic dynamics of culture, detailed analysis of which was neglected by the Frankfurt School theorists, particularly regarding the peculiarities of the cultural commodity. Further-more, it is important to consider how cultural change in the late twentieth century is related to industrial change in general, especially with reference to the theme of a transition from Fordism to post-Fordism in the older industrial economies of the West. These considerations raise a number of matters regarding the scope and limitations of specifically governmental power in the industrial restructuration of culture, locally, nationally and internationally.

COMMODIFYING CULTURE

Adorno and Horkheimer (1944/1979) were not only disdainful of the narrative predictability of Hollywood B movies, the commercial speech of American radio and the apparent senselessness of jitterbugging: they were alarmed at the transformation of Enlightenment ideals into instrumental reason. In their estimation, with the advent of monopoly capital, the scientific and administrative imaginations had become a totalising system governing all forms of representation and action. This had achieved a nightmarish intensity in Nazi Germany, yet the Frankfurt School exiles also found it immanent in the 'free market' institutions of the mid-twentieth-century USA. According to Adorno and Horkheimer, 'enlightenment' had turned into 'mass deception' through the machinations of 'the culture industry'.

In his essay of 1967, 'Culture Industry Reconsidered', Adorno (1991) reflected upon why he and Horkheimer had replaced the concept of 'mass culture' with 'culture industry' in their original 1940s essay on the topic. 'Mass culture' was named by them in the early 1940s to refer to the way in which a standardised and meretricious culture was imposed on the masses by modern technological media and entertainment businesses. However, they came to believe that the term could too easily be misconstrued as referring to an authentic cultural emanation of the active masses rather than something passively consumed by them. To put the word 'culture' together with 'industry' seemed much more unambiguously damning. Ever since the Romantics had severed art and culture from the values and practices of industrial capitalism, the prospect that art and culture should succumb to these very values and practices had been, for neo-Enlightenment intellectuals like Adorno and Horkheimer, a fearful one. The point about genuine art and culture was that by means of aesthetic form they transcended the grubby operations of the factory system and the marketplace, functioning as the imaginative transcendence of mundanely instrumental reason. Furthermore, the authentic work of art had a uniqueness and 'aura' that distinguished it fundamentally from the mass-produced commodity. In this respect, the archetypal case is probably oil painting: to stand before the *Mona Lisa* itself is a quite different experience from seeing an otherwise technically excellent photographic reproduction of it, as Benjamin (1936/1973a) had pointed out in the 1930s, an insight hardly denied Adorno in his role as Benjamin's tough-minded mentor (Bloch *et al.*, 1977).

Yet, there was an inherent problem here: how could the uniqueness and auratic qualities of the singular work of art compete with modern technologies of reproduction that made cultural products so widely available? Since the invention of printing the book had ceased to be a unique artefact. Its words might still be deemed the expression of an individual mind but, as a material object, the book was now multiply reproduced: it was no longer the work of handicraft. Prints from woodcuts had a comparable function. Modern photographic and recording techniques, from the turn of the nineteenth and twentieth centuries, had further extended the capacities of multiple reproduction immensely, bringing other forms, old and new, into roughly the same category as the book and the print: industrially produced artefacts with potentially limitless audiences.

Adorno and Horkheimer are frequently said to have been prejudiced against technologically reproduced and mass-distributed culture *per se*; and, clearly, such an interpretation is not wholly inaccurate nor is it indefensible. However, as the original formulations on 'the culture industry' indicate, their position was somewhat more complicated than a purely Romantic refusal of the modern age, as inevitably it would be for once professedly Marxist intellectuals. For them, the particular applications of technological reproduction to culture were determined by the economic and ideological interests of monopoly capitalism, serving as means of profitability and mass-market organisation. These interests manipulated and, indeed, manufactured the tastes of social majorities, according to Adorno and Horkheimer, delivering the same multiply reproduced cultural commodities to all, thus exploiting the economies of scale and, perhaps, thereby denying the potential diversity that truly liberated social and political arrangements would, in theory, enable. Everything was reduced to easily replicable formulas and commodity status. Despite claims about increasing consumer choice, in effect the culture industry administered the commercial exploitation of the mass consumer with, in reality, quite a limited range of products, however much they were distinguished according to brand.

These arguments concerning the mass standardisation of culture are historically rooted in relation to the Fordist moment of industrial capitalism when the system of assembly-line manufacture and the formation of a mass-consumer market came to predominate in comparatively wealthy societies. Allied to this was central government intervention to regulate the economy in Franklin D. Roosevelt's USA as well as in European countries where some form of social democracy achieved a measure of governmental power. These developments, stretching in one way or another from socialism and communism through liberal democracy to the fascist state, presented to the Frankfurt School critics the spectre of a totally administered society and a general homogenisation of culture. In the USA, the individual was revered yet conformity was demanded from everyone. For example, the Hollywood star system set up fantasy role models to follow and 'keeping up with the Joneses' level of consumption became a widespread obsession. The Frankfurt School were not alone in identifying these trends and their ideas were to echo in various currents of criticism, including the French Situationists of the 1960s, who sought to challenge what they called 'the society of the spectacle' in which all meaning was subsumed under the significatory processes of mass consumerism (see Plant, 1992; Debord, 1994).

It is modish to believe that the homogenising tendencies of capitalist culture were interrupted and indeed reversed by the 1980s revival of free-market economics, the decline of nation-state regulation and the growth of individuated 'lifestyle' cultures. Some would argue, however, that the Frankfurt School's pessimistic imaginary has never been so relevant as it is today. What critics like Adorno and Horkheimer were particularly astute at pinpointing were the contradictions between promotional ideology and the evidence of actual conditions. Endless propaganda concerning individualism and choice, which is not new in consumer culture, vastly exaggerates the power that 'consumers' exercise over their everyday lives. From this point of view, the 'post-Fordist' transformation of the older system of mass production and consumption, with its much vaunted 'flexible specialisation' geared to rapid changes in product line, which is very often merely repackaging and minor modification to product,[1] may not be so radically different in practice from the standardising operations of monopoly capitalism that were excoriated by Adorno and Horkheimer in the 1940s and may even suggest that 'neo-Fordism' is a more accurate description than 'post-Fordism'. Moreover, it should be noted that Adorno and Horkheimer, in a sense, anticipated the collapsing hierarchies and the blurring boundaries, brought about by the commodification of all culture, which is said to characterise the textures of postmodern experience generally.

The key figure representing a counter-point to Adorno and Horkheimer's pessimism in the German tradition of critical theory is Walter Benjamin, a marginal associate of the Frankfurt School. He was supposed to join them in US exile, but before embarking upon his intended voyage across the Atlantic Benjamin committed suicide on the Franco-Spanish border in 1940 when he mistakenly thought he was just about to be captured by the fascists. Encouraged by his friendship with the playwright and poet Bertolt Brecht during the early 1930s (Benjamin, 1973b), Benjamin had developed a much more optimistic attitude towards modern technological media than the one held by Adorno and Horkheimer. Brecht was especially enthusiastic about radio's talkback potential and cinema's entertainment value, though he had little opportunity to work satisfactorily in these media himself (Willett, 1964). Unlike theatre, radio and cinema addressed millions simultaneously. As means of communicating with the people in general they had great advantages over the pre-industrial media that were seemingly favoured from a patrician point of view by the leading members of the Frankfurt School. Also, the necessarily *industrial* structures and processes of modern technological media had the further advantage of demystifying cultural creation as the expression of individual genius and the like. These media brought art and work back together again; and their collective modes of production and consumption appealed to the collectivist politics of Benjamin and Brecht.

Under Brecht's influence, Benjamin proposed a theory of the democratising qualities of modern communications media, the very media that Adorno and Horkheimer were later to dub 'the culture industry'. In his seminal essay written in 1936, 'The Work of Art in the Age of Mechanical Reproduction', Benjamin argued that multiple reproduction destroyed the aura of the work of art, but this was no bad thing. Popular attitudes to art in modern experimental forms were quite reactionary, as writers like Adorno and Horkheimer and other advocates of the *avant-garde* complained, yet modern culture was not so much about cubism and atonal music but, instead, principally about the newer media, most notably photography and cinema, which were having much greater impact on representational discourse and popular consciousness. For example, parallel narrative and montage techniques in cinema spatialised time and produced shock effects that corresponded to the textures of modern urban existence. The everyday mode of consuming such culture, in relaxed distraction rather than intense concentration, enriched the experience of people in general, enabling them to become cultural experts without formal aesthetic training in a way which undermined the role of academic critics and mediators such as Adorno and Horkheimer. Ordinary cinema-goers acquired a certain expertise, a knowledgeability and critical nous denied most people before the modern media made so much culture widely accessible and open to popular judgement. Cultural consumption was, in effect, becoming democratised: it was no longer confined to the privileged and highly educated.

Benjamin was writing about these matters before the Second World War. Since then there has been a further expansion of popularly accessible media on a global scale, a veritable 'explosion of culture' that accentuates the processes of 'democratisation' at the point of consumption. Even for optimists of a similar persuasion to Benjamin, however, glaring discrepancies between access to the consumption of mass-distributed cultural commodities and access to cultural production persist. Hans Magnus Enzensberger (1974), writing in the 1960s during his radical youth, enunciated a typical and resonant view on the cultural Left that the democratic potentials of modern media were blocked because power over the major means of communication was held in so few hands and was, in any case, unnecessarily centralised, owned and controlled by major corporations in both the private and, then more so, public sectors. Most people are unable to transcend their allotted stations as consumers. They are rarely in a position to talk back or produce original public meanings for themselves. Such thinking from the 1960s has since been manifest in a series of political movements for democratising communications and culture, including various community arts and media uses of press, radio, photography, film, video and computer-mediated communications.

What is now so striking about the original German thinking on 'the culture industry' and its revival in the 1960s and 1970s, either from the pessimistic perspective of Adorno and Horkheimer or the optimistic perspectives of Benjamin, Brecht and Enzensberger, is how romantic it was. Adorno and Horkheimer wanted to resist the monolith of mass-distributed culture, whereas Benjamin argued that it democratised consumption, while Enzensberger stressed the possibilities of democratic production. Benjamin's view has been the closest to cultural actualities. Most people, most of the time, get their aesthetic pleasures from consuming mass-distributed culture. The unqualified pessimism of Adorno and Horkheimer has little resonance now outside the shrinking coteries of artistic refusal of mass-popular culture. And Enzensberger's youthful belief that everyone could and should become a cultural producer in relation to the major media of public communication was hopelessly utopian. Nevertheless, the leisure practices of photography, video, music-mixing and computing have spread enormously, thus demonstrating both the capacities of the commodity-producing system to pioneer new technological products and the enduring popular desire to be creative and to engage in active symbolic play.

Bernard Miège (1989) has produced the most telling critique of Adorno and Horkheimer's 'culture industry' thesis, a critique which cuts across the for-and-against politics of cultural industry and technology mapped out by the tension between the 'optimistic' and 'pessimistic' dialectic of the German tradition. Miège identifies three main limitations of the original culture industry theorisation. First, and most obviously, there is the attachment to 'a limited and rigid idea of artistic creation' which results in a 'distrust for technology and artistic innovation' (Miège, 1989: 10). Second, '[r]eference to the "culture industry" – in the singular – misleads one into thinking that we are faced with a unified field, where the various elements function within a single process' (p. 10). Third, according to Miège, Adorno and Horkheimer 'paradoxically took a greater interest in markets than in the industry' (p. 11). Miège goes on to argue that 'the capitalization of cultural production is a complex, many-sided and even contradictory process' (p. 12).

Adorno and Horkheimer failed to unravel the internal complexities and differentiations of 'the culture industry'. Miège himself identifies three competing logics of capitalist cultural production: a publishing logic, a flow logic which is especially characteristic of broadcasting and, finally, the logic of the press. The first of these logics, that of publishing, refers to the tasks of distributing cultural products of an ostensibly autonomous status to audiences, involving problems of copyrighting and marketing in particular. The flow logic of broadcasting involves problems of sustaining a steady output of serial product and maintaining audience loyalty. The logic of the press is to sustain regular consumer purchase of product with a rapid and routinely built-in obsolescence. Of special interest is the conflict between the logics of publication and of flow with regard to their differential constructions of the role of the cultural producer. 'Flow' is much more comprehensively 'industrialised', in the Fordist sense, than is 'publishing', though there is unrelenting pressure on the latter to conform to the logic of the former. Miège also provides a tripartite model of types of cultural commodification in relation to his distinction between, on the one hand, artistic professionals and cultural workers proper and, on the other hand, industrial workers in the cultural industries. Type 1 products are reproducible but they do not involve the direct involvement of cultural workers proper: this category includes equipment, such as cameras, and materials, such as celluloid and videotape, manufactured like any commodity and with nothing necessarily to do with their eventually aesthetic rather than simply technical function of bearing meaning. Type 2 products are cultural commodities proper, by definition involving the participation of cultural workers proper, though rarely salaried workers, and infinitely reproducible in Benjamin's sense, such as films, television programmes and recorded music. Type 3 products are semi-reproducible, such as repeated live performances and limited print editions of artworks. The fundamental objective of the cultural industries is to ensure financial valorisation and capital accumulation with regard to products of particularly the second type, the demand for which is either inherently unpredictable or, at least, relatively difficult to predict.

SOCIALISING THE MARKET

From the mid-1980s, the concept of 'cultural industry' was linked increasingly to various social-democratic projects of urban regeneration in British cities. These strategies were inspired by theoretical developments in the political economy of communications and culture. The rationale for cultural industries strategy was theorised by Nicholas Garnham for the 1981–6 Labour Party administration of the Greater London Council (GLC) and implemented to a limited extent by the Greater London Enterprise Board. This politics of socialising the market under conditions of rapid economic and cultural change can be taken to illustrate some of the main problems of democratic regulation in the cultural field.

When the Labour Left took command of the GLC in 1981 they had no fully worked-out cultural industries policy. The dual aim at first was simply to widen access to the established arts, the orthodox social-democratic orientation, and to stimulate community arts in inner-city districts. The GLC's financial commitment to the 'national' institutions in London, such as the National Theatre and English National Opera, continued to swallow up most of the arts budget but additional funds were also made available through the Community Arts Sub-Committee for more modest 'grass-roots' projects.[2] Towards the end of its existence, the Labour GLC commissioned Comedia Consultancy to evaluate the results of the community arts policy. The findings and interpretations, published as *Art – Who Needs It?* (Lewis *et al.*, 1986), were devastatingly critical of a 'grass-roots' activism that saw community arts as the key to progressive cultural policy. It was found that community arts facilities were used very largely by highly educated middle-class people who were not wholly dissimilar in social origin from the core audiences for the 'traditional arts', though many of them were unemployed and politically disaffected. A similar picture emerged with regard to subsidised cinema, the films and ambience of which were found to appeal mainly to the tastes of the petit-bourgeois cinemagoer. Working-class people were typically put off by the 'arty' image of such venues. Mulgan and Worpole (1986) took up this issue of the apparent failure of community arts and similar public cultural provision. They attacked the workshop ideology of 'process', whereby doing it, making something of satisfaction to the producer, was considered more important than actually building audiences for the products thus made. Both the Comedia report and Mulgan and Worpole castigated community arts for lack of financial skill, organisational incompetence and, in practice, comparative indifference to potential constituencies and audiences. These criticisms signified an emergent commercial attitude to subsidised art and culture, coming not from Conservative free marketeers but from commentators and activists on the Left.

However, the critique of the GLC's original social access policy should be qualified by recording success as well as failure, especially with respect to 'ethnic' and 'Black' arts. An Ethnic Arts Sub-Committee, with its own budgetary allocation separate from Community Arts, was established following the GLC's conference on ethnic arts in 1982, at which event interested parties came together to discuss policy. Kwesi Owusu reported on this in his book *The Struggle for Black Arts in Britain* (1986), Owusu, like many 'Black arts' activists, was critical of the liberal term 'ethnic arts' but, none the less, he wrote appreciatively of the manner in which the GLC developed its policies from the initial conference, particularly by including arts constituencies in the decision-making process of the sub-committee. A specific outcome was the vital role the GLC played in the formation of a Black film culture and practice in Britain, which had been put on the agenda at the 1982 conference. GLC funding, combined with the ACTT (Association of Cinematic and Television Technicians, now BECTU) workshop agreement and Channel Four's contribution to investing in and exhibiting independent production, created the conditions, albeit fragile, for Black film-making. A major theme of the 1982 conference had been that Black arts practices, including theatre as well as film and video-making, should not be confined to a woolly, compensatory notion of community arts but, instead, serious professional training was required to enable Black people to enter the industry and make careers on an equal footing with whites.

The example of Black film-making and the GLC's enabling role illustrates a progression of thought through the social-democratic discourse of 'access' towards a policy model of the cultural industries but it does not fully demonstrate the reasoning behind cultural industries strategy in London. During the early phase of the 1981–6 GLC administration, the discourse of social access was pushed to a logical limit which inevitably raised questions about the economics of cultural production and distribution. It became evident that facilitating alternative forms of cultural production was not enough if the alternative cultural products thus made were not distributed efficiently, if they did not reach their intended audiences or failed to create new audiences. Until it was addressed by the GLC the problem of distribution had been comparatively neglected, leading to the failure of innumerable radical alternatives in the cultural field (Landry, et al., 1985). The problem of distribution and the fact that a major part of London's economy is to do with the production and distribution of cultural commodities are crucial to understanding the shift that occurred in the GLC's approach to cultural policy. This shift can be described as moving away from an idealist arts patronage model, which was qualified to some extent by community arts, towards a materialist model of cultural exchange, signified by the terminology of 'industry' and 'markets'.

The basic framework for a cultural industries strategy was stated by Nicholas Garnham in position papers that he prepared for the GLC cultural policy conference of November 1983.[3] It is important to note that Conservative central government had already declared its intention by this time to eventually abolish the GLC. There was a popular yet unsuccessful campaign against abolition: so what Garnham had to say was 'theoretical' in more senses than one. As Franco Bianchini (1990: 219) observes, 'The cultural industries strategy was more important for its conceptual innovations than for its practical achievements.' Garnham (1990) argued that the community arts critique of 'elitism' in public arts patronage was inadequate because it remained within the dominant cultural policy paradigm, in effect acquiescing with the marginal role ascribed to public agencies in the cultural field. It failed to address the real power structures of culture, which are 'private' rather than 'public', capitalist-controlled and not dependent upon the interventionist policies of the national and local states. The idealist tradition of arts patronage and its radical opponents had unwittingly conspired together, then, in keeping public policy comparatively irrelevant. As Garnham said:

[W]hile this tradition has been rejecting the market, most people's cultural needs and aspirations are being, for better or worse, supplied by the market as goods and services. If one turns one's back on an analysis of that dominant cultural process, one cannot understand either the culture of our time or the challenges and opportunities which that dominant culture offers to public policy-makers.

(1990: 155)[4]

Unqualified opposition to the cultural market was seriously unrealistic and self-defeating. Although the market has many questionable features, including the exploitation, objectification and commodification of labour power, it is also a profoundly efficient means of communication, registering popular tastes and aspirations much more effectively than state-planned arrangements. This was a reality that even the most dyed-in-the-wool socialists had to recognise. Garnham's now classic paper 'Public Policy and the Cultural Industries' (reprinted in Garnham, 1990) went much further, however, than these elementary observations concerning economic power in the cultural field by making several useful analytical distinctions. He interrogated 'cultural industry' as a 'descriptive term', distinguishing, as did Adorno, between cultural goods that are circulated industrially but are not necessarily the product of industrial technology in the first instance (such as writing and musical performance) and those that are (such as newspapers, films and television programmes). These two modes are frequently conflated together in the arts administration usage of 'cultural industry', although it is debatable quite to what extent the distinction still holds with the advent of word-processing and electronic music-making technology. There is, nevertheless, an insight here for grasping why a stubborn distinction persists between 'the arts' and 'the media' on grounds to do with residual differences of 'creative process'.

Garnham insists on how essential it is to analyse the cultural field as an integrated whole in which there is competition for limited consumer income, limited advertising revenue, limited consumption time and limited skilled labour. Limitations of time are especially pertinent for understanding how the cultural industries operate. The use of cultural products tends to be very time-consuming, particularly regarding narrative forms, which is, in any case, one of the principal functions of cultural consumption. Time is limited and, therefore, scarce; so is money. Competition for scarce time and money is very acute in the cultural industries. This gives rise to the emphasis on home-based consumption in product design and marketing. The aim is to achieve maximum exploitation of leisure time and spending power.

To appreciate the peculiarities of the cultural commodity it is necessary to consider both how commodified culture exemplifies capitalist production and circulation in general and, also, the particular features of meaning-bearing products. The market constantly exerts pressure towards a universalisation of exchange value as the only significant calculus of worth, cultural or otherwise. However, the cultural commodity has certain distinctive characteristics that create problems for the general process of valorisation and, furthermore, that distinguish the cultural commodity from commodities that are not primarily bearers of meaning. It is exceptionally difficult to market cultural commodities. According to Garnham (1990: 160), 'There is a contradiction at the heart of the cultural commodity.' The continuous production of novelty so as to expand market share is an insistent drive, yet the difficulty with cultural commodities is that they are not typically used up during consumption. In order to stimulate consumption of new product and to cope with endemic uncertainties concerning demand there are powerful tendencies, then, in favour of monopolistic and oligopolistic control, concentration on hardware, packaging audiences for advertisers and producing commodities that both gain and lose novelty very quickly (the newspaper is a perfect example). The sheer volatility and unpredictability of the cultural commodity's use values and its subtle status as a positional good present acute problems of business management that have to be dealt with by strategies such as the repertoire, whereby overproduction, backlisting and re-release are deployed to overcome the inevitability of failure in many cases: hits have to pay for misses.[5]

Garnham (1990: 161–162) observes,

> the drive to audience maximisation, the need to create artificial scarcity by controlling access and the need for a repertoire bring us to the central point in this analysis. *It is cultural distribution, not cultural production, that is the key locus of power and profit.*
>
> (1990: 161–162)

Distribution is connected to the pivotal 'editorial function' in the cultural industries which selects and channels material and tends, however dispersed the production process, towards geographical concentration of distributive power: for example, in London as a major hub of the national and international circulation of cultural commodities. Garnham's reasoning fed into the London Industrial Strategy of the GLC and the Greater London Enterprise Board (GLEB). Regional government could have little impact on the large transnational firms operating in London but it might, however, have strategic influence over the development of smaller and medium-sized enterprises, the scale of enterprise that proliferates around the power centres of the cultural field. With investment and loan programmes, the GLEB sought to plan socially useful production and, by providing common services, to enable new cultural enterprises to market their wares. Also, when faced with almost certain abolition for the last three years of its existence, following the vindictive 1983 Conservative general election pledge to rid the capital of socialist government, the Labour GLC was committed to aiding organisations founded in 'communities of interest', representing subordinate cultures of one kind or another, to become self-financing and commercially viable. The GLC's cultural industries strategy helped to found, for instance, community recording studios, a Black publishing house and a radical book distribution network (Bianchini, 1987). The GLC also created a festive atmosphere in London with a number of popular events, particularly around the Thames. Its practical achievements were limited, though, by time, money and central government hostility. An urban renewal strategy levered by socialist cultural and industrial policy had insufficient time to develop beyond a few indicative experiments in London. The GLC's strategic innovations did survive well beyond 1986, however, in their enduring influence upon a number of Labour-controlled local governments around the country.

Manufacturing cities such as Birmingham, Newcastle and Sheffield had suffered the full blast of de-industrialisation, unlike London, and were cities in which political leaders were looking around for new ways of regenerating their local economies. Cultural industries, in one form or another, presented a possible source of growth to these Labour administrations. The greatest effort to implement a specifically production-based cultural industries strategy was made in Sheffield, where a once-dominant steel industry had collapsed with devastating consequences, particularly for male employment. In Sheffield, hope was invested most notably in popular music. Red Tape studios, funded by Sheffield City Council as one of the first building blocks of a 'cultural industries quarter', were opened in 1986 by the then Labour Party leader, Neil Kinnock. Simon Frith remarked upon this initiative seven years later:

> There is no doubt about the subsequent success of Red Tape in its own terms – its expansion has continued as planned, and the Cultural Industries Quarter does now consist of a variety of subsidized and commercial businesses which feed off each other: the private studios are available for trainee placements, and trainees are available as flexible studio labour. It is certainly arguable that as well as providing much needed resources (which have been used by a wide spectrum of musical and community groups), Sheffield has also succeeded in establishing a musical identity. An Employment Department memo in November 1990 noted that thanks to WARP and Modo records relocating from London, Sheffield had achieved a 3.2 per cent share of the British singles market, an indication that 'the City is on target to register as a major music production centre, increasingly recognized as such by the Media and Record industry'.
>
> (1993: 17)

Sheffield's small-scale success and the perspective formed by the National Federation of Music Projects illustrates how the logic of a cultural industries strategy unfolds. The initial aims tend to emphasise representation:

86

creating conditions for cultural experiment, opening up fresh opportunities for participation and the articulation of local identities. As time passes, however, economic goals and job training are increasingly stressed. The logic of a cultural industries strategy, then, becomes rather more industrial than cultural, often unrealistically so. As Frith notes (1993: 22), there is 'a contradiction between local culture and culture industry policies', which is especially evident in a global music market in spite of the marketing of a 'local' sound. Frith, however, does not question this apparent diminution of expressive intent, the demise of a distinctly *cultural* programme. He concluded his contribution to the 1991 British Arts and Media Strategy debate with the following slogan, 'Support hucksters! Develop spaces! Build structures! Challenge consumers!' (Frith, 1991a: 11). Support for entrepreneurship and unabashed commercialism in local cultural policy resulted in a strange coalescence of Left and Right perspectives by the beginning of the 1990s.

Another aspect of this coalescence is to do with the industrially vanguard qualities of the cultural industries, displaying features of post-Fordist vertical disintegration *avant la lettre*. In the popular music industry, for instance, 'research and development' in actual production is not conducted best by major companies but by self-employed individuals and groups operating in a cottage industry until the lucky few break into the contractual big time and get distributed by the majors. Frith points out:

> [T]he small/creative/marginal vs big/exploitative/central model is not a very helpful way of understanding how the cultural industries work. In the record industry, for example, the majors and the independents have a symbiotic rather than oppositional relationship, with small labels acting as the research and development departments of the majors, which, in turn, take on the task of marketing and promising 'discoveries' (and many independent companies are, in fact, part owned or bank-rolled by the majors). And one could point to the similar dependence of the theatrical 'fringe' on mainstream impresarios, of independent producers on the major broadcasting companies, of 'alternative' comedians on mass media exposure. To put this another way, even small businesses are 'market-led', even 'creative' independents are dependent for their livelihoods on the sale of their products, on their competitive edge in the market place where the rules of exchange are defined by the 'big' operators. This doesn't preclude their producing 'oppositional' work, but it does suggest that such radicalism is not, in itself, a matter of marginality – independent publishing companies mostly produce mainstream culture (their independence a reflection of market specialism rather than resistance); radical art and ideas are just as likely to emerge from the cultural bureaucracies.
>
> (1991b: 145–146)

VERTICALLY DISINTEGRATING?

While it is important to isolate the peculiarities of cultural-commodity production and distribution, in effect the micro-economics of the cultural industries, it is also necessary to situate these structures and processes in relation to the changing macro-relations of economy and culture. It is not just that the economic determines the cultural but, as a number of commentators have observed, economies are inflected culturally and industry in general comes to resemble cultural industry in particular. Scott Lash and John Urry (1994) argue that all industrial production is now more design-intensive than in the past and, as such, is increasingly similar to cultural production. In the cultural industries, a great deal of material resource and labour is devoted to the production of 'prototypes', in principle every copyrightable sound, word or image. The physical manufacture of multiple copies is comparatively easy and cheap. Also the costs of marketing and distribution in the cultural industries frequently exceed those of copying the product for sale, a cost structure which is also becoming a trend, according to Lash and Urry, for industries where the use value of the product is not first and foremost meaning. With accelerated rates of capital accumulation and volatility of tastes, the value-addedness of design, research and development, supported by marketing, provides a competitive advantage in the marketplace.

One of the virtues of an historical account of the transition from Fordism to post-Fordism is a renewed appreciation of the intimate relations between culture and economy (see Amin, 1994). The Fordist system of motor vehicle manufacture, unveiled in Michigan, USA, when the first Model T rolled off the assembly line on the brink of the First World War, was to become the paradigm of industrial production in general through to the 1970s, having reached its highpoint in the 1950s and 1960s after the Second World War. Fordism is characterised by product standardisation, mechanisation of production, division of labour tasks according to the principles of 'scientific management' and assembly-line flow. Fordism is not only a system of mass production; it is also a system of mass consumption. The pioneers of Fordism realised that, in order to reap the benefits of expanded production, consumption had to be expanded too, that there would need to be a 'democratisation' of consumption. An effective means of achieving this was to integrate production, distribution and exchange so as to organise the market. An archetypal instance of such vertical integration was the classic Hollywood system in which the majors, from the 1920s and 1930s, owned first-run cinema chains and were in a position to remain in command of distribution beyond the break-up of their own vertically integrated combines through ownership from the 1950s onwards.

The deeper reasons for the decline of Fordism (Harvey, 1989a) need not detain us here since the main object of this discussion is the affinity of post-Fordism with cultural industry. As Robin Murray (1989) points out, early signs of post-Fordism in Britain were in retailing, not in manufacturing. Supermarket chains introduced computerised stock-taking on a continuous basis in order to achieve a more flexible and efficient response to consumer demand. This indicates a fundamental feature of what is said to characterise post-Fordist culture and how it differs from Fordist culture. If the touchstone of Fordist culture was 'keeping up with the Joneses', then the touchstone of post-Fordist culture is being 'different from the Joneses'. The post-Fordist consumer is supposed to be more discerning, more sovereign, more choosey. Consequently, according to Murray (1989: 43), 'the emphasis has shifted from the manufacturers' economies of scale to the retailers' economies of scope'. The post-Fordist consumer is rather like F. R. Leavis's ideal literary reader, discriminating. A transition from Fordism to post-Fordism, then, represents not only a change in the 'regime of accumulation' but a rejigging of 'the mode of regulation', in the conceptual terminology of Regulation School political economy (Lipietz, 1987). Mode of regulation refers to the organisation and patterning of social and cultural life, for instance individuation and self-reflexity under late modern or postmodern conditions. Whether one is talking of Fordism or post-Fordism, a whole social process is under consideration, not only economic organisation.

Such reasoning on economy and culture is exemplified by the work of the Lancaster School of Sociology.[6] Their analyses of various cultural industries, including advertising, film, television, publishing and music, are located within a broad theoretical discussion of the postmodernisation of economy and culture, relating to globalisation and localisation, intellectual property rights and the contemporary fluidity of meaning, subjectivity and identity. For Lash and Urry (1994), the speed at which wealth and signs now circulate fatally disrupts traditional and oppressive ways of life while not, however, eliminating material and cultural injustice.

There is, according to the Lancaster researchers, an unevenness of development across the cultural industries, but the general trend historically is of Fordisation followed by post-Fordisation. For example, in comparison with cinema, publishing became Fordist late when the mass-market paperback was introduced. In the music business, coordination of production and recruitment through the major record companies' Artist and Repertory (A&D) departments disintegrated with the rise of 'indies' doing the job of R&D and talent-spotting, a characteristically post-Fordist 'outsourcing'. Instances of both Fordist vertical integration and subsequently post-Fordist vertical disintegration are cited frequently with regard to the movie and television businesses. The Lancaster authors draw on the path-breaking work of Christopherson and Storper (1986) here, who have traced these developments in the American film industry.

Susan Christopherson and Michael Storper's article 'The City as Studio;

the World as Back Lot' outlines how the movie business was at the forefront of organisational change in the cultural industries throughout the twentieth century:

> Over the past three decades, the motion picture industry has undergone a dramatic transformation. Until the 1950s, the industry was dominated by large vertically integrated firms which produced films via a routinized factory-like production process. In the contemporary motion picture industry, by contrast, production is carried out primarily by independent production companies which subcontract direct production activity to small specialized firms. The industry is vertically disintegrated and its production process is nonroutinized and designed to maximize variability of outputs and flexibility with respect to inputs. The numerous transactions required to produce the film product now take place on the market rather than within a firm. As vertical disintegration has proceeded, those firms providing services to producers have become smaller and more specialized. These specialized subcontractors reduce their own risks by marketing their services to other entertainment industries, including recording and television. As a result of these combined processes of vertical disintegration and cross-industry subcontracting, an entertainment industry complex has developed.
>
> (1986: 305)

There was a geographical dispersal of production and, simultaneously, a reagglomeration of coordinating practices in and around Los Angeles, where command over distribution is associated with the clustering of smaller firms that offer services to the major film companies and other parts of the cultural industry complex. Hence, the enduring centrality of 'Hollywood', reproducing the nodal position it attained under Fordism, complicated now by Japanese hardware manufacturers buying up American software manufacturers, a trend which, amongst others, begins to cast into doubt the longevity of the vertical disintegration moment. In Christopherson and Storper's account, there is a compatibility, indeed inevitability, between vertical disintegration and horizontal integration. They say, 'the reagglomeration of the industry means that Los Angeles is the headquarters and technological centre for an industrial complex that has the whole world as its back lot' (1986: 319).

Fordism in the movie business was originally pioneered at Paramount with Adolph Zukor's integration of production and distribution by building a nationwide exhibition network of eventually 6,000 cinemas; and by Thomas Ince's introduction of assembly-line methods into formulaic film production around 1920. It was Paramount, as the largest player amongst the majors, which eventually provoked the greatest resentment against oligopolistic barriers to competition in the movie business, resulting in the

1948 Federal Court decision to force Paramount to divest itself of its huge cinema chain. This legal reaction against vertical integration was accompanied by the spread of television-viewing in the 1950s and, between them, they sowed the seeds of post-Fordisation in the movie business long before Fordism was seen as an outmoded regime of accumulation in the older industrial nations generally. The studios became primarily distribution rather than production companies and rented out their facilities or turned them over to television, facilities that were no longer viable as in-house assembly lines for feature film production, and they shared out the risks by investing in 'independent' production. This long-run process was further accentuated during the cataclysmic 1970s, as Christopherson and Storper note. Also the idea of 'product differentiation', from the mundanity of television and between films, was linked to the diversification of production sources and intensive marketing campaigns.

Janet Wasko (1994) has disputed Christopherson and Storper's vertical disintegration thesis with regard to Hollywood. She says, 'rather than disintegration, the US film industry has experienced a process of reintegration in the late eighties' (p. 16). Although her critique of Christopherson and Storper is to do with their exclusive concentration on production, thereby missing the corporate orchestration of distribution and sales through cinema release, video, cable, television, computer games and spin-off products, the real issue seems to be whether Hollywood is conceptualised as a discrete set of rival companies or as an integrated system where oligopoly rather than competition is the driving force. The US government's attempts to resist European protectionist policies through GATT on behalf of the American audio-visual industry would suggest that the latter is the more accurate view of Hollywood and one with a long historical tradition. Yet also at the level of the firm there are pronounced tendencies towards vertical *reintegration*. The fate of Paramount Pictures, taken over by the conglomerate Gulf and Western in the 1970s, but rising like a phoenix to name the corporation as a whole in the 1990s *Paramount Communications*, traces a circuitous dialectic of disintegration and reintegration. During the 1980s, the Hollywood majors were yet again allowed to own cinemas, reversing a forty-year-old prohibition. Asu Aksoy and Kevin Robins are in no doubt concerning the integrative properties of 'Hollywood in the information age', including horizontal agglomeration and vertical command over the circuit of production and consumption:

> The major Hollywood companies are being turned into image empires with tentacles reaching down, not only to movies and TV programmes, but also to books, records, and even hardware. The feature film business no longer exists in its own right, but is increasingly becoming part of an integrated, global image business, central to the broader media strategies of entertainment companies and

conglomerates .... [T]he major studios are the fundamental building blocks of the emerging entertainment megacompanies.

(1992: 22)

That the whole world is the 'back lot' for the Los Angeles-based American movie business is not in itself the worst problem for the rest of the world's cultural industries: other countries are only too keen, on economic grounds, to attract and welcome US film production to their soil. What is a problem, however, is the kind of representation of the world and its cultures that this produces. Resistance to 'Americanisation' has been especially pronounced in French governmental policies and was a prime consideration for Jack Lang's Socialist ministries of culture in the 1980s and early 1990s (Wachtel, 1987). As Susan Hayward (1993) observes, Lang not only stressed *l'état culturel*: he was particularly concerned with *l'industrie culturelle* and awarded a privileged position to film and cinema. Lang's policy ran through the whole gamut of cultural industries strategy, providing subsidy for production and exhibition in a decentralised framework. The policy had some success in the early 1980s but, at the 1993 termination of Socialist government in France, it was obvious that 'Lang's efforts on behalf of the industry did not succeed in reversing the slow downward spiral of the French film industry' (Hayward, 1993: 388). Hayward dilutes her harsh judgement, however, by pointing out that the contest was unequal and that Lang's policies did at least manage to keep a once-powerful and popular national film industry going in the face of the overwhelming presence of Hollywood product.

Communications conglomerates, operating under flexible conditions of 'vertical disintegration', ultimately command the whole circuit of media production and consumption from a position of power over distribution. On the ground, many cultural workers are placed in a paradoxical situation. Outsourcing for product from smaller 'independent' companies, in British television, for instance, has provided a 'window of opportunity' for creative personnel whose aspirations were frustrated by the bureaucratic sclerosis of a fenced-off industry, yet at the cost of occupational insecurity and a weakened labour bargain. Jane Arthurs describes the Fordist structure of the television industry in Britain and its disintegration since the 1980s:

The classic model of a television company is a large vertically integrated company in which the workforce is ordered into a hierarchical pyramid; horizontal divisions are based on specialized skills. These demarcations between levels and types of job are sustained not only through the allocative power of management, but also through the closed shop system of union power which polices the wage differentials between grades of jobs and restricts entry to the industry through a system of control over who is allowed to do different types of work. This is the type of complex organization that dominated television broadcasting in Britain up to the latter half of the 1980s...

The large, vertically integrated companies described above are rapidly responding to political and economic pressures to be more flexible and cost-effective by shedding permanent staff (between 30 and 40% since 1988) and increasing the proportion of programme-making and attendant services bought in from independent companies and freelance labour. Even the BBC, in response to external pressures exerted by a dwindling licence fee and a need to placate government in the run up to the 1996 charter renewal are shedding staff at an equivalent rate.

(1994: 90, 98)

Vertical disintegration was heralded by Channel Four from 1982, funded by advertising and opening up space for new production entrants to television, including non-profit-making cooperatives. Although at its foundation Channel Four was seen as a significant *cultural* departure in British broadcasting, a national television channel that was legally required to be innovative and multicultural, it soon became evident that 'the channel' also represented, and with greater consequence, a new *industrial* departure, an experiment in vertical disintegration that could be applied throughout the industry (S. Harvey, 1994). This resulted in the loss of union power, particularly the closed shop in ITV. Margaret Thatcher had, in the 1980s, called the ITV system 'the last bastion of restrictive practices'. She was not mistaken since the unions, especially ACTT, had negotiated very high wages and extremely protective conditions of employment for members in commercial television. All this was broken down by legislation which required the regional ITV companies and the BBC to contract 25 per cent of programming from the new sector of independent producers. Casualisation, poor pay and overwork all grew apace. Colin Sparks (1994: 151) has likened the resultant labour market to that of a peasant economy: '[Independents] are the industrial equivalent of small peasants who work themselves and their families to death in order to hold onto the family plot after the realities of the market place have dictated that it would be rational to sell up to a large capitalist farmer and move to the city to find work'.

Is this, then, the 'refeudalisation of the public sphere' at the point of production? The robber barons themselves now raid on a much grander scale than in medieval times, organising neo-feudal relations of production and consumption in the burgeoning cultural and information industries across the globe. Advertising is the medium of reintegration, according to Armand Mattelart's *Advertising International* (1991), which is subtitled 'The Privatisation of Public Space'. Mattelart says there is '[n]o media without advertising' (p. ix), by which he means that much cultural production is dependent not only upon advertising finance and effective marketing but also upon the representational discourses and audio-visual formats of commercial speech, a view which is close to Janet Wasko's (1994) claim that *corporate synergy* gives rise to a corresponding *cultural synergy*. Corporate business plans and marketing perspectives call the shots. In the cultural and information industries, then, there is a 'double line of evolution . . . being drawn: on the one hand, the rise of global firms; on the other, that of small autonomous units, eventually inside the big structures' (Mattelart, 1991: 57).

5

URBAN REGENERATION

Urban policy in the late twentieth century is now inseparable from cultural policy.

Ken Worpole, 1991: 143

The trouble with all of this cultural emphasis is that it has directed attention away from the general problem.

David Harvey, 1993a: 14

The epigraphs at the head of this chapter appear to contradict one another. Ken Worpole's statement might be read as simply extolling the panacea of cultural policy for troubled towns and cities. David Harvey's 'general problem' is that of 'wealth creation'. It could thus be construed that the only realistic prospects for urban regeneration, in his opinion, are sound economic analysis and public policies aimed at resisting the harsher effects of foot-loose capital. These epigraphs suggest irreconcilable extremes: on the one hand, that cultural policy is *the* solution to the 'general problem'; and, on the other hand, that no amount of public investment in cultural leverage and related partnerships with the private sector can satisfactorily ameliorate the devastating consequences of de-industrialisation. It is reductive to argue that because culture is an economic force in its own right, a growth industry and source of wealth, therefore, cultural policy is nothing less or, indeed, more than economic policy. Such a view is unrealistic. However, there is no necessary contradiction between wealth creation and improving the qualities of urban life: they may even influence one another.

In the passage from which the epigraph is taken, Worpole adds, '[i]n any programme of urban and civic renewal, getting the economic base right is going to be a key ingredient', including, for him, cultural industry in the broadest sense. The difficulty here is that cultural industry can become an exceptionally elastic concept, ranging from the arts and crafts workshops discussed by Worpole himself all the way across to mass-market retailing, shopping as a creative pursuit. Attracting yet more chainstores to a rundown city centre is sometimes seen by local government as one of the few practicable means of improving the 'quality of life', by countering an ex-urbanisation process in which shopping and entertainment facilities are located increasingly on the outskirts of the city with damaging consequences for public transport and accessibility.

Harvey's position is more nuanced than is implied by the epigraph. In the same interview from which it is taken, Harvey (1993a: 16) remarks, 'one of the possible benefits from cultural industries in the centres of cities is that, insofar as you can bring back predominantly the suburban upper middle class into the city centre, you will involve them at some level or other with what's going on in the city, as opposed to them sitting out in the suburbs and saying: what's going on down there has nothing whatsoever to do with me'. He is concerned mainly with economic transformation in the crisis-ridden cities of Britain and the USA, crises brought about by de-industrialisation. Harvey's perspective meets up with Worpole's, however, on the question of recovering the practical sense of a public sphere under conditions not only of economic restructuring but also of cultural privatisation and social segregation.

Issues of urban regeneration and cultural policy are numerous and heterogeneous. This chapter concentrates on just three aspects at rather different levels of abstraction and complexity. First, the dual theme of globalisation and localisation is related to urban culture and economy. Second, urban renewal strategies conducted through cultural policy are outlined and examples of success and failure considered. Third, excessive civic boosterism is called into question with regard to civil unrest amongst the socially excluded.

LOCALISING THE GLOBAL

The most insightful commentators on globalisation stress its dialectical relationship to localisation. Anthony Giddens (1990: 64) defines 'globalisation' as 'the intensification of worldwide social relations which link distant localities in such a way that local happenings are shaped by events occurring many miles away and vice versa'. Annabelle Sreberny-Mohammadi (1991), meanwhile, stresses a 'dynamic tension between the global and the local'. David Harvey graphically depicts the double existence of everyday life situated in place and the sense of a larger global space in the following passage:

> [W]e live in a world of universal tension between sensuous and interpersonal contact in place (with intense awareness of the qualities of that place in which temporal experiences unfold) and another dimension of awareness in which we more or less recognise the obligation and material connection that exists between us and the millions of other people who had, for example, a direct and indirect role in putting our breakfast on the table this morning.
>
> (1993b: 15)

Giddens (1990) identifies four determinations of the late-twentieth-century process of globalisation. The first of these is a growing interconnectedness of the world capitalist economy. Transnational corporations are the key players, typically overriding the powers of the nation-state. Giddens, however, insists upon the enduring significance of the nation-state. The global system is still characterised politically by conflictual and cooperative relations between nation-states as the legitimate representatives of peoples in international affairs. The business rhetoric of globalisation and the reality of world markets have to be qualified, then, by this second feature of globalisation, the *interconnectedness* of nation-states. Third, there is the world military order which has survived the collapse of Soviet communism due to the economic imperatives of arms manufacture and trade, forever seeking wars to supply or threaten. Finally, there is the international division of labour which carves the world up into specialist territories: for instance, South-East Asia leading in the field of electronic goods, motor vehicle and steel production, shifting the fulcrum of economic power away from North America and North-Western Europe. Much of the story of urban regeneration as we approach the millennium is to do with strategies for reversing the economic consequences of declining heavy industry and manufacturing in the USA and Europe. At the same time, huge tracts of the South, in global terms, remain comparatively marginal to modern industrialism, never mind the development of informational and 'post-industrial' economies upon which 'the West' has staked its future.

The business rhetoric of globalisation and its myths (Ferguson, 1992) are closely related to instantaneous communications, resulting in what Harvey (1989a) has called 'time-space compression'. It is even claimed that the rapid circulation of market information and audio-visual news and entertainment are creating a 'global culture', a claim which routinely neglects local differences concerning command over and appropriation of communicational and cultural resources. Worldwide viewing of the same television programmes, for instance, may indeed contribute to longer-term shifts in peripheral cultures; this is likely to be so where television itself was not universally available until recently. Yet any reliable interpretation of such trends must be conditional upon adequate understanding of local religious, linguistic and other situational factors.

As Sharon Zukin says of global culture's home ground:

Swiftly fading from mind are the industrial prosperity that was guaranteed by U.S. dominance in the world economy and a shared middle-class way of life that was accessible by work and skill. In their place rise alternative images of great wealth, insecurity and fragmentation.

(1991: 3)

In a similar vein, David Harvey (1989a) has traced the transition from Fordism to a regime of 'flexible accumulation' in which the sheer mobility of capital leaves some places economically derelict while simultaneously developing productive capacity elsewhere, especially in places where labour is cheap or other favourable conditions prevail for accumulating wealth. Zukin calls this spatial restructuring of economies and places to live 'creative destruction'.

During the 1980s, in North America and Western Europe, a series of urban regeneration schemes emerged that were frequently led by flagship cultural projects, both permanent and transient, arts, leisure and museum complexes, festivals and spectacular events. These projects were accompanied by the postmodernisation of urban architecture and the built environment, buildings that quoted from the past construction of their surroundings and gave a glitzy look to city centres. Harvey (1989a) dates the origins of these developments from the early 1970s OPEC oil crisis and the coincidental reaction against the kind of modern architecture that symbolised a massified modernity and was functional to it. From that moment, the Fordist system of mass production and consumption went into sharp decline in the hitherto advanced capitalist world and capital shifted into a more flexible regime of accumulation and product specialisation. Large-scale factory production switched increasingly from comparatively high-pay countries and cities in the West to cheaper labour markets on the fringes of the First World and into the Japanese-dominated and high-tech Pacific Rim. Labour costs were reduced, computerised technologies were deployed intensively and stylistic differentiation of commodities became more fashionable than mass standardisation in the sphere of consumption. Some older industrial regions slid into seemingly terminal decline; others more or less swiftly adapted to the new economic and cultural conditions, particularly by applying the 'American model' of urban regeneration. This was pioneered by, for example, Baltimore's transformation from a blue-collar to a white-collar city with downtown financial institutions, luxury apartments, a plethora of restaurants, hotels and harbour marinas, only a short distance from dilapidated working-class housing and industrial districts (Harvey, 1993c), a spatial mix which was to be replicated in similar places, such as Northern English cities like Liverpool and Manchester.

Harvey (1989b: 259) sees these 'transitions in the urban process as a key point of integration of the political-economic move towards flexible accumulation and the cultural-aesthetic trend towards postmodernism'. Urban growth coalitions competed with one another to make their cities the image winners in a desperate battle for survival, resulting in 'socially wasteful investments that contribute to rather than ameliorate the over-accumulation problem that lay behind the transition to flexible accumulation in the first place', according to Harvey (p. 273). Harvey goes on to ask sardonically, 'how many successful convention centres, sports stadia, disney-worlds, and harbour places can there be?' Such urban regeneration, in effect, articulates the interests and tastes of the postmodern professional and managerial class without solving the problems of a diminishing production base, growing disparities of wealth and opportunity, and the multiple forms of social exclusion.

Zukin (1991) sees the landscapes of creative destruction not just as physical places but as mental representations, imaginary maps that organise desire and consumption in a post-productivist economy. She refines the general analysis of spatial fixes with a precise taxonomy of urban responses to economic and cultural change. In her book *Landscapes of Power*, Zukin presents five case studies that exemplify different forms of urban transformation in the USA, from the worker buyout of the steel plant at Weirtown, West Virginia, to the contemporary 'capital of symbolism' in Florida's Disney World. In between, there is the stark example of de-industrialisation in the old Motown of Detroit. Zukin (1991: 103) remarks, 'since the early 1970s, an influx of imported cars and a failure to meet qualitative changes in consumer demand had played havoc with Detroit, the auto city'. A similar scenario unfolded across the older industrial map of Britain, most dramatically in the once prosperous West Midlands of England, centre of the British car industry. These are among the paradigmatic cases of de-industrialisation, leading not only to high levels of unemployment but also to a sense of despair, hardly relieved by what Zukin calls 'quixotic' urban renewal projects. Detroit's corporate and governmental efforts, for instance, failed miserably: in spite of the downtown investments that were made, unemployment in Detroit stood at 36 per cent at the end of the 1980s.

While the urban core of Detroit continued to decline, growth occurred in its outlying districts, which is a typical pattern of 'Edge City' development in the USA:

The divided landscape around Detroit and most other large American cities indicates a major reversal of meaning between the city and its suburbs. Until quite recently we thought of cities as the economic heartland whose vast wealth nourished a surrounding, and clearly subordinate, regional culture. The city had smokestacks; the suburbs had tract housing developments. The city had sleek office towers; the suburbs had poky commuter trains. The city had theaters and concert halls for original performances; the suburbs had mass culture's derivative shopping centers and drive-in movies. This socio-spatial differentiation repeated the pattern of form following function, with 'suburbanism' considered a form of consumption derived from the city's productive functions. More critical, however, is the fact that the city has always financed the suburbs. Investment by the city's banks builds highways and shopping centers. Employment in the

city's offices pays mortgages on suburban homes. And the concentration of 'social problems' in the city fuels the exodus outward into
the suburbs of all those people who can afford to move away. Even
in the glossiest cultural representations, it was never imagined that
the suburbs would compete with the city as a source of productive
wealth, a landscape of economic power.

(Zukin, 1991: 135–136)

The shift of economic power to the suburbs is exactly what happened
to places like Westchester County, New York State, one of Zukin's case
studies, which she dubs 'a prototype landscape of consumption'. Westchester County is not only somewhere to live and consume, however; it is also
somewhere to work. IBM, General Foods and several other companies
located major business 'campuses' there in the 1980s. Joel Garreau's *Edge
City* (1991), subtitled 'Life on the New Frontier', is a prize-winning
journalistic account of ex-urbanisation and a paean to the escapologists of
the American Dream, professional-managerial groups that benefit most
from a post-industrial and information economy. Garreau stresses 'the
global importance of grasping Edge City' (p. xxii) because it is, according
to him, the urban trend of the future. The eruption of multiple urban
cores stretching many miles out from and in between established cities, on
the pattern of the Los Angeles conurbation, is occurring across the USA.
Garreau provides a minimal definition of Edge City, USA: it consists of
at least 5,000,000 square feet of leasable office space, 600,000 square feet
of leasable retail space, more jobs than bedrooms, and the sense of being
one distinct place that was not yet a city thirty years ago. Although Edge
Cities may be identifiable places to their inhabitants, they do not necessarily have names. The place-with-no-name is typified by the space
between Interstates 287 and 78 in New Jersey. Edge City does not only
represent the decentring of the traditional city, it is, at least nominally,
itself decentred. The residents of Bridgewater Township between 287 and
78 campaigned for a centre in the late 1980s, 'a kind of twentieth-century
village green' (Garreau, 1991: 42). Instead, they got Bridgewater Commons,
a gigantic shopping mall with ground-level parking. Garreau admits that
the closest thing to a public space that you find in Edge City is a parking
lot.

Garreau is well aware of the criticisms that are made of Edge City and
when he began studying the phenomenon he shared most of them. However, he was won over by their elusive charms or, perhaps, merely came
to accept the inevitability of such spatial patterning, impelled by the suburban values of middle America and the economic logic of an informational
economy and consumerist society. Garreau argues strenuously against the
one-dimensional view of Edge City as merely 'white flight' places, citing
developments around Atlanta, in particular, that are favoured by the grow-

ing black middle class. John Lichfield has questioned Garreau's apologetics for Edge City, including his claim that racism is not a significant motive for its inhabitants. Moreover:

> Edge City, according to Garreau, offers the best of both worlds. It preserves something of the 1950s American small-town culture of soda fountains and drive-in movies and high-school proms. It also has city comforts and city chic and well-paid, interesting city jobs. In truth, more often, Edge City has the worst of both worlds. It has the congestion and impersonality of a city, without the sense of community which people have in small towns or city neighbourhoods.
>
> (Lichfield, 1992: 9).

The most ominous feature of Edge City, USA, however, acknowledged by Garreau himself, is the way in which its indeterminate political status, ill-defined by official boundaries, results in the effective privatisation of government, comprising unelected public-private committees and the policing powers of companies that own and run shopping malls. Does this finally represent the secret wish and utopian solution of the anti-government and tax-mean American professional-managerial class?

In addition to the 'ex-urbanisation' of Edge City, Zukin (1992) has identified a second archetypal 'postmodern' landscape, that of 'gentrification'. In her seminal work, *Loft Living* (1988), she analysed gentrification in Manhattan, how vacant industrial premises were converted into roomy and elegant apartments by artists and lifestyle aesthetes, apartments that were subsequently to be occupied by advertising executives and stockbrokers. In Zukin's further observations concerning gentrification in *Landscapes of Power* (1991), on returning in one of her case studies to New York, she discusses the expenditure of cultural capital by 'a college-educated generation' engaged in 'reflexive consumption' (p. 202), our old friends the postmodern petite bourgeoisie. They represent 'a critical infrastructure' in the formation of taste and ideas of the good life. Gentrification of inner-city districts has had considerable impact on the housing market, not only in the USA, when larger houses are returned to single-family occupancy and artisanal cottages are refurbished according to a cannibalised notion of traditional style. With the consequential rise in house prices, in Britain at any rate, lower-income groups, who had not already moved to outer-suburban council estates, were banished once more, for reasons of financial incapacity, from the more exquisitely recoverable inner-city districts.

There is still a persistent romanticism of the city, originating no doubt with Baudelaire, and promoted most famously in the 1960s by Jane Jacobs's *The Death and Life of Great American Cities* (1961), which launched innumerable conservation campaigns, and has to an extent been reiterated with somewhat greater sophistication more recently by Richard Sennett (1990) in his advocacy of 'a city of deconstructions'. Disorientation and uncertainty, the pleasures of the *flâneur*, the surprise encounter, the cosmopolitanism of the great city, and so forth, remain the intellectual ideal, which does not ask too many awkward questions about the material interests involved in the reconstruction of urban life after industrialism.

The danger in concentrating exclusively upon the local 'effects' of globalising trends, the international relocations of industry and trade, the rise of the informational economy, the speed of communications, ex-urbanisation and gentrification is to reify 'the process' and to forget just how shambolic and crisis-ridden capitalism can be, has been and continues to be. This point may be borne out by referring to the fiasco of private-property-led urban regeneration along the Thames in the East End of London (Schwarz, 1991; Sudjic, 1993; Colenutt, 1994). The historically unfashionable, on occasion politically explosive and always working-class part of the metropolis, economically dependent upon the docks and devastated by its loss of function, was supremely ripe for redevelopment in the early 1980s. Local democracy could do little to influence the New Right solution promoted by the London Docklands Development Corporation, which was founded by the first Thatcher government in 1981. This unelected quango (quasi-autonomous non-governmental organisation) was entrusted with enormous and sweeping powers to appropriate land and to reconstruct the space of 'Docklands' in the image of a *laissez-faire*, information-based and financial-service economy, unrestrained by the traditional working-class and socialist politics of the area. There was considerable negotiation and manoeuvring in the early years, but once the Canadian company Olympia and York, which had developed the World Financial Center in New York, took control of the Canary Wharf project in 1987 the eventually complete yuppification of the East End looked assured. Cesar Pelli's office block rose up to be the tallest building in Britain in 1991, amidst wine bars, upmarket shops and expensive apartments, apartments that exceeded the spending power of the indigenous population – and indeed many of the incoming yuppies, as it turned out. The whole financial house of cards collapsed with Olympia and York in 1992, leaving a grotesque reminder of 1980s 'enterprise culture' and its deeply flawed agenda for the future. As Bob Colenutt (1994) has observed, one of the negative effects, amongst several, was to exacerbate the long-established scapegoating and racist resentment against the local Bangladeshi population by members of a white working class who were excluded from affordable housing and decent employment prospects in the once-to-be 'regenerated' Docklands.

RECLAIMING THE CITY

There are different levels for analysing where people live and make sense of their lives, from, for example, a focus upon the megalopolis, Deyan Sudjic's (1993) '100–mile city', linked into various globalising systems of fast communication, to the textures of everyday life in any particular place you care to name around the world. To what extent these different levels of analysis connect and how they mutually inform one another is a complex and open question. Doreen Massey describes the potential range of foci brilliantly in the following passage:

> Imagine for a moment that you are on a satellite, further out and beyond all actual satellites; you can see 'planet earth' from a distance and, unusually for someone with only peaceful intentions, you are equipped with the kind of technology which allows you to see the colours of people's eyes and the numbers on their numberplates. You can see all the movement and tune into all the communication that is going on. Furthest out are the satellites, then aeroplanes, the long haul between London and Tokyo and the hop from San Salvador to Guatemala City. Some of this is people moving, some of it is physical trade, some is media broadcasting. There are faxes, e-mail, film-distribution networks, financial flows and transactions. Look in closer and there are ships and trains, steam trains slogging laboriously up hills somewhere in Asia. Look in closer still and there are lorries and cars and buses, and on down further, somewhere in sub-Saharan Africa, there's a woman – among many women – on foot, who still spends hours a day collecting water.
>
> (1994: 148–149)

Massey stresses 'the power-geometry of time-space compression', by which she means that it does not affect everyone to the same degree: some are in command of space and time; others are caught in place with little or no control over temporality. Massey says:

> [A]mid the Ridley Scott images of world cities, the writing about skyscraper fortresses, the Baudrillard visions of hyperspace ... most people actually live in places like Harlesden or West Brom. Much of life for many people, even in the heart of the First World, still consists of waiting in a bus-shelter for a bus that never comes. Hardly a graphic depiction of time-space compression.
>
> (1994: 163)

This section concentrates upon urban regeneration and cultural policy in Western Europe and particularly in Britain where both American and European models of strategic renewal have been applied (Bianchini and Schwengel, 1991). The American model inspired Conservative central

103

government policies whereas the European model functioned as an alternative approach for the more ambitious Labour-controlled local authorities. Although no pure ideological and political distinction can be made, private-property-led redevelopment strategies and out-of-town leisure and retailing complexes are indicative of the American model, on the one hand, and Europeanism, on the other hand, is characterised by less immediately tangible attempts to recover the city centre for public culture. The European model is associated with 'café society', the city centre as a convivial and safe place to visit in the evenings for all sections of the population.

The Thatcher government set up urban development corporations to issue leverage grants to property developers, such as Olympia and York in the East End of London. Bianchini and Schwengel (1991) identify two features of this strategy. First, it seized control over urban development from local government and was undemocratic. Second, it resulted in the widespread privatisation of public space. Out-of-town developments are exclusively commercial space and city-centre shopping malls are locked up in the evenings when the customers have gone home. Such privatisation of public space erodes urbanity and social cohesion. The European model, in contrast, aims to foster employment in the cultural industries and seeks to revitalise 'the public realm':

> [W]hat do we mean by the 'public realm'? The public realm, or public sphere, certainly does not coincide with the public sector. The public realm is the sphere of social relations going beyond our own circle of friendships, and of family and professional relations. The idea of the public realm is bound up with the ideas of expanding one's mental horizons, of experiment, adventure, discovery, surprise.
>
> (Bianchini and Schwengel, 1991: 229)

Continental-European-style urbanity, for commentators like Bianchini and Schwengel, is connected to the city centre, the hub of transport and communications; where a sense of civic identity is inscribed in the physical environment. Furthermore, it is 'neutral territory', in principle nobody's and everybody's possession. There are a number of practical policy proposals flowing from this city-centre focus: adequate and cheap public transport; well-lit and sensitively policed streets where women are not frightened to walk; mixed development of residence with shops, restaurants and entertainment venues; imaginative and 'soft' urban design strategies; the formation of 'cultural quarters' with sufficient density to achieve a lively night-time environment.[1] Something rather like the myth of Paris, in fact, and sadly missing in the past from British conceptions of city life, with the notable exceptions of London's West End and central Edinburgh.

The social-democratic agenda for reclaiming the city centre responded to the 'retail revolution' of the 1980s, which was the main preoccupation of the influential Centre for Local Economic Strategy pamphlet *City Centres, City Cultures* (Bianchini *et al.*, 1988). It was also at the heart of much consultancy work done by Comedia for Labour-controlled local authorities. In addition to worsening problems of traffic congestion, Ken Worpole sees the retail revolution as having had extensively deleterious consequences for the quality of urban life:

> The [retail] revolution involved widespread physical alteration to the built fabric of most towns and cities, and changes in local economic leverage, involving: pedestrianisation of high streets; development of covered shopping centres; appropriation and ownership of town centres by pension funds and insurance companies; creation of closed, private spaces in town centres where public thoroughfares and pedestrian routes used to be; escalation of town-centre rents so that only multiples could afford to be there; requirement for large-scale dedicated car parking space; growth of the financial services sector in high-street premises (building societies, cash-dispensing machines); decline of secondary shopping areas; decline of town-centre housing and residential accommodation; and finally the marginalisation of town-centre districts where traditional facilities (libraries, museums, theatres) were sited, as shopping centres created new centres of critical mass elsewhere.
>
> (1992: 16–17)

Practical inspiration in Britain, as well as idealisation, was culled from continental Europe for retrieving the public domain of town and city centres from the privatising forces of the Thatcherite and retail revolutions. Franco Bianchini and Michael Parkinson's edited book of case studies, *Cultural Policy and Urban Regeneration* (1993), usefully charts and compares urban cultural policies across Western Europe. City-based strategies were facilitated in the 1980s by decentralising political trends. Contrary to Britain, a number of central governments on the European mainland devolved power and money to regions and cities, thus giving encouragement to the idea of a 'Europe of the regions'. France, where the state had been exceptionally centralised since Napoleon, quite different from the decentralised *Länder* system of the Federal Republic of Germany where national unification was always a problem, is the outstanding instance of decentralisation during the 1980s. When the Socialists came to power in 1981 they sought to develop communications and cultural industry in the regions. Patrick Le Gales (1993) reports on a typical French case in his study of Rennes in Britanny. In October 1982, Mitterrand's Minister of Culture, Jack Lang, signed a convention with Rennes city council agreeing to fund an expansion of spending on culture in the city and its hinterland. This kind of arrangement was not peculiar to Rennes. There is also a study of Montpellier (Negrier, 1993) in the Bianchini and Parkinson book.

105

Between 1978 and 1990 the major French cities' expenditure on culture rose from, on average, 8 per cent of their budgets to 15 per cent. This was intended not only to improve 'the quality of life' but to stimulate economic growth at local and regional levels as well.

Even in Britain, where regional and local democracy were reduced and spending was restricted by Conservative central government, significant developments also took place in the cities and regions. There was a devolution of funds from the Arts Council to the Regional Arts Associations, subsequently renamed Regional Arts Boards. The urban development corporations (UDCs) also supported cultural projects with a regenerative and economic purpose. These UDCs were established as quangos to assume responsibilities held previously by the metropolitian county councils that were abolished in the mid-1980s. For example, the Merseyside Development Corporation promoted the Liverpool Garden Festival and 'regeneration' of the Albert Dock to house the Tate Gallery in the North, bijou shops and restaurants. So, although Britain was backward by Western European standards, developments occurred similar to those of comparable countries like France and Holland; and this happened in spite of the fact that public cultural expenditure in Britain remained much lower than in such countries. In another important respect Britain was in step with the rest of Western Europe and, to some extent, ahead of it by shifting cultural policy out of an exclusively state-subsidised sector. Across Western Europe, during the 1980s, public-private partnerships arose, allying local governments closely with business interests in the formulation and funding of urban regeneration strategies. And whereas creative cultural policies had originated generally on the Left, often deriving from 1960s and 1970s counter-culture movements, the promise of cultural policy was appreciated increasingly by private business and the political Right, thereby forging a new consensus regarding culture, economy and polity at regional and local levels.

The striking thing, however, confirmed by a number of studies in the Bianchini and Parkinson book, is the paucity of evidence that direct economic benefit has accrued from cultural investment strategies in Western European cities. In their study of Hamburg, Jürgen Friedrichs and Jens Dangschat (1993: 132) say that 'economic growth can be induced without a clear cultural policy and spectacular new buildings for culture'. '[M]ost probably,' they remark, 'investment in culture is not a major factor for success in urban regeneration strategies.' However, as Friedrichs and Dangschat also note, a number of cities have succeeded in repositioning their images through cultural policy. The most commented-upon example is Glasgow, which went from a reputation for being a rundown and violent city through the 'Glasgow's Miles Better' campaign of the early 1980s to become European City of Culture in 1990. Other cities had similar but more modest success in re-imagining themselves, such as Rotterdam and

Bilbao. By investing in festivals, performance venues, galleries and museums, and by making general improvements to their built environments, these cities have, in effect, engaged in 'city marketing', which has indirect economic benefits that are difficult to measure. A few extra jobs in catering and occupations ancillary to cultural production, which are typically low-paid and casual, do not eliminate high levels of unemployment. New business may, however, be attracted to a city but not necessarily in the cultural industries. Evidence suggests that companies' relocational decisions are based more on local labour-market conditions, transport and housing than on the aesthetic ambience of a city. Servicing the tastes of an influx of young professionals and managers, moreover, may not be to the advantage of local working class, unemployed and marginalised groups, including ethnic minorities, whose spending power is not high. This is one of the main tensions in urban regeneration strategies conducted through cultural policy.

In spite of Bianchini's advocacy of cultural investment for local economic development, he is not troubled by the revelation that its effectiveness in wealth creation is unproven. Concluding *Cultural Policy and Urban Regeneration* (Bianchini and Parkinson, 1993), Bianchini outlines his 'holistic cultural planning' perspective, a perspective which is irreducible to instrumental reasoning and the accomplishment of economic goals. Economistic cultural policy is vulnerable to holistic criticism since it privileges the economic over aesthetic and social considerations with, ironically, dubious results in its own terms. Bianchini's holistic approach implies a more complex view of culture and citizenship than that of a reductive *homo oeconomicus*, adding cultural rights to T.H. Marshall's trio of civil, political and social rights. Traditional planning methods, legitimated by positivistic knowledge and powerful interests, are inadequate, not least because of the unintended consequences of post-Second World War reconstructions of the built environment. With Charles Landry, Bianchini recommends a creative, lateral and synthetic mode of thought and practice in urban and cultural planning which recognises the limitations of instrumental reasoning and the fallibility of 'scientific' expertise (Landry and Bianchini, 1995). Patsy Healey's (1989) 'planning as debate', inspired by Habermas's theory of communicative action, is also at the heart of a way of thinking that breaks with undemocratic and blinkered practice. Enabling procedures for public consultation and open negotiation, not restricted to the representatives of big business and official politics, are required if 'the creative city' is to be built. As Bianchini and Schwengel say,

> Cities will be re-imagined in democratic forms only by creating the conditions for the emergence of a genuinely public, political discourse about their future, which should go beyond the conformist platitudes

of the 'visions' formulated by the new breed of civic boosters and municipal marketers.

(1991: 234)

Kevin Robins is equally sceptical of civic boosterism. He observes acidly of the postmodernist and marketing hype that has characterised much urban regeneration rhetoric and strategy:

> With its emphasis on art, culture, consumption and a cappuccino lifestyle, the fashionable new urbanity seems to be shaped in the image of exactly the same social group that stands behind the wider political programme of post-Fordism . . . [I]t is only about revitalizing fragments of the city. It is about insulating the consumption of living spaces of the postmodern *flâneur* from the 'have-nots' in the abandoned zones of the city.

(1993: 321, 323)

The sense that cities are being transformed according to the postmodern imaginary of the professional-managerial class in a manner that exacerbates rather than diminishes social polarisation is also stated sharply in Manuel Castells's (1994) concept of 'the dual city'. Castells's speculative prognosis concerning the emergent 'informational society' is a far-reaching and, if accurate, challenging scenario for the future of urban life. The epochal transformation that Castells sees happening is located in four fundamental trends, viewed from a European perspective. First, there is the 'technological revolution' of computing and information transfer. This creates a worldwide infrastructure and intensified competition between cities. At once, the high command over message transmission is further concentrated in key centres while circulation and reception is greatly dispersed geographically. Communicational and cultural capacity, then, becomes increasingly vital for the economic success of cities and regions.[2] Second, the generic society which is emerging is 'informational', meaning that cultural, economic, military and political capacities are all increasingly knowledge-based. Third, the newly emergent 'global economy' is both related to and qualitatively different from the older world economy. Castells explains (1994: 21): 'By global economy we mean an economy that works as a unit in real time on a planetary scale.' Moreover, 'This global economy increasingly concentrates wealth, technology, and power in "the North", a vague geopolitical notion that replaces the obsolete West-East differentiation, and that roughly corresponds to the OECD countries' (p. 22). On this reckoning, Japan would be in 'the North'. 'The South' has become extremely heterogeneous, consisting of both, for instance, major growth centres in South-East Asia and stricken regions in Africa.

According to Castells, Western Europe remains, for the time being, 'a fragile island of prosperity, peace, democracy, culture, science, welfare and civil rights' (p. 22). European integration is the fourth fundamental trend analysed by Castells: 'the productivity and competitiveness of regions and cities is determined by their ability to combine informational capacity, quality of life, and connectivity to the network of major metropolitan centres at the national and international levels' (p. 29). Western European cities are, however, undergoing 'an identity crisis', particularly as a result of migration and racism. Class divisions are widening: 'Because the informational society concentrates wealth and power, while polarizing social groups according to their skills, unless deliberate policies correct the structural tendencies we are also witnessing the emergence of a social dualism that could ultimately lead to the formation of a dual city' (pp. 25–26). Members of the 'new professional-managerial class' are as far removed from the rest of the population now as the bourgeois household and exclusive places of recreation were in the nineteenth century. They are, however, 'torn between attraction to the peaceful comforts of the boring suburbs and the excitement of a hectic, and often too expensive, urban life' (p. 27). The privileged are mobile both physically and informationally in a social world where 'the space of flows' gains pre-eminence over 'the space of places'. '[T]he fundamental dualism of our time', then, says Castells, is between 'the cosmopolitanism of the elite' and 'the tribalism of local communities' (p. 30). In Castells's estimation, only local government can overcome the social and spatial tensions of contemporary urban life. He particularly stresses the need for cooperation between cities across Europe and he sees the traditional civility of European culture as 'a fundamental antidote against tribalism and alienation' (p. 32).

RIOTING PLACES

In 1992, the BBC televised an excellent Open University documentary on Los Angeles, City of the Future, made the previous year with the aid of Edward Soja, Professor of Urban and Regional Planning at UCLA and author of the influential Postmodern Geographies (1989). On screen, Soja described the symbolic and material 'regeneration' of a downtown that had never been great, illustrated by the Bonaventura Hotel, which was made legendary in social and cultural theory by Fredric Jameson's (1984) original observations on its postmodernist confusions of space and the place of the person within it. The programme also examined the multicultural world of the African-American and Latino inner-city poor, the siege mentality and guarded apartment blocks and shopping complexes of middle-class residents in the city, including the black middle class; and, finally, the 'communities', spatial apartheid and incipiently totalitarian neighbourhood conventions of Edge City developments on the outer rim of LA. There was no sense of anticipation in the programme, however, of anything like the impending riots of 1992, which indicates just how difficult

109

it is to hold together, in any satisfactory account, the many contradictory, fragmenting and perilous forces that traverse contemporary urban life.

The most spectacular sign of urban unrest is rioting, whether it takes place in inner-city ghettos or on suburban council estates, as happened in Britain during the early 1990s. As a form of popular protest, rioting has a long and honorable history preceding the modern industrial city. Rural protests before the advent of capitalism, like many an urban riot since, were sparked off by crises of popular consumption and production. People have rioted when food was denied them and their means of livelihood were taken away. Rioting is also a form of cultural expression, not much like chamber music but, nevertheless, meaningful. The messages issued by rioters are open to differences of interpretation, from anarchic disorder that must be dealt with by tougher policing and punishment measures to the most dramatic mode of protest available to the dispossessed: in that sense, rioting is an extreme demonstration or manifestation of grievance. Rioting articulates a deep malaise in the current state of culture and society, signifying social injustice and resentment.

When, in the spring of 1992, a white suburbanite jury acquitted four white police officers for the brutal beating up of the black Rodney King for drunken driving, an offence that was seen by all the world on televised amateur video footage, south-central Los Angeles went up in flames. Anger was channelled, in a displaced manner, not only on the perpetrators of the outrage, the LAPD and the 'justice' system, but upon Korean shopkeepers and innocent white motorists unfortunate enough to be there, thus giving vent to diffuse and pent-up resentments. Looting and murder were not a peculiarly black response, nor were these the favoured tactics of black people in general. Race was indeed a factor, however, along with class. There was a certain intellectual sophistry around amongst commentators concerning the questionable 'truth value' of any moving images captured on video. A more disturbing possibility to consider, though, was that the white jurors on the case were perfectly clear about what they saw, never doubting for one moment the veracity of the video record, and what they saw was deemed all right. At a deeper level, the protection of their standard of living, their quality of life and their sense of security was being served by the summary treatment dished out to Rodney King, who was obviously a dangerous figure from the black 'underclass'.

Why should city and town centres be seen as such 'dangerous' places routinely, places that are prone, at the extreme, to flare-ups like the Los Angeles conflagration of 1992? Of the LA riots, the journalist Alexander Cockburn observed, 'Everyone knows why the riots began: 27 years after the Watts rebellion, 12 years after Ronald Reagan took office, south central LA has been drained of jobs, services and hope' (*New Statesman & Society*, 8.5.92). If everyone knows why these problems arise, then surely the solutions must be clear enough? Not at all, because what we see on the surface is the manifestation of deeply embedded problems that are stubbornly resistant to clear-cut political solutions.

John Kenneth Galbraith's (1992) analysis of middle-class 'contentment' and the anguish of 'the underclass' provides an incisive account of the deadlock. In his book *The Culture of Contentment*, published just before the LA riots, Galbraith pointed to the structural relation of comfortably-off majority populations in rich countries like the USA and Britain to a deprived minority that is often distinguished by race and ethnicity as well as by an insecure socio-economic position. This is the same structural division that Goran Therborn (1989) has dubbed the 'two-thirds, one-third society'. 'The culture of contentment' has four distinguishing features. First, there is 'the affirmation that those who compose it are receiving their just deserts' (Galbraith, 1992: 18). Second, 'short-run public action . . . is always preferred to protective long-run action' (p. 19). Third, for the comfortable majority, 'the state is seen as a burden' (p. 22). Fourth, there is a remarkable 'tolerance shown by the contented of great differences in income' (p. 26). Using a term that frequently appears in right-wing social commentary to denote the allegedly wasteful destination of the culture of contentment's taxes, 'the underclass', Galbraith proffers a radical thesis:

> [T]he underclass is integrally a part of a larger economic process and, more importantly, . . . it serves the living standard and comfort of the more favored community. Economic progress would be far more uncertain and certainly far less rapid without it. The economically fortunate, not excluding those who speak with greatest regret of the existence of this class, are heavily dependent upon its presence.
>
> (1992: 31)

The classical Marxist model of a proletarian majority struggling with a bourgeois minority does not account for the material 'contentment' of modern majority populations and the suppression of class struggle in richer countries. Standards of living for such majorities have risen so high comparatively and the rewards of their life situations have become so appealing globally that resentment is inevitable. Exploited and excluded minorities are, however, weak politically. Low-paid work in what remains of the factory system and even lower-paid 'service' work, insecure and part-time, especially for women, remains to be done, usually by children of the Diaspora. Alternatively, there is unemployment and what the New Right like to call 'welfare dependency'. The contemporary underclass recalls Marx's 'reserve army of labour', a 'flexible' workforce that is recruited and discarded at ease. It is little wonder that members of the underclass, which has to be loosely defined as a residual category (Morris, 1994), opt out entirely, living on their wits in a shadow economy or resorting to a life of crime. The underclass's citizenship rights are substantively less, either formally, as in continental Europe, or informally, as in the USA and Britain, than those of the contented majority.

Consistent with his broadly social-democratic politics, Galbraith proposed public expenditure solutions to the problems of the underclass in the year of the LA riots:

> Life in the great cities in general could be improved, and only will be improved, by public action – by better schools, by strong, well-financed welfare services, by counseling on drug addiction, by employment training, by public investment in the housing that in no industrial country is provided for the poor by private enterprise, by adequately supported health care, recreational facilities, libraries and police. The question once again, much accommodating rhetoric to the contrary, is not what can be done but what can be paid.
>
> (1992: 180–181)

These solutions have been distinctly unappealing to the contented majorities of the 1980s and 1990s since it would be their money, their increased income taxes, that would be spent on improving the life chances of the discontented minority. Yet the interests of the contented majority might be better served in the end by ameliorating the grievances of those beneath them sooner rather than later, according to Galbraith, which was so with such measures in the not-too-distant-past.

The political voice of the LA rioters, following the riots, seemed to speak otherwise. Much of what happened has been mythologised, particularly the claim that the two leading gangs, the Bloods and the Crips, established a truce directly after the riots, inspired by the 1978 Camp David accord between Egypt and Israel. Mike Davis (1993b) has shown that the truce actually occurred three days *before* rioting broke out for local reasons unrelated to the first verdict on Rodney King's assailants. 'The Plan' that these gangs later drew up was revealing. Commenting on regeneration proposals in the gangs' plan, Martin Walker reported their content as '[t]exts of classic town planning orthodoxy mixed with utopian dreams and streetwise common sense and [with their] loathing of welfare dependency [they] would gladden the heart of Ronald Reagan or Margaret Thatcher' (*Guardian*, 30.5.92). In return for helping the police to maintain order in south-central LA, the gangs demanded policing powers for themselves to force the local drug lords to invest their ill-gotten gains in community building and small business. Public money was sought only as a supplement to private investment in capitalist solutions for enterprising members of the underclass. A leader of the LA Crips, Clyde, made proposals to information technology companies, IBM, Xerox, Apple Computer and Microsoft, demanding free equipment and training for his gang members.

The conditions that gave rise to the events of April 1992 in Los Angeles were identified prophetically by Mike Davis in his book *City of Quartz*, published two years before. After the riots, Davis argued that the private-enterprise solution, led by the Rebuild LA (RLA) coalition of business corporations, which was heavily publicised at the time, proved to be no real solution at all: 'RLA's hype has simply displaced attention from the savage hollowing out of public services and employment' (1993a: 6). In 1965, President Johnson's Democratic administration had come up with the Model Cities legislation and federal investment in response to the Watts riots. Nothing of that kind was forthcoming during the Reagan–Bush era. The urban underclass had, to most intents and purposes, been abandoned economically, at a time of mass unemployment, homelessness, AIDS, drug-trafficking and addiction, not only by the Republicans but also the middle-class populism of Ross Perot and Clinton's Democratic presidency. Main-stream politics was concerned, first and foremost, with addressing the Edge City constituencies. Federal contributions to big city budgets had, by the mid-1980s, plunged to less than half of their mid-1970s level in percentage terms (Davis, 1993a: 11), thus hastening 'the virtual meltdown of local government' (Davis, 1993b: 45). Urban programmes were slashed and there was no sign of a reversal of this trend after the 1992 LA riots.

Between 1970 and 1990, in the USA, the ethnic composition of metropo-lises changed radically, losing 8 million whites from the ten biggest cities, while gaining nearly 5 million Latinos, a great many unenfranchised, 1.5 million Asians and nearly a million blacks. Davis regards the Edge City developments as 'white flight' encampments that have been, in effect, subsidised by the federal state. Spatial segregation according to race and class since the 1970s has eroded common citizenship. Davis (1993a: 14) remarks, 'While Reaganism was exiling core cities into wilderness, it was smothering suburban commercial developers and renegade industrialists with tax breaks and subsidies.' Although American social and spatial inequalities are very definitely racialised, Davis sees the withholding of public-policy antidotes to the ravages of de-industrialisation and post-industrialisation as a vicious form of class politics.

Beatrix Campbell (1993) takes a similar view of the comparatively less racialised manifestations of urban distress in Britain, the first genuinely post-industrial society in the straightforward sense of an industrial society which is no longer so. Britain had its fair share of race-related inner-city rioting during the 1980s, from Bristol in 1980, through the Brixton, Chapeltown, Handsworth and Toxteth riots of 1981, to the clash between the police and local youth on Tottenham's Broadwater Farm estate in 1985. In the early 1990s, however, rioting places were not so much the black inner cities as the white suburban council estates, places that were originally supposed to relieve the urban working class from the misery of decaying cities. These estates became 'mono-functional' ghettos, dormitory zones without sufficient facilities to alleviate jobless boredom and loss of hope amongst the young. As David Harvey (1993d) insists, 'it's vital to get beyond the simple myth of an urban underclass incarcerated in an inner-city prison and waiting to break out at any moment. To begin with, the term "inner city" is a misnomer. In Sheffield and Glasgow the problems are found on the edge of the city.'

Suburban rioting around Cardiff and Newcastle in the early 1990s featured white working-class antagonism towards Asian shopkeepers, similar in certain respects to the resentment against the Koreans of LA. Another notable aspect of these British events was motor vehicle delinquency, TWOCing (taking without the owner's consent) and joy-riding, normally late at night, and 'auto-acrobatics', such as the hand-brake turn, around outer-town council estates. The Blackbird Leys estate, on the outskirts of the ancient and cultured university city of Oxford, became 'an alternative Silverstone' (Campbell, 1993: 38) during the early 1990s. When the police tried to crack down on these well-attended yet, for most of the neighbourhood, terrifying displays of masculine bravado in August 1991, rioting ensued. Many of the boys involved were the sons of redundant carworkers from the Cowley plant that was originally established by Morris, later Lord Nuffield, founder of an Oxford college. Employment there had dropped from 30,000 to 5,000 over the preceding twenty years. The masculine attachment to cars is of prime symbolic significance in these events. As Campell observes, 'where men's employment in making cars had given way to young men's enjoyment in stealing them, the car was the fetish, *par excellence*' (p. 45).

In her account of the British suburban riots of 1991 and 1992, *Goliath* (1993), Beatrix Campbell stresses the role of working-class masculinity in depressed neighbourhoods in opposition to Charles Murray's moralistic attack on single mothers in 'underclass' culture: 'The argument of this book is that neither manners nor mothers are to blame, but that there is an economic emergency in many neighbourhoods' (p. 303). Campbell speculates, furthermore, upon how the *Robocop* and *Terminator* films, for instance, may have encouraged fantasies of aggressive masculinity in distressed conditions, contrasting the muscular response of men and boys with the actually more robust and solidaristic coping strategies of women. Campbell discusses how inchoate masculine protest can lead to hurtful behaviour towards inhabitants of the immediate vicinity, including wives and neighbours. Her wish, however, to challenge the conservative version of underclass conditions is less insightful sociologically than Galbraith's structural account of the underclass, which avoids treating the underclass as simply the figment of the New Right's imagination. Galbraith's (1992: 31) observation that 'the underclass is deeply functional' evokes an articulation of the places of trouble with the spaces of power, a relational explanation of underclass conditions instead of description and counter-description of how the poor live today.

Campbell (1993) does, however, situate her account of the 1991 and 1992 suburban riots within a general discussion of 'the decline of Britain', a theme which is taken up in the next chapter of this book. She also identifies how such disorderly conduct differs from older traditions of popular resistance. According to George Rudé (1980), the distinguished historian of troublesome crowds, it is more satisfactory to view outbreaks of riotous behaviour in the past as rooted in rational protest against unjust conditions rather than meaningless 'mob' behaviour. Riots have expressed popular aspirations and the desire for better conditions, however callously destructive they have appeared. Still, according to Campbell, the suburban rioting of the early 1990s was difficult to read since the message had no transformative intent. She says:

> These extravagant events were an enigma. They made worldwide news and yet they seemed to be powered by no particular protest, no just cause, no fantasy of the future. However, even in their political emptiness they were telling us something about what Britain had become; the message in the medium of riotous assemblies showed us how the authorities and the angry young men were communicating with each other. The riots were the young men's way of speaking to their world.
>
> (Campbell, 1993: ix-x)

6

NATIONAL HERITAGE

Britain is the world's first heritage state.
Deyan Sudjic

In a global economy and culture, the autonomy of a national economy and culture is called into question. Yet the nation-state retains legitimate authority, for the most part, in politics. Legitimacy and power, however, are not identical. As Raymond Williams (1984: 5) once remarked, 'the nation-state, for all sorts of purposes, is too large and too small'. Transnational communication flows bypass the regulatory powers of the nation-state. At the same time, 'the nation' tends to restrict the expression of sub-national identities within the territorial domain of the overarching state. A sense of national belonging is not, though, the mere figment of a redundant political imagination in a global/local matrix. Williams satirised it as follows:

> There was this Englishman who worked in the London office of a multinational corporation based in the United States. He drove home one evening in his Japanese car. His wife, who worked in a firm which imported German kitchen equipment, was already at home. Her small Italian car was often quicker through the traffic. After a meal which included New Zealand lamb, Californian carrots, Mexican honey, French cheese and Spanish wine, they settled down to watch a programme on their television set, which had been made in Finland. The programme was a retrospective celebration of the war to recapture the Falkland Islands. As they watched it they felt warmly patriotic, and very proud to be British.
>
> (1983b: 177)

The combination of national identity and loyalty to the nation-state is a fairly recent historical phenomenon, a constitutive feature of modernity (Hobsbawm, 1990). Nations are imaginary constructs, not absolute structures that have been in existence since time immemorial, according to Benedict Anderson's (1991) theory of 'imagined community'. People feel

116

a sense of national belonging without ever interacting with more than a tiny fraction of other subjects and citizens. Commonality with many strangers must be imagined. Anderson has traced how modern nations were constructed by a symbolic process which created the impression they had actually existed for much longer than really was so, aided by 'the invention of tradition' (Hobsbawm and Ranger, 1983). In premodern times, sovereign power was founded upon dynasty and regional hegemony rather than on a nation-state with mutually agreed borders in the modern sense. Moreover, language did not simply define nationality. European ruling classes, for instance, communicated with one another in the international languages of Latin and French whereas ordinary monolingual people spoke languages of lowly and regional status.

Formation of the modern nation-state is linked to the rise of capitalism and the role of print media in facilitating trade and producing an imagined community. Long before the advent of broadcasting, newspapers stimulated a sense of simultaneous but not instantaneous eventfulness amongst dispersed peoples in a national territory who spoke and learnt to read the same language. Newspaper readership is still largely confined to region or nation, unlike the greater globalising propensities of audio-visual media. While it needs to be appreciated that nations are historically and culturally imagined, it is equally important to understand their resilience. The extraordinary thing about nations is how willing people have been to die for them. Patriotism has a necessarily symbolic dimension that is made concrete literally in monuments of a nationhood forged and safeguarded by war. Anderson (1991: 10) notes how difficult it is 'to imagine, say, a Tomb of the Unknown Marxist or a cenotaph for fallen liberals'. Only religion is so effective as nationalism in fostering and sustaining such widespread solidarity. Nationalism and patriotism have remarkable emotional force. That powerful interests should be so concerned, then, with securing their suasion over others by insisting upon respect for national culture and heritage is not surprising. For this reason, the historical imagination looms large in the cultural policies of all nation-states but especially so in 'old countries'. Post-imperial England and what has been its unusually stable multi-national British state, covering Scotland, Wales and part of Ireland, is a notable instance of how the past exerts tremendous ideological sway.

DECLINING BRITAIN

Deyan Sudjic's assertion that Britain is the world's 'first heritage state',[1] uttered on the occasion of the tenth anniversary of English Heritage, the quango charged with preserving and 'listing' historic properties, was both an incisive observation and a misleading exaggeration. It is true to say, however, that 'heritage' is a big deal in the British Isles. When the Conservatives won their fourth successive general election in 1992 they did

117

what Labour and the Liberal Democrats were proposing to do for several years: they founded a ministry of culture, a ministry with a conservative name, the Department of *National Heritage*. Ministerial responsibility for communications and culture had been distributed piecemeal around a number of departments of state: 'the arts' under Education during periods of Labour government and under the Treasury since the early days of Thatcherism, broadcasting in the Home Office with police and prisons, and film in the Department of Trade and Industry. More in keeping with European rationalism than with traditional British empiricism and its atomistic habits of administration, the new ministry assumed responsibility for sport, museums and libraries as well as arts, media and the hitherto narrower referent of 'heritage', the built and landscaped environment. That 'heritage' should be adopted as the generic title for a cultural ministry the very idea of which was previously held in contempt by British Conservatives as *dirigiste* and potentially Stalinist indicated a backward-looking rather than forward-looking set of governmental preoccupations. Coal mines and factories were already being turned into industrial heritage sites as the economy spiralled forever downwards. Meanwhile, English Heritage, Canute-like and too late, implemented its listing policy over-zealously in order to regulate improvements to old and not-so-old buildings. According to heritage critics like Sudjic, such obsession with the past deflected attention from a dismal present and an unpromising future. Although British attachment to heritage is not in itself exceptional, a strong case has indeed been made out for seeing excessive immersion in the past and its glorification as implicated somehow in long-term economic and political decline.

Heritage is an international phenomenon promoted by governments concerned with national identity and tourist revenue and, also, by the commercial exploitation of ubiquitous and popular fascination with the past in diverse forms of entertainment, including theme parks and the nostalgia mode in cinema, television, music, fashion, home decoration and furnishing. The bicentennial celebrations of the American Revolution in 1976 and the French Revolution in 1989, for instance, demonstrated how selective representations of great moments from national history are rearticulated in the present. Disney's Mainstreet USA is perhaps the most famous simulation of an imaginary past for entertainment purposes, one which combines national propaganda with infantile regression. The Australian writer Donald Horne (1984), in his critical treatise on historical tourism, dubbed the whole continent of Europe 'the great museum', and this is no doubt how many post-colonial visitors to Europe see it. Playing the history card in international tourism is not, then, in E. P. Thompson's (1979) resonant phrase, one of 'the peculiarities of the English'. Nowhere is unhistorical or entirely absent from the international 'heritage industry'. Belief in national exceptionalism is, nevertheless, part of the problem addressed by the critique of heritage Britain.

Thatcherism initiated a project of 'regressive modernisation' (Hall, 1988a). Welfare-state socialism was to be swept aside and an enterprising spirit revived, the very spirit that made Britain so great in the past. As John Corner and Sylvia Harvey comment:

> [I]n a number of contradictory ways, 'heritage' and 'enterprise' have been officially mobilized to provide the imaginative dynamics by which transition might be managed at the level of national culture and its attitudinal deep structure. Although both notions led an active ideological and political life before the 1980s, the decade saw them extensively reorganized as they were semantically recharged with the forcefield of national politics. More specifically, it saw them *interconnected* as related elements of Thatcherite reconstruction. One cultural aspect of this process was the emphatic projection of new perspectives upon the national past and future, involving new ways of relating imaginatively to *continuity*, while admitting new principles of economic and cultural *change*.
>
> (1991: 45)

Thatcherism eventually proved an abject failure yet, for a season, it achieved a clever sleight of hand on the terrains of national culture and of British Conservatism. The most fundamental strand of 'regressive modernisation' derived not so much from Conservative party tradition but, instead, from nineteenth-century Liberalism's veneration of free trade and sound money: this was a key source of the vaunted 'enterprise culture'. Of lesser consequence, 'heritage' retained a doctrinal connection to Disraelian 'one-nation' Conservatism. Thatcher had it both ways, in effect, by pursuing the economic logic of international business and finance while paying lip service to the historical nation. For instance, backwoods Tories were allowed to insist upon the English literary canon and imperial history for the national curriculum while 'the market' ran riot over the mass media. You do not need to be a conspiracy theorist to see how 'heritage' may have served as a convenient albeit potent distraction from the more lucrative action in the cultural field, a not-too-important topic for critics to debate in the Murdoch-owned *Sunday Times*.[2]

Patrick Wright's *On Living in an Old Country* (1985) and Robert Hewison's *The Heritage Industry* (1987) both linked 'heritage' to British national decline. Neither regretted the loss of imperial power. Instead, they criticised heritage discourse for diverting public debate from the real problems of modernising an archaic state and crisis-ridden economy. The strengths of such a critical perspective demand serious appreciation before the weaknesses identified in Raphael Samuel's (1994) more sanguine account of heritage can be properly assessed. The economic and political conditions of declining Britain also need to be sketched in so as to comprehend the gravity of the critique of heritage.

119

The decline of Britain has a one-hundred-year-old history, dating from when it peaked as top nation economically and was still amassing the largest empire ever known. 'The first industrial nation' had attained dominance over international trade and commerce. In the period immediately preceding the First World War, both Germany and the USA were challenging British command over world markets. Their technologies and production systems were more advanced. Following the Second World War, France and Japan also surpassed Britain. The *longue durée* of decline accelerated during the 1960s and 1970s. Andrew Gamble says:

> The course of the hundred years decline was shaped decisively by two momentous choices. The first was the continued adherence to free trade and to the institutions of the liberal world order long after the conditions which had originally recommended it had disappeared. The second was the decision to fight Germany rather than the United States. In two world wars Britain helped destroy German ambitions to become the dominant world power. But instead of Britain's power being preserved, that of the United States was established.
>
> (1994b: 58–59)

Britain's decline is fraught with irony. It was free trade that made Britain rich and powerful and it was free trade that brought it down. The British fought for democracy and became the poor cousins of the most powerful democracy in the world, the USA, after the Second World War. The British economic decline has, of course, been relative, not absolute. Living standards rose greatly if not so greatly as elsewhere, although income disparities widened in the 1980s and 1990s, pushing the poor downwards and not only in relative terms. General economic growth needs to be mentioned because nostalgia for Britain's 'greatness' forgets how miserable were the material conditions of most Britons at the height of empire.

Gamble examines how Britain's decline has passed through a series of different phases, diagnoses and renewal strategies. He identifies three recurring debates, concerning 'national efficiency', 'modernisation' and 'social democracy', cross-hatched by four themes to do with the empire, the culture, the economy and democracy. They have each been variously inflected by 'market', 'state' and 'class' perspectives. Through the constant anguishing over the state of the nation there is a discernible continuity of thematic concern and a striking persistence of habituated forms of institutional life in Britain:

> The success of the traditional governing class in avoiding overthrow during the period of industrialisation, either by a radical industrial bourgeoisie or by a revolutionary working class, permanently shaped civil society and state in Britain. The degree of social conservatism amongst all classes, the tenacity of antiquated institutions, the secrecy

surrounding central processes in government and the major institutions of civil society, the enduring liberal perception of the state's
role in the market order – all these are easily recognised features of
twentieth century Britain, and they stem directly from the exceptional
continuity which British institutions have enjoyed.

(Gamble, 1994b: 74)

Will Hutton (1995:1) remarks in *The State We're In*, '[t]he British are
accustomed to success'; and, one can only add, there have been major
problems in coming to terms with a reduced status and power in the world.
Hutton identifies the financial system, situated in the City of London, as
the prime source of Britain's economic woes, and the unwritten constitution, with an archaic and discredited monarchy at its symbolic apex, as
the source of political limitations. The crucial feature of finance in Britain
is the addiction to quick and high returns. Outward investment, international trade and commerce, most notably insurance, have been favoured
in the past and continue to be so. Investment capital for domestic production is much less forthcoming: the consequences for British manufacturing industry and the indigenous development of new technologies have
been disastrous. For a comparatively weak national economy, it is remarkable just how much British-originated investment there is in the rest of
the world and how many major companies, according to stock-market
valuation, are registered in Britain: 'the country's role is to be a free-
market, offshore financial centre and base for transnational production'
(Hutton, 1995: 23). The comparative absence of 'smart money', meaning
long-term internal investment, is at the heart of the matter for Hutton.
Britain's most deadly economic disease, then, is 'short-termism', which
makes sense of both the emphasis upon high-yield external investment and
apparently irreversible internal decline. Furthermore, Hutton castigates
'gentlemanly capitalism' for lack of economic patriotism:

> This gentlemanly ideal is difficult to define – that is part of its
> mystique – but there is no doubting its motivating power for gener-
> ations of Englishmen. A gentleman does not try too hard; is under-
> stated in his approach to life; celebrates sport, games and pleasure;
> he is fair-minded; he has good manners; is in relaxed control of his
> time; has independent means; is steady under fire. A gentleman's
> word is his bond; he does not lie; takes pride in being practical;
> distrusts foreigners; is public spirited; and above all keeps his distance
> from those below him. The gentleman is a human island, simul-
> taneously aware of the nuances of rank while recognising the import-
> ance of integrity and reputation in his relationship with his peers.
> The civilization fostered by such values is extraordinarily favourable
> to finance, commerce and administration – but not to industry.

(Hutton, 1995: 114)

It would be too simple merely to read Hutton's critique of British business culture and economic policy as a variant on George Orwell's (1941/1982: 54) depiction of England as '[a] family with the wrong members in control'. *The State We're In* presents a very complex, multi-levelled and challenging thesis.[3] However, it is interesting to note how reluctant the ruling class has been to 'bat for England' when out to make money. Attachment to their English heritage is another matter. Patrick Cormack, the Conservative politician, published his book *Heritage in Danger* in 1976, the year that Chancellor of the Exchequer Denis Healey's plan 'to squeeze the rich until the pips squeak', declared on the occasion of Labour's general election victory in 1974, finally ran into the dust. Instead of imposing a wealth tax, Healey introduced public expenditure cutbacks at the behest of the International Monetary Fund. Healey's threat had, though, at first seemed real enough. For the political and cultural Right, it was reminiscent of a similar threat to the rich and their property posed by the 1945 Labour government.

The *Brideshead Revisited* scenario of a landed gentry beleaguered by socialism symbolised the reactionary politics of much 'heritage' discourse, for critics like Hewison and Wright. A key theme of grass-roots Conservatism is the decline of graceful living amongst those who are said to have built up the nation, its state system, great traditions and institutions, castles, manor houses and landscaped parks and gardens. In the first half of the twentieth century many old country houses were indeed allowed to go to rack and ruin, and several were demolished, as was documented by the historian of the country house, Mark Girouard. A whole history of grace and civilisation, inscribed in the rural idyll of the British aristocracy and gentlemanly business, was seemingly imperilled. Voluntary organisations, most notable of which is the National Trust, founded in 1895 and of enhanced significance after 1945, and public bodies of the 1980s, the National Heritage Memorial Fund and English Heritage, were funded in order to save the aristocratic and aristocratically veneered national past. The state spent money on heritage properties for 'the nation', not only to preserve its past in aspic, however, but also to make buildings and sites accessible to the general public.

'Heritage' was to incorporate the industrial past as well during a period of acute de-industrialisation and rising unemployment in the 1980s. Robert Hewison (1987) attacked 'the heritage industry', a term which he coined, for exacerbating national decline by substituting 'real' manufacturing with trivialising and economically marginal leisure facilities. The Wigan Pier Heritage Centre, for instance, made cultural capital out of George Orwell's famous visit to Wigan in the 1930s to see how the Northern working class were coping with the Depression. Then, 'Wigan Pier' was a sardonic joke: now it is a popular heritage attraction with actors dressed up in nineteenth-century factory costume to invoke a quaint image of the Victorian working class. The Ironbridge Gorge Museum in Shropshire has been designated a 'World Heritage Site' for representing the origins of industrialism in Britain (West, 1988). There is also the North of England Open Air Museum at Beamish in County Durham (Bennett, 1988b). Beamish is not the actual site of an industrial settlement but was constructed from bits and pieces taken from elsewhere. For Hewison, it is an offensive fake, a postmodern pastiche of Britain's industrial working past. Situated near Consett, a town devastated by the loss of its steel works, Beamish seems 'more real than the reality it seeks to record' (Hewison, 1987: 95).

Hewison's *The Heritage Industry* places too much stress on 'manipulation': 'At best, the heritage industry only draws a screen between ourselves and our true past . . . . Hypnotised by images of the past, we risk losing all capacity for creative change' (p. 10). In contrast, Patrick Wright's critique of heritage, *On Living in an Old Country* (1985), seeks to account for its popular appeal, its complexities and its contradictions. In his later work, *A Journey Through Ruins* (1992), Wright explores the role of the socialist George Lansbury in the early conservation movement as well as the National Trust's reactionary James Lees-Milne. Wright (1985: 4) does argue, nevertheless, that 'the unity of the nation is achieved at the cost of considerable mystification'. Yet, he insists, it also has a 'popular basis in everyday consciousness'. According to Wright, 'the rags and tatters of everyday life take on the lustre of the idealised nation when they are touched by its symbolism' (p. 24). This sheds light, for instance, upon the Royal Family's peculiar charm for the British populace since Victoria Saxe-Coburg's public relations campaign in the late nineteenth century through to Elizabeth Windsor's 'annus horribilis' in 1992. The hegemonic power of national heritage, topped off by monarchy, requires popular consent in order to work its spell. 'Traditional' symbols and rituals evoke a vicarious sense of security in a country on the slide for a century, creating nostalgia for an imaginary past more splendid and enchanting than the gloomy present.

Wright (1985) discusses the myth of 'Deep England', a national substratum preceding the travails of urbanism, industrialism and welfare-state socialism. The raising of the *Mary Rose* in 1982 was a strangely literal instance of Deep Englandism. When it sank in 1545 the *Mary Rose* was the flagship of the most legendary of English kings, the bluff, beef-eating and much-married Henry VIII, whose father was Welsh. A number of unsuccessful efforts to salvage the *Mary Rose* from the deep had been made over the intervening years. Its eventual raising happened to coincide with the naval recovery of the obscure and distant Falkland Islands, or Malvinas, from Argentina in 1982. In these two events there was, notes Wright, an unmistakable symbolic correspondence, in effect a contingent yet compelling metaphor.[4]

It is generally believed that the brief Falklands War occurred at a convenient moment for Margaret Thatcher's first government.[5] Monetarist policies had brought about rapid de-industrialisation, spiralling unemployment and governmental unpopularity. Naval victory in the South Atlantic, however, made some Britons feel better about themselves and their nation, in spite of the scandalous manner in which international rules of engagement were broken over the sinking of the *General Belgrano* as it steamed away from the British fleet. The victorious fleet returned to be greeted by jingoistic crowds at Portsmouth, reminiscent of the days when British imperial might really did rule the waves. It gave the lie to English 'understatement' and reiterated, instead, national traits of self-congratulatory belligerence and bloated chauvinism.

BACKING INTO THE FUTURE

The critique of heritage Britain is disputed fiercely by Raphael Samuel in his *Theatres of Memory* (1994), the first volume of a trilogy on popular memory, history and discourses of the national past. Samuel dubs not only Hewison and Wright but also the *Independent on Sunday* columnist Neil Ascherson 'heritage-baiters' and he takes them to task for their alleged elitism. It is Samuel's contention that '[w]e live ... in an expanding historical culture' (p. 25), of which heritage is a mainly popular, rather than imposed from above, set of representations and practices. His general position on heritage is summarised by him in the following passages:

> The past in question – the 'heritage' which conservationists fight to preserve and retrieval projects to unearth, and which the holiday public or museum visitors are invited to 'experience' – is in many ways a novel one. Though indubitably British, or at any rate English, it departs quite radically from textbook versions of 'our island story'. It has little or nothing to do with the continuities of monarchy, parliament or British national institutions ....
>
> The new version of the national past, notwithstanding the efforts of the National Trust to promote a country-house version of 'Englishness', is inconceivably more democratic than earlier ones, offering more points of access to 'ordinary people', and a wider form of belonging. Indeed even in the case of the country house, a new attention is lavished on life 'below stairs'.
>
> (Samuel, 1994: 158, 160)

Samuel contrasts the populist heritage industry with professional history, which, when it denounces 'heritage' for being false and superficial, is only defending a vested interest, keeping the past within a narrowly circumscribed academic frame. There is a direct line of continuity, according to Samuel, between the disdain shown for heritage on the part of professional historians and 'heritage-baiting' in broadsheet journalism. The term 'heritage' itself, denoting inheritance from the past, has a range of different connotations that are not reducible to either 'conservative' or 'commercial' meanings. Even in the sophisticated critique of heritage mounted by Wright, which is recognised by Samuel, there is a basic methodological error, that of 'expressive totality' (p. 242), the old complaint made by Althusserian Marxism of holistic interpretation. Wright does indeed seek to read a general message in particular cases, as in the example of the raising of the *Mary Rose*, which he holds to be 'expressive' of Deep Englandism. Furthermore, both Hewison and Wright do indeed treat the 1980s heritage industry as in some sense 'expressive' of British conservatism. Wright, however, is careful not to dismiss heritage simply as a reactionary conspiracy and he relates its appeal to popular consciousness in conditions of an unsettling late modernity. Samuel clearly has a higher opinion of Wright's arguments than he does of Hewison: *The Heritage Industry* is derided unfairly as a 'squib'. Nevertheless, Samuel fails to register the full subtlety of Wright's critique, much to both Wright's (1995) and also Ascherson's (1995) chagrin, so keen is he to distance himself from 'heritage-baiting'.

Samuel points to how hard-pressed Labour authorities have used heritage in urban regeneration schemes and he argues, with justification, that the revival of older styles and architectural conservation meet with widespread popular approval. In spite of this, '[h]eritage has ... emerged as one of the principal whipping-boys of Cultural Studies ... [and] [h]eritage-baiting has become a favourite sport of the metropolitan intelligentsia, the literary end of it especially' (1994: 259–260). Most elitist of the critics, for Samuel, is the Scot Neil Ascherson, whose articles on heritage in the *Observer* during the 1980s challenged what he called its 'vulgar English nationalism'.[6] The very word 'vulgar' betrays elitism, in Samuel's judgement. *Theatres of Memory* is a very substantial work of scholarship yet its attack on Ascherson, Hewison and Wright is more akin to journalistic polemic than scholarly disputation. Samuel's counter-criticisms are rarely substantiated with alternative evidence and interpretation, although there is an important argument made concerning what Samuel sees as a 'perceived opposition between "education" and "entertainment" in the critique of heritage Britain, 'and the unspoken and unargued-for assumption that pleasure is almost by definition mindless' (p. 271).

Wright and Ascherson both replied to Samuel's book, questioning his caricature of their arguments and his own apparent loss of critical sense. Wright (1995) was perplexed by the political shift that had occurred in Samuel's version of 'people's history':

> The late E.P. Thompson may have set out to rescue the working class from the condescension of posterity, but with Samuel the whole argument is apparently now shifted over onto the heritage trail. Those he wants to rescue from condescension are the metal detectorists and

historical re-enacters, the steam engine freaks and the 'living history' audience. There are still caricatured baddies in his picture, but in place of the old class enemy, we find the academic historian who arrogantly presumes to a higher truth than the popular enthusiast or theme park designer, and almost everyone who has had the nerve to criticise the British heritage industry.

Also responding to Samuel's attack, Ascherson (1995) raised the thorny question of historical truth. It is perfectly reasonable, remarked Ascherson, for Samuel to seek to interpret 'New Age' interest in 'leylines, astro-archaeology, Odinism, white witchcraft, Merlin ecology, megalithic trigo-nometry and so forth', as he does in one part of *Theatres of Memory*. There is no justification, however, for treating them as equivalent to valid historical knowledge. Analysing myths and recycled myths in their own terms is necessary yet, Ascherson (1995) insists, 'at some point, the truth or untruth of myth does matter'.

In passing, both Ascherson and Wright accuse Samuel of populism, 'evasive' for Ascherson and 'sour' for Wright. The populist assumptions embedded in Samuel's work need further probing in order to clarify the issues at stake in this particular debate over heritage. It would be difficult for the present writer to avoid commenting upon the way in which Samuel's *Theatres of Memory* conforms to my own critical description of 'cultural populism' (McGuigan, 1992 and 1996). Cultural populism is anti-elitist by definition: it calls into question established hierarchies of value and seeks to interpret the meanings of popular culture appreciatively. Mainstream cultural studies can still be characterised largely in these terms, regardless of Samuel's claim that cultural studies has a closer affinity to 'heritage-baiting' than to his own position. At one time, cultural studies saw popular culture as the product of 'the people' in creative tension with, though not necessarily direct opposition to, mass-consumer culture. In the later development of cultural studies there was a discernible switch from interest in the historical production of popular culture from below, which included, for example, youth subcultures, to mainstream practices of consumption; although consumption, in this sense, is theorised in a productivist frame-work, stressing the role of the reader, the active audience and the discerning shopper. What people do with cultural commodities and the meanings they make for themselves out of consumption is where the action has been for a great deal of theorising and research in cultural studies since the 1970s. I have argued previously, in short, that this exclusively consumptionist perspective ceases, quite irresponsibly, to be at all critical of mass-popular culture and it has become, in many respects, virtually indistinguishable from the free-market ideology of sovereign consumption. Moreover, cul-tural populism is insufficiently explanatory, hardly ever addressing the political economy of culture or satisfactorily locating cultural circulation within historical contexts and institutionalised systems of power.

The drift into uncritical populism is replicated by Samuel's recent departure from the original aims of 'history from below', inspired by writers like E. P. Thompson, and, indeed, from the tenor of Samuel's own collaborative project with History Workshop,[7] towards a mere celebration of 'heritage' consumption which is made possible by an abrogation of critical responsibility. My argument is not that 'heritage' should be roundly denounced, for whatever reason and in whatever form, but that critical questions should be posed concerning how the past is represented and used politically. Samuel does himself reflect upon the erstwhile radicalism of conservation movements and of popular historiography. He expresses regret at their deradicalisation:

> It is for anyone, like the present writer, who is a socialist, an unfortunate fact that these resurrectionary enthusiasms, emanating very often from do-it-yourself historical projects, popular in their sympathies and very often radical in their ancestry or provenance ... have been subjected to Conservative appropriation, and have strengthened the Right rather than the Left in British politics.

> (Samuel, 1994: 162)

And yet, despite his excellent analyses of 'retrochic', old photography and the dramatic representations of the past in contemporary film and television, Samuel (1994) persistently evades critical discussion of the at least debatable ideological meanings and political displacements that can be found in many 'heritage' representations. For instance, he has nothing but praise for Jorvik, the York Viking 'museum'. Jorvik is a telling example of what is at stake in the debate over heritage since it is genuinely controversial and has, for good reason, been much criticised. Ostensibly derived from local archaeological excavation, in effect Jorvik is nothing other than a theme-park ride through an environment that owes precious little, so far as I can see, to archaeological knowledge of Viking settlements and a good deal more to a certain style of children's storybook illustration turned into three-dimensional models of people and huts – and accompanied by the smell of fish. As the ride commences, the voice-over of Magnus Magnusson announces the freezing of history. The ride ends, as the rider leaves 'history', with a cordoned-off hole in the ground, meant to represent 'the dig'. When I visited Jorvik, most of the 'time-travellers', once they had been taken for a ride, dashed past the few shadowy relics displayed on the way out in order to reach the souvenir shop before it became too crowded. Jorvik is an over-priced and over-hyped yet comparatively modest theme-park ride, much inferior, in my admittedly subjective estimation, to theme-park rides that have no archaelogical pretensions. That many people, especially children, enjoy the entertainment supplied by Jorvik while learning nothing of archaeology is not at all surprising. What is surprising, however, is Samuel's comment on Jorvik: a 'brilliantly executed' simulation (p. 182).

Such 'heritage' attractions are now very common and many of them are privately owned and run for profit as lucrative forms of entertainment. They vary in quality, no doubt, and their meanings are open to differential interpretation like any complex message. For example, there is the Tetley Brewery Wharf museum in Leeds, West Yorkshire, opened in 1994. I enjoyed my visit there immensely because I am rather interested in beer, yet, in the end, I was also disturbed by the story it tells not so much about the past but about the future. The main attraction, in addition to stables, the display of beer-mats and trays, videos extolling the virtues of the drayhorse and of Joshua Tetley's enterprising spirit, and a trip around the brewery, is a series of dramatic tableaus telling the story of the English pub in history. Having passed through the Middle Ages, Eliza- bethan, Georgian, Victorian and Second World War England, and having been regaled by a Cavalier plotting the restoration of the monarchy during Oliver Cromwell's brief Commonwealth, the tour reaches the recent past and a representation of the future but no present. Visitors are seated in a small movie theatre with a screen not much bigger than a television set to watch a black-and-white promotional film ostensibly dating from the 1950s about the gravitational problems of beer-drinking in future space travel. It is always amusing to see how foolish were past representations of the future, actual or pastiche; this is all done for laughs in any case. When the video ends the spectators are then jolted back into their seats as they are swung around to see an altogether more dazzling and multi-coloured display of computerised video-imaging of a yet-distant future. We are now in the year 7823 at the Star and Crater pub where the robotic barmaid, Beveridge D. Spencer, introduces herself: 'You can call me Bev.' The cus- tomers, who are robots and various strains of mutant, are not drinking beer: they are drinking cocktails (screwdrivers and nuts for the robots). This very familiar collection of Hollywood-style grotesques are suddenly hurried into ordering and downing their last drinks: 'Last orders?', 'A bit more final than that!' The Universe is just about to end. Bev wishes us to 'Have a nice day – it's your last!' It is interesting and I believe significant that, on the end of a mildly diverting journey through a series of clichéd and entertaining moments from Ye Olde England, the future, however dimly imagined, has to be represented as a nightmare.

SELLING THE PAST

Heritage criticism is challenged not ony on populist grounds of political interpretation but also for failing to grasp the economic relationship between 'heritage' and 'enterprise', for missing 'the connection between the celebration and marketing of a selective past and a real, if limited, economic and commercial expansion' in the late 1980s (Corner and Harvey, 1991). Such an observation is inaccurate if applied to Hewison since his concern is exactly with the selling of the past, tourism and day-tripping. For example, Hewison (1994) has commented upon the re-presentation of the Crown Jewels at the Tower of London, which was done in order to increase throughput and raise admission charges. Commercialisation of 'heritage' is a feature not only of private enterprise but also of 'public culture' (Horne, 1994). It has been of increasing preoccupation to arts marketing and heritage management within the state-subsidised sector since the 1980s. To quote from a *Marketing Week* article of 1988:

> Ten years ago the very idea of linking the words 'museum' and 'marketing' would have seemed too crass to contemplate. Museums, after all, are seats of learning, and repositories for the wisdom and beauty of the ages. The New Enlightenment of 'fend for yourself capitalism', however, which has been sweeping the Western world, was eventually bound to reach into even these hallowed halls and after the initial shock, most people seem to agree the results have been decidedly beneficial. It isn't confined to Britain either. All over Europe, governments are saying that there is a limit to the public purse, and that museums must look for ways to raise as much money as possible, and become more 'user friendly' in the process.
>
> (Crofts, 1988: 48)

The *Marketing Week* article goes on to praise Saatchi and Saatchi's advertising campaign for the Victoria and Albert Museum, Britain's public museum of art and design, which repositioned its image from a musty and scholarly haunt to a popular tourist attraction during the 1980s. Heritage tourism has mushroomed everywhere over the past twenty years (see Urry, 1990). Priscilla Boniface and Peter Fowler (1993: xi, 1) declare unreservedly, 'Tourism is fast becoming the biggest industry in the world . . . [and] in the area of tourism, countries have courted a world market; their chosen object of enticement, more often than not, heritage.'

Clichéd versions of the nation and of particular places are inevitably used to attract foreign tourists[8] and the clichés of other nations are absorbed and rearticulated for internal consumption as well. In the USA, for instance, there are a number of displays of 'America' and of other nations. While Sharon Zukin (1991: 223) observes of the original Disneyland in Southern California that it offers 'a multidimensional collage of the American landscape', at Disney World's Epcot Center in Florida there is also a lakeside tour around a selection of national pavilions, thus incorporating a selective version of the whole world into the Disney Corporation's American landscape. Busch Gardens at Colonial Williamsburg similarly enables indigenous and foreign tourists to sample England, France, Germany and Italy at a distance (Rojek, 1993: 163).

The export of American popular culture to the rest of the world has frequently been cited as the main contemporary form of cultural imperialism: the siting of EuroDisney near Paris, for instance, was seen as such by critics, although the comparative failure of that venture has illustrated, instead, the limits to American cultural imperialism. Because the 'Americanisation' thesis usually over-simplifies what actually happens, there is a fashionable inclination to discard the very notion of cultural imperialism entirely in favour of a loose idea of cultural globalisation (Skovmand and Schrøder, 1992). A further complicating factor is the role of Japanese 'hardware' manufacturers in the global media industry seizing control of American 'software', exemplified by Sony's takeover of Columbia Pictures and Matsushita's of MCA/Universal, which, in the USA, despite the rashness of these Japanese business decisions, raised the question: who exactly is the cultural imperialist? Mitsuhiro Yoshimoto, a Japanese academic working in an American university, has explored this question with reference to Tokyo's Disneyland, established in 1983:

> [T]he idea of cultural imperialism becomes meaningful when the following two conditions are satisfied: (1) the basic unit of world politics is a nation-state constantly trying to reinforce its imaginary identity; and (2) imperialism or the economic domination of the periphery by the metropolitan states precedes or simultaneously occurs with the unidirectional overflow of foreign cultures from the latter to the former.
>
> (1994: 191)

Although Yoshimoto believes that '[t]he ideological objective of Disneyland is to equate the commodification of daily life with the narrativisation of American nationalism as a world economic power' (p. 192), he finds, in the case of Tokyo Disneyland, that if there is cultural imperialism going on it is the Japanese who are doing it, not the Americans. He points out that, unlike at EuroDisney, the name of 'Mainstreet USA' had to be changed to 'the World Bazaar' so as not to offend Japanese national sensibilities. This is only one manifestation of a much deeper process. Yoshimoto notes, following Donna Haraway, that 'nature' is closely associated with 'native' in Japan, which makes sense of the Japanese incorporation of other cultures into its own 'natural' environment. Japanese culture is eclectic yet totalising and comfortable with hybridity. The most 'Japanese' of American cultural institutions, Disneyland, was adapted to Japanese conditions. There are several more theme parks in Japan that simulate 'foreign monuments, villages, cities, or simply landscapes' (Yoshimoto, 1994: 193). 'Foreign villages' eliminate the negative features of American and European places of interest that Japanese tourists have to endure when they actually visit the USA and Europe. Simulated translations of them are, in certain respects, preferable to the real thing and consistent with a Japanese sense of self-identity.

Boundaries have been blurring between theme parks and museums, with museums becoming more like theme parks, particularly in the case of open-air museums, and vice versa. 'The museum experience' now, according to the conventional wisdom, has to be entertaining, not just educative, in order to draw in the crowds and make money. Although the popularisation of museums can certainly be seen as a positive development, it is also seen as a threat to the functions of conservation and scholarship, replacing serious curatorship with frivolous marketing. Issues concerning the museum 'renaissance' are many and varied, according to Robert Lumley's (1988) survey, not least of which is, first, the postmodernist wave of 'nostalgia', the retreat from the present, that greater enthusiasm for museum-visiting implies.

Second, there is the question of 'bias' or, better still, 'representation'. How museums signify the past and what is included and excluded are controversial. 'Bias' is too crude a concept for analysing what is at stake, however, because it suggests a simple divergence from 'objectivity', which in itself is a contested idea. A more satisfactory approach is to frame the issue in terms of negotiation and struggle over representation, an approach that does not presume to know the objective truth in, say, quantitative terms. From a feminist perspective, for instance, it ceases to be a question only of whether or not women's lives are represented but how they are represented, the narrative discourses and images that are deployed. A key stimulus, historically, for the formation of museums and connected disciplinary knowledges, such as anthropology, was European imperialism. Artefacts collected from 'the colonies' provided collections for ethnographic museums where 'Otherness' was conveyed through ethnocentric and, indeed, racist discourses. The ideological depiction and marginalisation of Native Americans in the museums of the USA pose similar problems for which progressive curators and pressure groups have sought to develop solutions through dialogue and debate (see, for instance, Karp and Lavine, 1991; Karp et al., 1992).

Third, there is the issue of what Lumley (1988) calls 'the public's point of view', concerning audience and interpretation. It is all very well for historians and curators to discuss what public museums should be like and what should be in them. But what does all this mean to visitors and potential visitors? Because all textual meanings differ according to who is interpreting them and how they are received and used in context, it is naive to assume a one-to-one fit in any communication. Museum curators used to be complacent about the meaning of their collections and rarely asked visitors what they thought of them. The stress on marketing has, however, brought about a greater concern with visitor research (see, for example, Merriman, 1989). An important consideration here is whether the museum visitor is conceived of as a customer to be persuaded or as a citizen with a voice in the representation of the past. This connects with the fourth issue identified by Lumley: 'commercialization'. Public museums are now required increasingly to perform like private businesses, adopting a 'proactive' visitor strategy, selectively charging for admission, marketing their wares and selling sundry commodities in gift shops.

Fifth, there is the issue of 'realism', once believed to depend exclusively upon displaying authentic objects from the past that were supposed to speak for themselves: the chair that Lenin sat upon or the crown that Queen Victoria wore. It has become disputable to what extent merely seeing such objects makes sense of Bolshevism or the British Empire. A fuller explanatory context needs to be provided so as to facilitate the learning experience. An outstanding example of such didacticism is the Bayeux Tapestry museum in Northern France. It has one authentic artefact, the Bayeux Tapestry itself, telling the story of the events leading up to and including the Norman Conquest of England in 1066. The visitor is not permitted to see the tapestry until properly educated about it. This involves passing through a tape-slide presentation, a documentary film show and a facsimile of the artefact annotated in several languages. It is a learning experience, no doubt, yet not exactly a re-enactment of the Battle of Hastings with actors dressed up in eleventh-century martial costume or a 'virtual' realisation of events by hologram and computer, the kind of standard of 'realism' or, rather, 'hyperrealism' that is finding its way into museums as well as theme parks.

The sixth and final issue listed by Lumley is 'the impact of the media'. Because the museum's role in representing the past and other places is now shared to a much greater extent with the modern visual media and particularly television, the rationale for public museums has become more problematical. A typical response is to emphasise 'what *only* they can do': for example, fine art museums with pictures, scupltures and installations that visitors can scrutinise at their leisure. Even this function can be replicated electronically, to a degree, by CD-ROM and virtual museum programmes. Another response is the rise of the 'multi-media museum', which, if it cannot beat electronic media, seeks to join them. A very successful example of such a public museum in Britain is Bradford's National Museum of Photography, Film and Television, a regional branch of the Science Museum in London. It is largely devoted to media technology and has been criticised for constructing a technological-determinist history of the modern visual media. The Bradford museum, however, also pioneered interactive displays in the early 1980s, including push-button photographic techniques, television-editing and special effects, such as a magic-carpet ride simulated by colour separation overlay.

Museums not only represent history: they are historical institutions (Walsh, 1992). The modern museum is very much the product of Enlightenment thought and capitalist modernity. Enlightenment philosophers of the eighteenth century trusted in the perfectibility of knowledge. In principle, they assumed, human beings could know everything worth knowing, make sense of the world and control it. Such thought is too casually derided today for its manifest and self-deluding pretensions. The ideal of perfect knowledge and control is now, of course, properly discredited as a delusion. Yet the European Enlightenment was itself demystifying, in seeking to dispel religious prejudice and fostering rationalism. The Enlightenment ushered in modernity with its systems of classification and analysis, application of scientific knowledge to industry, public institutions and culture.

In the most industrious and powerful state in the world, Great Britain, a linear and teleological conception of history became educated common sense during the nineteenth century. The Victorian belief in progress included the assumption that industrial civilization was far in advance of all other societies, exemplified by the backwardness of the colonies in which Enlightenment was to be introduced. There was also a deep fascination with other cultures. It became a pastime and later a profession for inquisitive members of the progressive bourgeoisie to collect artefacts from older civilizations, such as Lord Elgin's Athenian Marbles at the British Museum, and from 'primitive' lands. A classic example of a nineteenth-century bourgeois and British imperialist version of history is the Pitt Rivers Museum with its 14,000-item collection. The museum was originally established by General Pitt Rivers at the Bethnal Green branch of the South Kensington Museum in 1864 and subsequently moved to Oxford, where it remains surrounded by cloistered colleges. Pitt Rivers has been described as 'the father of scientific archaeology' by Mark Bowden (1984). Fascinated by technological progress and its material culture, he first began collecting firearms and ordering them in chronological sequence of production and, hence, sophistication. Then, he moved on to other weapons and tools, taking in a great many artefacts of material culture. Pitt Rivers had read Charles Darwin's *Origin of Species* soon after it was published in 1859 and was won over by the evolutionary perspective on biology. As well as becoming personally acquainted with Darwin himself, Pitt Rivers also came under the influence of Herbert Spencer, the sociologist who applied Darwinian evolutionary theory to the development of society, from 'simple' traditional societies to 'complex' societies like that of Great Britain, the foremost imperial power in the world and at the height of what the Victorian bourgeoisie thought of as civilization. Social Darwinism still frames the display of material artefacts at the Pitt Rivers Museum, for instance tracing the evolution of money from tokens of barter to valuable metals and paper currency. The 'primitivism' of subjected and colonised peoples is represented most notoriously by a gruesome collection of shrunken heads from Borneo.

In the nineteenth century the museum became an object of state policy consequent upon William Ewart's Museums Act of 1845. Museums had previously relied upon private benefactors and philosophical societies operating on a voluntary basis. Their collections were transferred to new publicly funded museums. Alongside the national museums, local government took responsibility for providing access to the past and other cultures at the municipal museum, as it did with providing access to books and knowledge in the public libraries and in the schools. These were the kinds of public cultural institution that were put under enormous pressure to conform to managerialist and marketing imperatives during the 1980s.

Kevin Walsh's *The Representation of the Past* (1992) gives an incisive account of how the recent history of museums and the burgeoning heritage industry relates to broader processes of postmodernisation. It is not just that de-industrialisation and the dislocations that characterise the present make the past seem more attractive in a general sense, as both Hewison and Wright contended. Walsh argues convincingly that heritage very largely appeals to the professional and managerial 'service class', the PMC. For these mobile people, the past is yet 'another country' to tour around. While the number of museums and heritage sites have increased and attendance has risen, the general social profile of visitors is very similar to Bourdieu's findings of the 1960s, according to survey evidence quoted by Walsh. Members of the service class, then, are the major consumers of a freshly commodified past with its postmodern play of signifiers and pleasures.

Like Hewison and Wright, Walsh questions how the past is represented and sold in accord with the hegemonic neo-conservative and free-market ideologies of the recent period. He calls for a renewal of public responsibility towards the past and the principles of a critical 'new museology' (Vergo, 1989) to be applied. From Walsh's perspective, it is essential to develop further the educative functions of the museum. In this respect, Walsh is influenced by Fredric Jameson's (1984) advocacy of 'cognitive mapping', which is meant to counter the 'postmodern' disruption of a personal sense of place in time and space. Museums must be facilitators of learning, enabling people to understand the physical and social world in which they live and how it has been constructed over time. That involves a much more active conception of museum visitors as individuals and in groups than was so in traditional museology's fetish of the artefact. Yet Walsh also resists a wholesale switch towards entertainment to the detriment of education. He praises the virtues of interactive video disc on which archives of information and images are stored and ready to be accessed selectively for study. The 'ecomuseum', which enables us to make better sense of ourselves and how others locate themselves geographically and historically, is Walsh's ideal. Furthermore, he insists, such public learning must be based upon free and open access at the point of consumption.

7

IDENTITY, 'RACE' AND CITIZENSHIP

I've been puzzled by the fact that young black people in London today are marginalized, fragmented, unenfranchized, disadvantaged and dispersed. And yet, they look as if they own the territory.

Stuart Hall, 1987: 44

Stuart Hall's observation of the late 1980s captures a paradox of the 'black' condition in Britain which had, by the mid-1990s, been further confirmed.[1] Black Britons were apparently more at ease in the cityscapes of a predominantly white society than was so in the early and mid-1980s when a series of bitter clashes between the youth and the police had occurred. Black popular culture with Afro-Caribbean connections, but also occasionally crossing over with Indian subcontinental elements in a syncretic mix, was flourishing and continuing to influence youth culture in general, which had for some time been part of its historic mission in any case. There was an ever greater confidence in the identities of black and Asian Britons, especially the young. Yet the indices of social deprivation, unemployment, criminalisation, educational underachievement, psychological breakdown, and so forth, associated with the Afro-Caribbean British, in particular, had not significantly changed for the better since the confrontations of 1981 in Brixton and 1985 on the Broadwater Farm estate in Tottenham. Moreover, a certain enhanced visibility and ameliorative presence in the mass media and the professions had only partially masked over enduring forms of injustice, oppression and exclusion.

The issue of 'race' as a discursive and subjectivising construct rather than a biological essence is poised between two concepts with heavily contested meanings, identity and citizenship. Contemporary social and cultural theory views self-identity as no longer fixed once and for all; instead, identity is forever in flux across the span of life's time. As Anthony Giddens (1991) has argued, the late modern self is a reflexive project, in perpetual process of becoming instead of being. Moreover, a number of complex theoretical formulations signify a definitive break with the Cartesian *cogito*, the full and rational subject of knowledge. In effect, the modernist subject is undercut by a catalogue of modern ideas, but now

135

often labelled 'postmodernist', that include the Marxist demystification of the individual, the Freudian discovery of the unconscious, the symbolic interactionist socialising of the self, the Foucauldian historicisation of 'Man' and various other anti-humanist, structuralist and post-structuralist decentrings of the subject (Burkitt, 1991; Hall, 1992; Larrain, 1994). Identities are destabilised, according to current thought on social subjectivity, perhaps most fundamentally those of gender and sexuality but also including those of class and nation. That 'race' has acquired a measure of indeterminacy is consistent, then, with a wider field of dislocations.

With the premature announcement of the eclipse of the nation-state, the retreat from a welfare-state model of social entitlements and the accelerated migration, frequently illegal, from poor to rich nations, the status of citizenship has similarly been dislocated. Universalism and particularism vie with one another to define the role of the citizen. Again, modernist pieties are called into question. Simultaneously, demands are made to extend the scope of citizenship beyond the economic, political and social rights that have been 'won' over the past two hundred years to the cultural, the assumption being that in some way or another we may speak of the cultural rights of citizenship. This clearly meets up with 'race' insofar as it raises questions concerning 'naturalisation' and 'integration', whether in terms of assimilating 'the Other' to a host community or respecting 'difference' in a more or less official manner. Cultural policy may seek to address these matters in a desperate attempt to keep abreast of shifting conceptions of identity, 'race' and citizenship. Although attempts to do so are often made with good intentions, there is always the suspicion that cultural politics vastly outpaces the lumbering discourses of cultural policy. Cultural politics puts itself at the cutting edges of theoretical dispute and practical intervention in the processes of representation. The official agencies of cultural policy can only track these unruly trends as best they can in a world where conventional politics is increasingly subordinated to economics.[2]

POLITICISING DIFFERENCE

In this section I shall consider the shift in Britain from 'multiculturalism'[3] and 'anti-racism' towards what the African-American critic Cornel West (1993) has named 'the new cultural politics of difference'. To clarify the meaning of that particular line of development in black cultural politics, specifically within the British context of Afro-Caribbean diaspora, a series of important essays by Stuart Hall will be discussed.

James Donald and Ali Rattansi (1992) have outlined the strengths and weaknesses of both the multi-culturalist and anti-racist policies that were developed and implemented within the British educational system during the 1970s and 1980s. Multiculturalism emerged in Britain as an alternative to older 'assimilationist' policies. The domain assumption of 1950s and 1960s assimilationism was that immigrants from colonial and post-colonial territories would ultimately become absorbed into 'the British way of life', learning to use the standard language and adopting the customs and habits of the host community. In comparison with biological notions of racial superiority and inferiority, such assimilationism was liberal, at the time, albeit ethnocentric in the extreme.

The assimilationist position did symbolic violence to peoples of other cultures, denying the validity of their beliefs and forms of life. Multiculturalism, then, was a necessarily relativising move which gained ground from the 1960s, and, while questions of English language competence and educational attainment remained of prominent concern, the rituals, religions, food and dress of 'ethnic minorities' were increasingly respected and no longer automatically denigrated, at least not so according to official policies. As Donald and Rattansi (1992) put it rather cynically, however, this relativistic, multicultural position resulted in the 'saris, samosas and steel bands syndrome' of special events in schools and festive occasions in the locality. Its cosy civility came under fierce attack from those who considered multiculturalism far too soft and misplaced a strategy for dealing with racial and ethnic injustice. The day-to-day experience of people with Afro-Caribbean and Asian origins remained that of racial discrimination in an inhospitable social environment; and this was worsening in spite of the well-intentioned multiculturalism of schools and community relations agencies.

The alternative, anti-racist case insisted that racism was deeply institutionalised in the hierarchical and exclusionary makeup of post-imperial Britain. Instead of putting energy into the display and appreciation of cultural diversity, the real political task, anti-racists argued, was to challenge educationally, and through a range of oppositional cultural practices, the ideological structures that underpinned institutional racism. To an extent, such a stance was adopted controversially by a number of Labour-controlled local authorities during the 1980s, including the Inner London Education Authority (ILEA) and the Greater London Council (GLC). The right-wing populist press had a field day exaggerating, inventing and mocking the anti-racist strategies that were said to be deployed with excessive zeal in schools and inner-city localities (no more 'Ba Ba Blacksheep' in Brent, for instance). More serious than this, however, was the judgement made by the 1989 MacDonald report, *Murder in the Playground*, on the unintended consequences of anti-racist policies (see Rattansi, 1992). The murder of the 13-year-old Ahmed Iqbal by white boys at the exemplary anti-racist Burnage School in Manchester was taken to signify the failures of an approach that tended to engender resentment rather than mutual understanding.

Notwithstanding its lack of subtlety regarding the play of cultural difference, the anti-racist position did expose the deficiencies of a purely cultural-ist discourse on 'race'. By the 1980s, racism was rationalised less on biological grounds, as it had been in the past, and more on cultural grounds (Barker, 1981). Cultural racism stressed absolute differences of culture which, while claiming to respect other cultures, resulted in a defence of the essential qualities of British and most particularly *English* culture. Such reasoning runs right through to the example that has been cited most tellingly by Stuart Hall, the Tebbit Test. The right-wing Conservative politician Norman Tebbit posed the question of whether or not a British Commonwealth immigrant was prepared to support England at cricket against his or her place of origin, India, Pakistan or the West Indies. If they were not prepared to support England, how could they claim to be British?

It became evident to leading black social and cultural critics that neither simple respect for cultural diversity nor a vigilant anti-racism worked. This was not, however, just a response to the practical failures of policy but had a great deal to do with a switch from modernist to postmodernist discourses of theory and politics (see, for example, Perryman, 1994). Such discourses, inspired by post-structuralism and deconstruction, share a critique of essentialism in all its manifestations. Specifically, notions of essential race or ethnic identity are rejected. Social reality is fluid and provisional from this perspective, which has inspired 'the new cultural politics of difference', so admirably theorised in the USA by Cornel West and which has a powerful resonance with the work of British writers like Stuart Hall, Paul Gilroy and Kobena Mercer. In the first instance, West (1993) sees the cultural politics of difference as the response to a set of challenges facing a new generation of black cultural workers and critics. He characterises its attitude in the following manner:

> Distinctive features of the new cultural politics of difference are to trash the monolithic and homogeneous in the name of diversity, multiplicity and heterogeneity; to reject the abstract, general and universal in light of the concrete, specific, and particular; and to historicize, contextualize, and pluralize by highlighting the contin-gent, provisional, variable, tentative, shifting, and changing.
>
> (West, 1993: 203–204)

The challenges are intellectual, existential and political. The intellectual challenge itself is further broken down into three parts by West. There is, first, the problem of dealing with 'the ambiguous legacy of the Age of Europe'. West criticises yet does not dismiss modern thought as Eurocen-tric ideology: its rhetoric of citizenship is still compelling despite inade-quate realisation. Second, there is 'the emergence of the United States as *the* world power', again a contradictory formation with a dual legacy of democracy and slavery. And, finally, black intellectuals in 'the First World' are still working through their complex relations to 'decolonization of the Third World'. One feature of a 'world-historical process' which is of immense significance for the identities of people of colour is the global presence of black-originated popular culture, most recently in the spreading influence of hip-hop. It is, for West then, a matter not only of bemoaning victimisation but also of engaging in an ongoing struggle for representation which involves a demystificatory impulse: 'The modern Black diaspora problematic of invisibility and namelessness can be understood as the condition of *relative lack of Black power to present themselves and others as complex human beings, and thereby to contest the bombardment of negative, degrading stereotypes put forward by white supremacist ideologies*' (p. 210). The existential challenge is for black cultural workers to create a viable political practice that avoids a number of familiar pitfalls such as 'the Booker T Temptation' of absorption into the mainstream or its equally problematical polar opposite, 'the Go-It-Alone option'. Another mistaken option identified by West is one which is uncomfortably close to what may well be the actual role of some proponents of the new cultural politics of difference, 'the Talented Tenth Seduction' of an elite, self-referring group. Recalling Gramsci's 'organic intellectual' is West's own favoured option of 'a Critical Organic Catalyst' mediating between the mainstream and oppositional currents, a practice for which he cites several exemplars, including Louis Armstrong, W. E. Du Bois and Martin Luther King, to illustrate the pragmatism of his position.

Symptomatic of the post- and even anti-Marxist flavour of the new cultural politics of difference, especially in its American form, Cornel West does not view the political challenge as at all anti-capitalist. Rather, it is an ethical and alliance-based politics with limitedly attainable objectives inspired by a 'prophetic' rhetoric: 'This challenge principally consists of forging solid and reliable alliances of people of color and white progressives guided by a moral and political vision of greater democracy and individual freedom in communities, states and transnational enterprises – i.e., corporations, and information and communications conglomerates' (p. 217).

Reflecting upon the apparent centrality of black youth on the London streets, Stuart Hall (1987: 134) asks, in 'Minimal Selves', 'Is this centring of marginality really *the* representative postmodern experience?' In so doing he begins a disquisition on the constitution of contemporary identity. Somehow the diasporic experience has become emblematic of the present and, arguably, an enviable position to occupy. Those who are more fixed in their identities are caught off-balance by 'this centring of marginality'. Where the narratives of the self and history intersect there forms identity. To be de-nationalised in a world of dissolving boundaries is to be in tune with forces that destabilise identity, released from the compulsion to defend a shrinking patch. Hall interprets this as a movement from 'nationalism' to 'ethnicity' in the formation of identity, a theme which he picked up and developed further the following year in 'New Ethnicities'.

Hall (1988b) discusses the shift into the new cultural politics of difference. In an earlier phase, black people challenged their racialisation and marginalisation from the mainstream of cultural production and representation, which involved the construction of a strong self-identity – 'black is beautiful', 'black pride', etc. – against a pervasive misrepresentation. The demands flowing from such a position were that black people should be more accurately represented, stereotyping should be eliminated, and blacks should have more power to represent themselves. Attendant upon these demands was the totalisation of 'the black experience', an attempt to unify all 'black' people, in the political sense of 'non-white', in a common history and common sociality. That imaginary unification was always questionable since not all blacks of Afro-Caribbean descent shared exactly the same historical and social experience, quite apart from the fact that Asians had very different trajectories in relation to the British Empire and migration to Britain.[4] The political category of 'black' never closed over the fissures between the variable forms of migrant ethnicity and racial marginalisation.

The shift into a new phase does not, as Hall insists, eliminate the earlier phase entirely: its critique of injustice remains valid. However, changing conditions require fresh responses. Hall (1988b: 27) describes the shift taking place 'in terms of a change from a struggle over the relations of representation to a politics of representation itself'. What is meant by this? First, it is a recognition of and willingness to live with difference. And, second, it is an appreciation of the arbitrariness of signifying processes. 'Race' is not an essential category of being; it is, rather, a cultural construct applied through a discursive process of becoming. Hall (1987) himself has remarked upon how he came to be defined as an 'immigrant' from Jamaica to England (by his mother!) and he draws attention to how someone comes to see him- or herself as 'black' in relation to the otherness of 'white' (and, also, to experience oneself as 'other'). The very condition of 'blackness' is unstable and the fluidity of identity is made yet more complex by the interlocking of gender, sexuality, class, or whatever socially constructed categories are applied to the self. Hall finds this processual and relatively indeterminate formation of identity to be explored refreshingly in a wave of British-made films during the 1980s with black, in the political sense, authors, including Hanif Kureishi's script for *My Beautiful Laundrette* as well as in the work of directors of Afro-Caribbean descent such as John Akomfrah and Isaac Julien.

Hall (1988b and 1990) appropriates Jacques Derrida's concept of *différance* with an *a* to invoke the play of signifiers and hence multiplication of differences which operate in the kaleidoscope of identity and its representation. Derrida (1975/1992: 112) identifies two meanings of *différance* in its Latin origins: first, 'the action of putting off until later, of taking into account, of taking account of time and of the forces of an operation that implies an economical calculation, a detour, a delay, a relay, a reserve, a representation' (to defer); second, 'the more common and identifiable one: to be not identical, to be other, discernible, etc.' (to differ). It is the deferral in differentiation which undermines any absolute fixing of identity: it is always slipping away from definite meaning. To appreciate the radicality of this conceptualisation, one only has to think of the fixed and oppressive forms of identity that are insisted upon dogmatically, such as Britishness or Englishness, with their connotations of 'nationalism, imperialism, racism and the state', to quote Hall. For Hall, then, it is vital to recover 'ethnicity' from fast-frozen versions of it that are supposed to dominate everyone's sense of self and identity. Quite specifically, he is concerned with diasporic identities, what the experience of migration does to identity. Nobody moves from one place to another or inherits and appropriates from a mix of cultures without being changed by the experience. In effect, identities become multiple rather than singular for the person or the group. A 'new ethnicity', in consequence, is one which is constructed out of cultural differences, the experience of difference, not the repetition of similarity.

In the third essay of Hall's under consideration here, 'Cultural Identity and Diaspora' (1990), he examines the two kinds of identity involved in the shifting cultural politics of race and identity. The first is summed up in the phrase 'one true self'. The second cannot be reduced to one self but is the product of an intersection of actual and potential selves. This kind of identity is not fixed but in process, not stuck in the past but oriented towards the future. Hall argues that the historical experience of colonisation, to have been colonised and, for some, to have moved from 'the periphery' to 'the centre' of the once or present empire, can only be understood satisfactorily with this much more nuanced conception of identity as inherently in flux. Colonial regimes, he remarks, 'had the power to make us see and experience *ourselves* as "Other" ' (1990: 225). The colonialists and colonisers rarely, if ever, experienced themselves as other: they were and probably remain the people who hold onto the illusion of one fixed and unchanging identity. The view of identity that Hall proposes is hybrid, made up of different bits. This stress on hybridity makes complete sense with regard to the diasporic identities of the Caribbean (see Hall, 1995) and the experience of Afro-Caribbeans in Britain. It is perfectly encapsulated by Dick Hebdige's (1987) telling phrase, 'cut 'n' mix'. The new cultural politics of difference, then, is about cutting and mixing in music, film, the adornment of the self, and anything else that is meaningful.

Hall's arguments greatly illuminate the contemporary politics of identity in general and in the particular cases from which he usually reasons, those concerning Afro-Caribbean/British identity. His view, consistent with the evident creativity of youth and popular culture in this context, is upbeat and optimistic. Yet, it does not readily lend itself to a satisfactory interpretation of all forms of response to post-colonial and diasporic experience, such as, for example, the reaction of leaders within the British Muslim community to the perceived affront to Islamic sensibilities made by Salman Rushdie's *Satanic Verses* (Parekh, 1989; McGuigan, 1992). Even on that issue, however, Hall (1992) adopts a comparatively sanguine view of how 'the empire strikes back', judging such a defensive and, indeed, culturally purifying response as in some sense a reasonable retaliation to the dominance of 'the West'.

CRISS-CROSSING THE ATLANTIC

Kobena Mercer (1994: 3) sees 'the emerging *cultures of hybridity*, forged among the overlapping African, Asian and Caribbean diasporas', as symptomatic of a 'crisis of authority' in Western culture and redolent of contradictory yet improved conditions and prospects for 'subaltern speech' (Spivak, 1988). Moreover, 'In a world in which everyone's identity has been thrown into question, the mixing and fusion of disparate elements to create new, hybridized identities point to ways of surviving, and thriving, in conditions of crisis and transition' (Mercer, 1994: 4–5). Hybridity, the intermixing of disparate elements associated with 'cross-breeding', and diaspora, the space of dispersed populations originally referring to wandering Jews from Israel, have become key terms in relation to what Paul Gilroy (1993a) dubs 'the black Atlantic'. In conversation with bell hooks, Gilroy (1993b: 208) says the black Atlantic is 'a concept that emphasises the in-between and intercultural'. He goes on to explain that '[i]nvestigating the black Atlantic diaspora means that you have to reckon with the creolization process as a founding moment, a point in time when new relations, cultures and conflicts were brought into being' (p. 209).

The historical experience and scars of slavery, the shipping of Africans across the Atlantic to the Americas in the eighteenth and nineteenth centuries, the stories of black sailors, and the migration back across the Atlantic from the Caribbean to Britain in the second half of the twentieth century, trace a criss-crossing movement and a triangular formation. It is a space across which there has been much exchange and dialogue, only one aspect of which is the current intellectual exchange between black America and black Britain. This international space transcends nationalistic public spheres and sets up a series of identifications and mutualities for a people with a common though variegated history of oppression, exclusion and struggle, where 'routes' are as important as 'roots' (Clifford, 1992).

'Double consciousness' (Du Bois) is the characteristic frame of mind of those in-between cultures, Black and British, Black and European, Black and American, and, in some sense, African. Gilroy is hostile to notions of cultural purity, whether white or black. They are dangerous and they are wrong. The world is not like that and to suggest it is so neatly divided up is to create false barriers and to legitimate rationales for excluding and oppressing others. Culture is fluid, forever changing, picking and mixing. This has always been so and it is further confirmed in a rapidly communicating world where messages and bodies are moving about with great speed.

The 'central organising symbol' of Gilroy's *The Black Atlantic* (1993a) is that of ships in motion on the high seas and, for him, the most moving picture in the European canon of fine art is J. M. W. Turner's *Slavers Throwing Overboard the Dead and Dying: Typhoon Coming On (The Slave Ship)* (1840). *The Slave Ship* was painted deliberately as an indictment of the international trade in bodies, market capitalism in one part of its early mercantile phase. John Ruskin, treated unproblematically by Gilroy as a founding figure of the British Left, owned the picture for a while and then sold it to an American. It now hangs in Boston. Ruskin's ambivalent attitude to the painting – he found it painful but not a great work – signifies, for Gilroy, a general failure of the British Left since then to face up sufficiently to the appalling legacies of slavery and empire.

There is a sense in which Gilroy's *The Black Atlantic* can be read as a black political response to Raymond Williams's founding classic of cultural studies, *Culture and Society* (1958). In that book, Williams, a Welshman, constructed an intellectual tradition of opposition on the cultural terrain of the English. Read now, it may seem parochial and blinkered. Gilroy constructs his own tradition, pantheon of great authors and canon of seminal works, in the space of the black Atlantic. The writers he discusses include W. E. Du Bois, the author of *The Souls of Black Folk*, Richard Wright, author of *Native Son*, C. L. R. James, also a contributor to 'a hermeneutics of suspicion and a hermeneutics of memory' (Gilroy, 1993a: 71), and lesser figures such as Frederick Douglass. However, he does not confine his reconstructions to a black high cultural tradition. The role of popular music is, of course, central to any discussion of the black Atlantic.

It has been suggested by Gilroy, Kobena Mercer and others that the various streams of black music running through Western and, indeed, global popular culture represent a particular kind of public sphere which is not reducible to the commercial mechanisms of their circulation. Rooted in the cultural rhythms of slavery and suffering, and infinitely productive of new combinations, black popular music, the modes of speech and the styles of dress and deportment associated with it carry the sign of 'authenticity', according to Gilroy. During the nineteenth century, with the Jubilee Singers' visit to Europe, 'Black people singing slave songs as mass entertainment set new public standards of authenticity for black cultural expression' (Gilroy, 1993a: 90). Gilroy finds a fashionable, 'postmodern' anti-essentialism that loses any sense of this connection similarly inadequate to an exclusive emphasis on unchangingly 'authentic' culture and identity, a position which is in danger of mirroring racist absolutism. This relates to the wider issues of black culture and politics that Gilroy has discussed through-out his writings (for instance, 1987 and 1993b). He holds to a view of culture 'which accentuates its plastic, syncretic qualities and which does not see culture flowing into neat ethnic parcels but as a radically unfinished social process of self-definition and transformation' (1993b: 61). Gilroy illustrates this perspective with a discussion of rap, its origins, transform-ations and questionable aspects:

> Rap is a hybrid form rooted in the syncretic social relations of the South Bronx where Jamaican sound-system culture, transplanted during the 1970s, put down new roots and in conjunction with specific technological innovations, set in train a process that was to transform black America's sense of itself and a large portion of the popular music industry as well. How does a form which glories in its own malleability as well as its transnational character become interpreted as an expression of some authentic Afro-American essence? Why is rap discussed as if it sprang intact from the entrails of the blues? What is it about Afro-America's writing elite which means that they need to claim this diasporic cultural form in such an assertively nationalistic way? Hip-hop culture has recently provided the raw material for a bitter contest between black vernacular expression and repressive censorship of artistic work. This has thrown some black commentators into a quandary which they resolve by invoking the rhetoric of cultural insiderism and drawing the distinc-tive cloak of ethnicity even more tightly around their shoulders. It is striking, for example, that apologists for the woman-hating antics of 2 Live Crew have been so far unconcerned that the vernacular tradition they desire to affirm has its own record of reflection on the specific ethical obligations and political responsibilities which constitute the unique burden of the black artist.
>
> (1993b: 125–126)

One of the great strengths of Gilroy's position is the willingness to ask awkward questions about black popular culture, for example concerning the misogyny of some rap lyrics and the pervasive, though often perhaps parodic, glorification of macho violence. There clearly was, at one time, a problem in discussing these matters at all, as Sherley Anne Williams's (1992) experience of questioning the meaning of rap at the Dia Center's conference on Black Popular Culture (Dent, 1992) in the early 1990s would suggest. She was challenged for condemning, in her words, 'one of the few things of value that unempowered black people have managed to create for themselves' (1992: 171). Since that Dia Center conference the issues have become much more openly debated amongst black people themselves, apart from and regardless of both Bush and Clinton's cynical denunciations of fighting words in rap during the 1992 presidential election. Black women's angry response to routine expressions of misogyny, in particular, has sparked constructive debate concerning bad relations between black men and black women. Moreover, rap is, in any case, an internally complex, highly differentiated and politically enraged, albeit frequently contradictory, space of the black public sphere in the USA and elsewhere: after all, rap is about rapping. As Douglas Kellner quite rightly says:

> [R]ap itself is best seen as a cultural forum for urban blacks to articulate their experiences, concerns, and politics. As a cultural forum, rap itself is a contested terrain between different types of rap with competing voices, politics, and styles. It is thus a mistake to generalise concerning rap as the differences between different rappers are extremely significant ... [W]hereas some rap glorifies a gangster lifestyle, drugs, and misogynistic attitudes, other rap artists contest these problematical interventions, using rap to articulate quite different values and politics.

> (1995: 176)

Isaac Julien's *Arena* documentary for BBC television, *The Darker Side of Black* (1994), looked at issues to do with hip-hop, dancehall, ragga and gangsta rap in Jamaica, New York and London. He argued that the young Jamaican DJ Buju Banton's homophobic 1993 lyric of 'Boom Bye Bye' symbolised 'the shutdown of ... political hopes', the belief in any possibility of changing the world, in Kingston, the capital of reggae music. Celebrating the body, and specifically the expressive heterosexual body, in dancehall had come increasingly to the fore because it is 'the only place where the powerless can exercise their power in a world indifferent to their sufferings'. The call to shoot 'batty boys' (gays), the obsession with the gun and the liberal use of 'bitch' in hip-hop lyrics have all been condemned in one way or another, although as Julien showed in his film, there is a debate over whether all this is to be understood as an aesthetic response to and a representation of lived conditions or, indeed, an incitement to act in ways that exacerbate the already desperate lived conditions of many young blacks. In *The Darker Side of Black*, Cornel West described the direction that much hip-hop culture had taken as 'a nihilistic response to nihilistic conditions'. Elsewhere, West (1992: 40) has defined the 'nihilism' he refers to in the following way: '*Nihilism is to be understood here not as a philosophic doctrine that there are no rational grounds for legitimate standards of authority; it is, far more, the lived experience of coping with a life of horrifying meaninglessness, hopelessness, and (most important) lovelessness.*'

According to West, there are two principal explanations that are advanced for the underclass conditions of many black people in the USA: the first, the liberal view, stresses 'structural constraints' on the life opportunities of blacks; the second, the conservative view, stresses the 'behavioural impediments' of urban black culture. Both are partial and neither of them is adequate to the complexities of the situation. The liberal view is correct to emphasise economic and political conditions but this is not enough and it is caught out by the cultural acuity of the conservative view. To go beyond these perspectives, it is necessary, says West (1992: 38), to 'delve into the depths where neither liberals or conservatives dare to tread, namely, into the murky waters of despair and dread that now flood the streets of black America'. Black civil society has been shattered, West argues, by the intensification of market calculation and cost-benefit analysis. Ironically, much of this involves the production and circulation of pleasure, to which the styles and forms of black culture contribute immensely. If the cost of black cultural creativity, however, is the despair and dread engendered by straitened and disorganised social conditions that are related to multiple deprivations, joblessness and the drug economy, then it is a very heavy price to pay.

West's advocacy of a 'politics of conversion' addressed to the task of transforming the nihilistic conditions of much black urban life in the USA runs the risk of treating economic and political problems in an excessively culturalist manner, which is exactly the approach that has been taken by New Right theorists such as Charles Murray. This is the major weakness of a cultural politics of identity which pays too little attention to the political economy of exploitation (Meiksins Wood, 1995) and, I would also add, the defence and extension of citizenship rights under liberal-democratic capitalism. Ellen Meiksins Wood has attacked an inordinate concern both with identity and, indeed, with citizenship as effecting a distraction from the critique of capitalism and the persistence of class inequalities in a 'free world' no longer threatened by 'communism'. According to her, 'the new pluralism' is seriously limited analytically and politically by its concepts of identity and difference. She puts it wickedly with regard to class:

> The 'difference' that constitutes class as an 'identity' *is*, by definition, a relationship of inequality and power, in a way that sexual or cultural 'difference' need not be. A truly democratic society can celebrate diversities of life styles, culture, or sexual preference; but in what sense would it be 'democratic' to celebrate *class* differences?
>
> (Meiksins Wood, 1995: 258)

Are not the problems of the American black underclass, then, at least partly those of class? This is certainly the view of William Julius Wilson, the black inventor of the underclass concept. Wilson (1994: 48) does not, however, deny the importance of culture: 'Poverty, like other aspects of class inequality, is a consequence not only of differential distribution of economic and political privileges and resources, but of differential access to culture as well.' But this should not be used as an excuse for 'blaming the poor' for their poverty. Nor, according to Wilson, will cultural action alone solve the problems of the black poor. His analysis of the worsening black underclass situation emphasises the effect of white flight from city centres in the USA and federal policies that abandon the racialised underclass to a dismal fate. Against the recent political tide and similarly to Mike Davis (discussed in chapter 5), Wilson (1994: 59) argues for 'race-neutral programmes to address the plight of the disadvantaged segments of the minority population'. This is politically very important because it is not only members of 'the minority population' who experience disadvantage; and, for that reason, such programmes can command support across a coalition of 'races'.

CIVILISING SELVES

It should be clear that there is a certain dissatisfaction with a politics of identity which celebrates the play of identity amongst black people and others to the neglect of the material conditions of life and power struggle over resources. In Hazel Carby's (1992: 193) words, 'The theoretical paradigm of difference is obsessed with the construction of identities rather than relations of power and domination and, in practice, concentrates on the effect of this difference on a (white) norm.' Kobena Mercer (1994) has raised the issue of 'sameness', what we share in common, not only what differentiates us from one another. This includes the very languages and concepts we use to articulate and debate our differences, express ourselves and seek redress for grievances. For Mercer (p. 284), speaking from a position *within* the cultural politics of difference, 'The concept of citizenship is crucial because it operates in the hinge that articulates civil society and the state in an open-ended and indeterminate relationship'. Mercer's argument suggests that citizenship is the key concept for connecting politics with a small 'p', the micro-politics of the self and social interaction, to Politics with a large 'P', the official terrain upon which rights are or are not recognised in ways that frequently seem very remote from day-to-day existence yet, none the less, have determinate consequences for the lives of individuals and groups. The relationship between identity and citizenship, then, is at the heart of the matter whether we are talking about the cultural constructions of the self or the rights to cultural resources that contribute to the politics of changing material conditions. Cultural rights should also, however, and much less instrumentally, be about our sense of human dignity and meaning, the pleasures and knowledges that make life tolerable.

Commenting on the ancient Roman introduction of the legalistic idea of the self as citizen, John Forrester identifies how a separation between the public and the private person was initiated:

147

With the introduction of the legal conception of the citizen, the concept of person became split: on the one hand, the citizen defined by rights, duties, prerogatives, by the public position in a polis; on the other hand, the notion of mask, of role, of theatrical self, bound up with imposture, hypocricy, deceit – the dialectic of the intimate and the foreign to the self.

(1987: 13)

It is understandable why some speak of identity and some of citizenship. Although both are related to the self, they appear to refer to very different orders of reality, the personal and the political. However, if, as feminism has it, the personal is political, somehow they have to be spoken of together. Membership of a city is the classical definition of citizenship. More broadly it has a connotative linkage with 'civilization' and 'civility'. As Raymond Williams (1983c) pointed out, 'civilization' only came to reference an achieved state of society after a complex etymological transformation from 'civility', behaving properly to one another. Along these lines, Norbert Elias's *The Civilizing Process* (1994) analysed how certain forms of civility, habits and manners, developed over a lengthy historical period in Europe. Such an analysis should be read not as a normative account of how European society became more 'civilised' but, instead, as Elias himself insisted, as a description of the formation of taken-for-granted social norms. Never the less, the term is loaded. In addition to the ethnocentric and imperialist opposition to 'barbarism' or 'primitivism', the mechanics of 'civilization' were themselves defined negatively in contrast with organic and creative 'culture' by the Romantics. There is, however, also a well-established, neutral and descriptive usage of the term 'civilization', justifying Elias's mode of analysis, that became widely accepted in the twentieth century: the relativistic reference to different 'civilizations', but this usage is already somewhat dated. Williams made the following interesting observation at the end of his entry on 'civilization' in *Keywords*: 'its sense of an achieved state is still sufficiently strong to retain some normative quality; in this sense **civilization, a civilized way of life, the condition of civilized society** may be seen as capable of being lost as well as gained' (1983c: 57–58). Recalling how consequential that normative connotation can be, though not using the actual word, Paul Gilroy (1993b: 161) has said '[t]he descendents of slaves have known for some time who the real primitives are'. In effect, then, the relation between identity and citizenship is very much to do with problems of civilised living, how to live with civility towards one another.

The cultural politics of difference casts into sharp relief the working fictions of a liberal-democratic rationale for citizenship, most pointedly because it is founded in individualism whereas demands for cultural recognition are collectivist demands. The basic Marxist critique of citizenship was focused upon this tension: it is all very well for individuals to have rights but this evades the injustice of structural inequalities between economic classes that are legitimated only by 'the rights of egoistic man' (Marx, 1843/1975). The social-democratic concept of social citizenship went some way to addressing that problem and provided theoretical grounds for the citizenship entitlements of the welfare state (Marshall, 1950/1992). This did not resolve the problem of economic citizenship and, for that reason, could still be criticised by Marxists for sustaining the illusion that capitalist social relations were fair and above board rather than realising the emancipatory demands of the workers' movement. In 'the real world' of politics, however, the tension between social democracy and Marxism pales into insignificance when confronted with the widespread delegitimation of social citizenship since the 1980s, the safety-net rights that were held to be necessary, until very recently, for maintaining social cohesion and preventing civil strife. The abandonment of a black underclass in the USA is a sharp instance of a capitalism which no longer trusts the soft apparatuses of the state to keep order. Bizarre as it may seem, however, just as social citizenship is systematically undermined, the issue of cultural citizenship comes firmly onto the agenda.

In his discussion of 'the politics of recognition', Charles Taylor (1994: 37) says, 'What is to be avoided at all costs is the existence of "first-class" and "second-class" citizens.' From such a thoroughly modernist perspective, citizenship is universal and indivisible. Universality actually underlies the demands of cultural citizenship, that no group should be assigned the status of second-class citizens. However, this principle has, of necessity, depended upon 'difference-blindness', that everyone should be treated equally. To claim a special dispensation for 'difference' complicates matters, to say the very least, from the point of view of liberal-democratic theory. Taylor gives the example of Francophone rights and obligations in Quebec, to illustrate how a collectivist and particularistic concept of citizenship modifies the individualist and universalistic conception of citizenship, in effect creating a state within a state. In his commentary on Taylor, Michael Walzer (1994) clarifies the argument by distinguishing formally between 'Liberalism 1', the rights of individuals, and 'Liberalism 2', the rights of collective survival. Without the exceptional provision of Liberalism 2, justified by a presumption concerning 'the equal value of different cultures' (Taylor, 1994: 66), Francophone culture in Canada might not survive.

Taylor and Walzer side-step rather than solve the problem with their philosophical shuffle. Responding to Taylor, Jürgen Habermas (1994a: 107) posed the question again and more directly: 'Can a theory of rights that is so individualistically constructed deal adequately with struggles for recognition in which it is the articulation of collective identities that seem to be at stake?' Habermas provides a much more radical answer to the

149

question than Taylor. This may be as much to do with the concrete issue which preoccupies him, German citizenship rights, as it is to do with purely theoretical disagreement. Taylor's concrete issue is the survival of Francophone culture in Quebec, to which he is himself committed politically. Habermas is concerned with the treatment of 'guestworkers' in contrast with the treatment of 'ethnic Germans'. People who can lay claim to German ethnicity are automatically entitled to German citizenship, an opportunity of which many Poles, for instance, have availed themselves since the collapse of Eastern European communism. For workers from Turkey, on the other hand, who have contributed immensely to the German 'economic miracle', it is much harder to become German citizens even after many years of residence in the country. The implications are unjust and racist.

According to Habermas, citizenship demands are about social emancipation in order to rectify injustice. They are not to do with special treatment so as to survive the drift of history. Various progressive movements come into the reckoning here, each with rather different emancipatory claims. Feminism, for instance, is 'not a minority cause, but it is directed against a dominant culture that interprets the relationship of the sexes in an asymmetrical manner that excludes equal rights' (Habermas, 1994a: 117). How feminist claims differ from '[t]he struggle of *oppressed ethnic and cultural minorities*' is significant. The latter kind of struggle does not affect 'the point of view of members of the majority culture' to anything like the same degree, being a less fundamental challenge to everyone than the universalistic claims of gender equality, and, besides, the potential range of particularistic claims, in comparison, is literally endless due to the sheer diversity of ethnic-cultural differences. Habermas states his general position on questions of cultural recognition and citizenship precisely:

> The ecological perspective on species preservation cannot be transferred to cultures. Cultural heritages and the forms of life articulated in them normally reproduce themselves by convincing those whose personality structures they shape, that is, by motivating them to appropriate productively and continue the traditions. The constitutional state can make this hermeneutic achievement of the cultural reproduction of lifeworlds possible, but it cannot guarantee it. For to guarantee survival would necessarily rob the members of the very freedom to say yes or no that is necessary if they are to appropriate and preserve their cultural heritage. When a culture has become reflexive, the only traditions and forms of life that can sustain themselves are those that bind their members while at the same time subjecting themselves to critical examination and leaving later generations the option of learning from other traditions or converting and setting out for other shores.
>
> (1994a: 130–131)

Multicultural societies need to develop satisfactory forms of co-existence, providing conditions for the reproduction of cultural heritages and, also, realistic openness to change, for '[t]he accelerated pace of change in modern societies explodes all stationary forms of life' (Habermas, 1994a: 132). Elsewhere, Habermas has reflected upon the conditions of political culture that are necessary for citizenship to operate in ways respectful of cultural difference. These conditions are those of a communicative rationality in a polity that is sensitive to the informal features of cultural difference and where democratic procedures of conflict resolution are not rigged from the outset:

> Citizenship can today only be enacted in the paradoxical sense of compliance with the procedural rationality of a political will formation, the more or less discursive character of which depends on the vitality of the informal circuit of public communication. An inclusive public sphere cannot be organized as a whole; it depends rather on the stabilizing context of a liberal and egalitarian political culture. At the same time, such a kind of communicative pluralism would still be ineffective unless further conditions could be met. In the first place, deliberations within the decision-making bodies need to be open for and sensitive to the influx of issues, value orientations, contributions and programmes from their informal environments. Only if such an interplay between institutionalized processes of opinion and will formation and those informal networks of public communication occurs can citizenship today mean anything more than an aggregation of pre-political individual interests and the passive enjoyment of rights bestowed upon the individual by the paternalist authority of the state.
>
> (1994b: 32).

In a debate occasioned by the Rushdie affair (Parekh *et al.*, 1990), Bhikhu Parekh sought to give substance to the necessarily uneven relation between democratic system integration and the cultural integration of, in his preferred terminology, 'a multi-communal or *plural* society'. Parekh himself comes from India and his observations generally have more to say about the situation of British Asians than do the observations made by Stuart Hall, whose attention is mainly fixed upon Afro-Caribbean Britishness. Theoreticians are not immune from the effects of cultural difference, nor should they be. Writers of an Afro-Caribbean descent tend to be more comfortable with notions of syncretic identity whereas writers from the Indian subcontinent, perhaps with the famed exception of Salman Rushdie, typically focus upon communities that have a more fixed sense of their own identities and on their self-conscious negotiations with the 'host' society. This mainly reflects the different trajectories of Afro-Caribbean and Asian Britons, not least relevant an aspect of which is the more problematical status of the English language for Asians, especially older women. For Afro-Caribbean Britons, in comparison, the issue is not so much to do with cultural 'survival' in conditions of communicational difficulty as the relationship between cultural syncretism, derived historically from slavery, and the sense of self-worth in a 'white' society. Both, however, are involved in cultural dialogue, whether across highly delineated positions, particularly associated with religious belief, in the case of Asian communities, or in the more fluid identifications across the moments of a diasporic history associated with Afro-Caribbean/British identity. Speaking from his own position, then, Parekh tried to spell out the conditions for a dialogic mode of integration, which are worthwhile quoting at length:

> First, cultural differences are a valuable national asset. Second, since they are ethnically grounded and remain fragile and fragmented outside their base in the ethnic communities, they cannot be preserved without preserving the latter. Third, the communities not only do not threaten Britain's social cohesion but positively strengthen and nurture it. Fourth, the widespread belief that British society is made up of, and only values, self-determining individuals and cannot tolerate self-conscious communities is fundamentally mistaken.... Finally, the minority communities are an integral part of British society and entitled to have a say in shaping its public culture.... Integration requires movement on both sides, otherwise it is an imposition.
>
> (1991: 194–195)

Flowing from these conditions are a further five principles for framing the 'rights' and the 'obligations' of cultural citizenship:

> First, cultural diversity should be given public status and dignity.... Second, minorities can hardly expect to be taken seriously unless they accept the full obligations of British citizenship.... Third, the minority communities must be allowed to develop at their own pace and in a direction of their own choosing.... Fourth, like individuals, communities can only flourish under propitious conditions.... Fifth, the distinct character of ethnic communities needs to be recognised by our legal system.
>
> (1991: 197–199)

Parekh puts a rather idealistic and Habermasian gloss on 'Britishness'. It is not a system of substantive beliefs as such: instead, it is about 'a specific way of talking about and conducting common affairs' (p. 203). Perhaps it takes an Indian to praise British civility thus, however guardedly, without cynicism, irony or the remotest hint of hypocrisy.

Parekh confines his discussion of multicultural citizenship to the space of the nation-state. However, it might be argued that his approach is already outdated since the nation-state is a dissolving entity. Bryan Turner (1993 and 1994) has propounded a speculative view along such lines. He argues that citizenship should be rethought in terms of human rights: 'The nation-state is not necessarily the most suitable political framework for housing citizenship rights.' Moreover, 'The point about the concept of *human* rights is that they are extragovernmental and have been traditionally used to counteract the repressive capacity of states' (1993: 178). The post-modernisation of culture and the globalisation of politics have deconstructed the modernist nexus of citizen and state. Cultural authority is collapsing, cultures are fragmenting and power dynamics are increasingly transnational. So: 'one might expect a convergence between the idea of global human rights, which are not tied to any specific nation-state framework, and postmodern cultural complexity, which recognises the incommensurability of world-views, the fragmentation of political discourse and the contingency of social science perspectives' (1994: 166). Turner is probably right about the broad drift of history and his views would seem to be consistent with the internationalising qualities of the cultural politics of difference. It is, however, rather too soon to tell what the actual outcomes of these trends will be. And while global citizenship is a fine ideal, it is only a little less fanciful now than when Kant first proposed it two hundred years ago. For the time being, at least, locally placed struggles and the spaces of negotiation with national governments are likely to remain key sites of action.

8

CENSORSHIP AND MORAL
REGULATION

> censor . . . *n*. an official with the power to suppress parts of books, films, letters, news, etc., on grounds of obscenity, risk to security, etc., – *v.t.* to treat (books, films, etc.) in this way. – **censorship** *n*. [L, = magistrate who registered citizens and could exclude from public functions on moral grounds].
>
> *Oxford English Dictionary*

The question of censorship is an extremely deceptive one and a good deal more complex than is usually appreciated. According to much conventional wisdom, censorship is a bad thing. Even official bodies that are responsible for censorship and, also, censorious public campaigns avoid using the term. For instance, the British Board of Film Censors now calls itself the British Board of Film Classification: so it is not really *censoring* movies; it is only *classifying* them.[1] Another example is the British wing of the radical feminist campaign against pornography calling itself the Campaign Against Pornography *and* Censorship (Itzin, 1992). The argument put forward for so doing is that pornographic combinations of sexuality and violence are a proven threat to women's freedom, dignity and safety.[2] Campaigning against pornography is said, therefore, to promote citizenship rather than censorship.

Why this anxiety about the nomination of censorship? Why censor 'censorship'? Either you are for or against censorship, according to the over-simplications of binary thought. Liberal democracies are supposed to favour freedoms of information, speech and expression. That official or quasi-official censorship does exist, however, and provokes public debate is an occasional embarrassment for the state. When censorship is openly disputed, it tends to be justified, if at all, on grounds of public protection, protecting state security or vulnerable people, particularly children, not in order to prohibit freedom. Official justifications can be hypocritical and they are frequently cloaked in euphemism. Censorship of a euphemistic and dishonest kind is insidious: this censorship which refuses to speak its name.

An adequate treatment of censorship must break out of the crude for-

and-against way of framing the issues. Leftist, liberal and libertarian opponents of censorship, on political, artistic and anti-moralistic grounds, in practice, typically prevent themselves from talking of moral regulation; for, in the end, that is what a great deal of censorship is about. By moral regulation, I mean modes of conduct and expression that are sanctioned by the community.[3] Particularly relevant here is Michel Foucault's (1977) research on modern disciplinary powers and techniques that regulate the self as a moral entity, as we shall see in this chapter.

According to Chris Rojek (1995: 43), 'Strategically speaking . . . , moral regulation is concerned with constructing normality.' How are the 'normal' modes of personal conduct shaped by the operations of power? Not in a direct and unmediated fashion. Power is rarely transparent in the self-understanding and everyday lives of individuals. On the relationship between censorship and moral regulation, therefore, it is important to explore the underlying psychic and social forces at work; and not confine attention exclusively to the most immediate and manifest issues of communicational and cultural control. Moreover, censorship is not only to do with the powers of the nation-state, as is most commonly supposed. It is at least as much to do with the powers of the international marketplace.

CONSTITUTING CENSORSHIP

Discussion of censorship very quickly becomes trapped in either-orism. Sue Curry Jansen's *Censorship – The Knot that Binds Power and Knowledge* (1991) makes a valiant attempt to rethink questions of censorship by refusing that liberal choice. She cites Michel Foucault on the dialectic of power and knowledge as a prime source of her ideas. Less fully acknowledged, yet just as important for her general argument, is the influence of Jürgen Habermas's theorising of communicative action and the ideal speech situation. To suggest that power and knowledge are bound up together not only invokes the truism that knowledge brings power but suggests, further, that power and knowledge are in a dialectical relationship with one another. Power generates knowledge and, in deploying censorship, defines what can and cannot be said as much as what can or cannot be done.

Curry Jansen distinguishes usefully between 'constituent' and 'regulative' censorship. *Regulative censorship* is deliberately prohibitive and official. A notorious historical instance of such censorship was the Roman Catholic Church's *Index Librorum Prohibitoreum*, which banned the reading of listed texts from 1564 to 1967. It was legitimated in the name of God and administered by the papal apparatus in God's corporeal absence. Such overt censorship is supported by threats and punishments, in this example to scare Catholics into complying with the Church's judgement. Secretive restrictions, such as governmental suppression of information, also fall within the category of regulative censorship. *Constituent* or *constitutive censorship*, on the other hand, is a more diffuse concept. It refers to how human communities establish rules of discourse in order to function socially. Constituent censorship has very deep psychic and cultural sources and resources. For instance, the Freudian theory of how the psyche functions censoriously, repressing and storing traumatic materials in the unconscious, suggests how such censorship may not be at all intentional or deliberate. According to psychoanalysis, in effect, we censor ourselves routinely without knowing how or why. Similarly, from the anthropological point of view, social symbolism, including totems that define the group or community, distinguish the sacred from the profane, and separate insiders from outsiders, is structurally underpinned and not necessarily a matter of conscious deliberation.

For Curry Jansen, then, constituent censorship is to do with latent, subterranean and taken-for-granted rules and operations of discourse. Because censorship in this sense is so fundamental, the libertarian wish that all censorship should be abolished would seem unrealistic. The most difficult questions politically, in practice, are connected to how regulative modes of censorship touch upon the deep mechanisms of constituent censorship, thereby exercising much greater control than overt prohibition, which is always an invitation to transgression.

In a liberal democracy, where censorship is said to be minimal, censorship routinely occurs behind the backs of the public. Information that is suppressed, voices that are not heard, views that are not aired, are silenced by the mechanisms of constituent censorship functioning through particular regulative techniques. With regard to such censorship, Curry Jansen introduces her normative concept of 'reflexive power-talk', a critical programme for reducing distorted communication and bringing to light the operations of censorship. Systems of discursive control should be revealed to intense public scrutiny and good reasons must always be given for censorship decisions. Censors should not only be accountable for their actions, which sometimes they are in any event, but space should be opened up so that different criteria of cultural and moral regulation, other than those working currently to oppressive effect, are enunciated and debated. Curry Jansen is not just making a liberal plea for wider public discussion: her remarks are directed specifically at the ethical responsibilities of knowledge workers in recognition of their key role in 'the information society'.

What Curry Jansen proposes for a more open and accountable censorship policy is, incidentally, supposed to happen already to an extent, according to the precepts of 'Enlightenment liberalism'. Curry Jansen (1991: 10) says the 'Good Lie' of the eighteenth-century Enlightenment was that it abolished censorship. Yet liberal democracies repeatedly contradict their founding principles by suppressing critical knowledge and wielding power arbitrarily. Furthermore, the Enlightenment fatally underestimated psychological, sociological, economic and political obstructions to achieving the procedural consistency of a rational society. This is not only a matter of hindsight. Anti-censorship liberals trace their descent from the great pre-Enlightenment tract of free speech, the Puritan poet John Milton's *Areopagitica* (1644). Milton's assumptions concerning who exactly should be able to speak freely were hardly faultless. He spoke very specifically on behalf of a male intellectual elite against monarchical power. Most people were excluded from Milton's free-speaking intellectual universe: the poor and disabled, the propertyless and ill-educated, women, Roman Catholics, Jews and Muslims. Such contradictions abound from the Ages of Reason and of Enlightenment. 'There's no such thing as free speech,' in any case, according to Stanley Fish (1994). It is used to justify all manner of oppressive discourse, most notably sexist and racist discourses. Anti-pornography feminism in the USA illustrates the point clearly, having come up against the First Amendment of the constitution, which campaigners see as functioning wrongly to defend the 'free speech' of pornographers.

Manifest and state-sanctioned censorship should not, however, be neglected. Plenty of actual suppression of information occurs, less so in the USA than in Britain, which still lacks a Freedom of Information Act. However, my main concern here is with comparatively inovert forms of censorship, two principal apparatuses of which are the *panopticon* and the *market*. The office of censor in ancient Rome was combined with that of census-taker, collecting information on the population. This connection between the gathering of information about people, surveillance, and control over the flow of information and knowledge, censorship, is crucial. It can be seen operating in the modern panopticon. The concept of the panoptic, seeing-all-around, as a technical apparatus of control, was an invention of the British utilitarian philosopher Jeremy Bentham in the 1790s and exemplified in his plan for a prison that was originally intended for the site beside the Thames in London where the Tate Gallery of modern and British art now stands. Guards were to occupy a central viewing platform whence they could see into the prisoners' cells without the prisoners seeing them, thus putting into effect an asymmetrical and efficient means of ocular power. This carceral principle has not only been applied to prison design; it has been applied ubiquitously to a multitude of social organisations where discipline and control are paramount aims, including schools and workplaces.

Foucault studied panopticism in *Discipline and Punish* (1977), where he traces the transition from 'classical' to 'modern' types of punishment, from treating the criminal body with spectacular violence to the creation of 'docile bodies' with refined techniques that work upon the subjectivity of the punished. As Foucault (1977: 201) says, '[t]he major effect of the Panopticon . . . [is] to induce in the inmate a state of conscious and permanent visibility that assures the automatic functioning of power'. Further, the panopticon is 'a generalizable model of functioning' that defines 'power relations in the everyday life of men [*sic*]' (p. 205). Panoptic techniques, then, characterise the modern exercise of power, according to the Foucault of *Discipline and Punish*.

The sovereign consumer of market capitalism, for instance, so frequently extolled as a natural state of being, may also thus be viewed as an effect of power and knowledge from a critical Foucauldian perspective. Curry Jansen (1991) follows Foucault in this respect by claiming that the 'wired society' of electronic culture is panoptic, joining surveillance with dissemination of information and entertainment to a subject population. The state makes use of panoptic power; so, however, does the market, gathering and collating information on consumers incessantly. Curry Jansen remarks, 'today nearly every citizen of an enlightened society is wired to the Tower and yet remains only marginally aware of the attachment' (p. 23).

Panopticism is a potent source for information technology paranoia, yet Foucault himself did not actually relate his own theorising directly to the spread of computing and computer-mediated communications.[4] David Lyon (1994: ix), however, has asked the cardinal question: 'At what points, under what circumstances, and by what criteria is the current computer-aided surveillance undemocratic, coercive, impersonal and even inhuman?' The problem identified here is usually stated as one concerning protection of privacy, assuming that our private lives are being invaded by information and media technologies, collecting data on us and manipulating our desires. The protection of privacy, however, is not fully adequate to formulating the problem since it is rooted in what has become an extremely questionable distinction between the public and the private, as constituting some absolute difference of kind. Many feminists have argued that the private cannot be separated from the public and from public scrutiny so sharply. There are, in addition, the complex relations of state and market power, how the public and the private intermesh in social management, which further supports the need for an interactionist rather than binary model.

Of particular interest here is how Lyon (1994: 109) contrasts the 'two faces of surveillance' that are associated with 'the electronic eye' of information technology: one tilted comparatively benignly towards equitable governance of the welfare state, for instance; the other tilted, much less overtly, towards social control linked to consumer exploitation. The market has come increasingly to usurp the powers of the welfare state and, in an even less democratically accountable manner, makes extensive and arcane use of information technology in ways undreamt of by 'Big Brother' as the icon of the surveillant state.

Like all technology, information technology is more determined than determining. Technological determinism, which maintains that social change is caused primarily by scientific discovery and technical invention, is a recurrent and pervasive ideology that obscures the complex web of cultural, economic and political forces influencing the development and use of technologies (see Williams, 1974). It is more satisfactory to examine how economic and political power, embedded in historical conditions and decision-making procedures, determine how technologies are pioneered and applied than to hold attention exclusively to the level of the technology itself. Research and development in information technology was originally funded by the US government for military purposes at the height of the Cold War during the 1950s and 1960s. Information technologies were only applied in general to routine tasks of business administration later, particularly in order to facilitate surveillance and marketing for purposes of consumer management. The adaptation of information technology to domestic and leisure goods has also, of course, opened up a very lucrative consumer market. To quote Lyon on the priority issues:

> Consumer surveillance entails a massive intensification of surveillance throughout society, and technological innovation is constantly enhancing its capacity. Subject transparency is especially augmented. Connections with the nation state and with the capitalist workplace – Social Taylorism – should be pursued, but consumer surveillance must also be viewed as part of an emerging set of social arrangements, articulated with consumption, that is also a departure from what we already know about surveillance. Similarly, the Orwellian and panoptic metaphors still offer insights but cannot be expected to tell the whole story.
>
> (1994: 156)

Linked to issues of consumer surveillance and information technology is an enduring debate over the capitalist market. Although market freedom is said to be aligned with political, personal and cultural freedom, according to critics like Curry Jansen such alignment is by no means guaranteed. Curry Jansen complains that 'the consciousness industry' as a whole is first and foremost concerned with profitability instead of democratic communication, which was very much Habermas's meaning when he first complained about 'the decline of the public sphere'. What Curry Jansen calls 'market censorship' has a great deal in common with Edward Herman and Noam Chomsky's (1988) 'propaganda model' of the American news media. Their model aims to demonstate how and why free-market communications are not immune from censorship and propaganda.

Walter Lippmann's notion of 'the manufacture of consent', stated in his famous book *Public Opinion*, published in 1922, is taken very seriously by Herman and Chomsky. Lippmann believed that political and business leaders had no reason to be complacent about public opinion and consumer choice. 'The public' were not to be relied upon to think and act spontaneously in a manner conducive to the smooth operations of liberal-democratic capitalism. Journalism, public relations and advertising must, then, assume responsibility for engineering mass consent. In one sense, Lippmann was merely describing the tasks of an emergent professional grouping, the information managers. Seen from the critical perspective of Herman and Chomsky, however, Lippmann was the guru of censorship and propaganda under conditions of liberal democracy.

Herman and Chomsky's account of media manipulation has provoked accusations of 'conspiracy theory' from industry spokespersons, information managers of the Lippmann tradition who are keen to discredit the critics as simple-minded and prejudiced. Yet Herman and Chomsky are careful to point out that deliberate conspiracy to deceive the public is not an independent variable of their model. Instead, the propaganda function of American news media is wholly explicable in terms of how the 'free-market' system works. There are five key 'filters' in the construction of news, according to Herman and Chomsky:

> (1) the size, concentrated ownership, owner wealth, and profit orientation of the dominant mass-media firms; (2) advertising as the primary income source of the mass media; (3) the reliance of the media on information provided by government, business, and 'experts' funded and approved by these primary sources and agents of power; (4) 'flak' as a means of disciplining the media; and (5) 'anti-communism' as a national religion and control mechanism.
>
> (1988: 2)

Censorship and propaganda have been salient features of totalitarian, state-dominated and blatantly unfree societies. It is much harder to apprehend something similar happening 'where the media are private and formal censorship is absent'. Herman and Chomsky's five filters provide a straightforward account of why this might be so. First, there is the elementary point that a free market in communications and culture does not actually exist. If you can see what you are looking at in the mainstream media, it is evident that ownership and control are highly concentrated; and, in consequence, it is hardly surprising that the interests of the wealthy and of profit maximisation take precedence over other actual and potential goals of communication. Second, the fact that commercial media rely heavily on advertising inevitably puts the interests of the advertisers before the public. Media products that do not attract sufficient advertising revenue and that disrupt the ideological universe of the advertisers and their clients are clearly at a comparative disadvantage even where a viable audience for such products does exist. Third, the news media rely routinely upon official governmental and corporate business sources for a regular flow of stories. Moreover, these powerful organisations employ legions of information managers themselves to ensure that their messages are put across properly. Fourth, there is what Herman and Chomsky call 'flak'. When news media occasionally transgress implicit boundaries and break tacit agreements, they are frequently attacked for misrepresentation and irresponsibility by political and corporate leaders. This is particularly so in times of war when an injudicious attachment to 'objective' reporting is likely to be met with allegations of being unpatriotic and disloyal to the nation.

Fifth, there is 'anticommunism'. As a key filter, this was in no doubt in 1988, the year Herman and Chomsky published their *Manufacturing Consent*, the year before the fall of the Berlin Wall. In the USA, anticommunism had indeed become a national religion, a crusade against the epitome of evil, and accentuated during successive Cold Wars with the Soviet Union. Dissent from conventional wisdom and received opinion, no matter what views were expressed, was habitually met with the slur of communist subversion when communism still seemed to represent a serious and threatening alternative to the capitalist economic and political system. Anticommunism legitimated disinformation concerning the military-industrial complex, support for genocidal dictators and umpteen instances of US-sponsored covert action around the globe. The collapse of European communism and the dramatic intellectual eclipse of Marxism-Leninism created a vacuum for scaremongering, but only up to a point. The possibility that communism and socialism might revive to the extent of their former glory anywhere is one saving grace for the scaremongers along with 'political correctness' and 'multiculturalism' in the USA itself. Another redeeming factor, from the point of view of a Bismarckian politics that requires a necessary enemy, is the threat posed to the flow of oil and Western values by the likes of Saddam Hussein and, more generally, the hostility engendered by Islamic fundamentalism.[5]

REGULATING MORALITY

During the 1960s, that still legendary decade of 'permissiveness', an apparently irreversible process of 'decensorship' in the arts and popular culture was set in train (Sutherland, 1982). For instance, the notorious Hays Code, which had prohibited positive representations of 'evil, wrongdoing and sin' in Hollywood movies since 1930, to greater or lesser effect, was finally abolished in the 1960s by an industry that no longer required its fig leaf for protection. The abolition of official and regulative forms of censorship normally happens late, as in the case of the Hays Code, when the rules are already so much out of kilter with current mores that they are broken habitually or when control has simply become inoperable for, say, technological reasons. It would be mistaken, however, to assume that the dialectic of regulative censorship and moral regulation is moving inexorably in the direction of libertarianism. In 1992, the American movie critic Michael Medved called for a return to the morality of the Hays Code and he was heeded, albeit not officially so.

Standards of taste and decency were never so firmly established in history as conservative nostalgia for supposedly moral times typically asserts. The desire to turn the clock back depends upon a pervasive historical amnesia. Perhaps it is true to say, however, that culture and morality are no longer so convincingly and securely founded now, either in abstract principle or in social consensus, as they were in the past. Yet moral regulation has not ceased to be an object of power. It is no less an object of power than it was during the nineteenth century in Britain when the liberal and modernising project of 'rational recreations' challenged the 'irrational' forms of leisure that were then defended by conservatives on grounds of tradition (Clarke and Critcher, 1985; Henry, 1993).

In *Unpopular Cultures*, Steve Redhead (1995) cites the following British legislation of the late 1980s and early 1990s: the Entertainment (Increased Penalties) Act 1990, setting constraints on the organisation of 'raves'; the Football Spectators Act 1989, controlling access to football grounds; the Football (Offences) Act 1991, outlawing racist abuse and pitch invasions; the Licensing Act 1988, used for closing down clubs; and the 1994 Criminal Justice and Public Order Act, aimed at restricting the activities of 'New Age travellers' and 'ravers', which was met with a popular but unsuccessful campaign of resistance amongst a youth population that, with the partial exceptions of ecology and animal rights, is generally thought to be indifferent to politics. Redhead (p. 8) comments: 'These regulatory regimes all exhibit familiar features of the relationship between law, market and the state in the 1990s and illustrate contemporary attempts to regulate, discipline and police popular culture.'

Redhead views such measures not only and exclusively as repressive but also, in particular instances, as enabling, which can be seen especially with regard to action against racism. Just as significant, however, is that these measures were enacted by a Conservative government wedded to a politics of 'de-regulation' rather than state control. Consumer sovereignty and the state's moral regulation of cultural consumption are not easily reconciled with one another. Proscriptions against hardcore pornography beamed into Britain from the European mainland, the Danish Red Hot channel in 1993 and TV Erotica from Sweden in 1995, indicated just how difficult it is to square the circle of 'freedom' and 'control'. In the same period, John Major's abortive 'back to basics' campaign sought to leaven 'market imperatives' with 'family values' (Hall, 1993). Public order and control are clearly to do with moral regulation. Yet 'the market' is also a normalising force, defining appropriate forms of subjectivity, most notably that of 'the sovereign consumer', and regulating modes of conduct, especially in organisational practice.[6] According to market morality, history flows one way. Current market freedoms are said to correspond somehow to the freedoms of the postmodern subject, released from ethical and aesthetic constraints. Depending upon the particular angle of vision adopted, however, selfhood, culture and morality may thus be seen as either in joyful free flow or, alternatively, as spinning perilously out of control. Reacting against market morality, conservative fundamentalists and communitarians in the USA have, in different ways, both expressed a pervasive sense of cultural and moral crisis, for instance in Michael Medved's deliberately controversial book *Hollywood Vs. America* (1992) and in Amitai Etzioni's equally tendentious *The Spirit of Community* (1993).

Medved's *Hollywood Vs. America* exemplifies a very resilient strain of American conservatism, the periodic call for a return to 'morality', a call that even encompasses the speculative recovery of 'Victorian values' and 'virtues', inspired by Margaret Thatcher (Himmelfarb, 1995). Medved, however, is a little more streetwise and up-to-date: he would like to see a rerun of the 'wholesome' movie values of the 1950s, ideally westerns like the ones in which Gary Cooper starred. A series of 'Moral Majority' themes are woven together in Medved's criticisms of '*the* popular culture', with his characteristic definite article. At the heart of the matter, for Medved, is a contradiction between the values of 'Hollywood' and the values of the majority American public. Hollywood, he argues, tends to undermine its own purpose, profitability, by releasing nihilistic movies that meet with widespread public disapproval and result in falling box-office takings. Medved blames this self-defeating tendency on the adolescent trace of 1960s counter-culture in the sensibility of middle-aged leaders of the entertainment business. '[T]he dream factory has become the poison factory' (Medved, 1992: 2) with its disrespect for organised religion, the family and marriage, America and American values. Whereas the majority of the American public are religious, the movies espouse atheism. Movies depict the family and marriage as failed institutions while the majority of married Americans stay married and enjoy family life. Hollywood is reluctant to make films about the 1991 Gulf War and the Vietnam War has been vilified in several movies. Medved's particular observations on American culture and morality are highly contestable but do not for the most part really merit close criticism. His general account is flawed, in any case, by a crude reduction of representation to reality and a simplistic conflation of aesthetics with morality. However, some of the questions Medved asks are worth asking:

What are the values which today's movies, TV, and popular music transmit to America and the world?

How are Hollywood's messages affecting our society and our children?

What are the underlying motivations of the moguls and creative artists who control the media culture?

What can be done to make the entertainment industry more responsible and responsive to the public it is supposed to serve?

(1992: 16)

These are reasonable questions and they represent the kind of question that critics on the opposite end of the political spectrum to Medved are loath to ask. This is partly due to the immense and perhaps intractable methodological problems they pose. However, critical reluctance is also to do with an endemic aesthetic and ethical uncertainty. Conservatives who cleave to a dogmatic standard of value put themselves in a comfortable position for asking evaluative questions with confidence. Very often, in comparison, the best that radicals seem capable of doing is to question all values, in a Nietszchean manner, including their own. Todd Gitlin's radical criticisms of American television are a striking exception in this respect:

> [I]n the remotely foreseeable future we can anticipate more of Aldous Huxley's soma than Orwell's You-Know-Who. We have more to fear from the endless production of triviality and a deep popular addiction to it than from propaganda; more to fear from a glut of images and stories than from ideological bias. Alongside some excellent work, we will see a thin, soulless, nihilist standardization of culture overriding nominal 'diversity'. At the same time, the deep cleavage between class cultures will persist, the wonders of channel-glut being affordable by what might be called a two-thirds society. Heavily (but far from exclusively) because of the televisualization of everyday life, we will continue to be flooded by glibness in speech and style; dazzled by a convergence of information and entertainment; yet at the same time, suspicious and preternaturally savvy.
>
> (1993: 351).

Gitlin's critical remarks on 'the popular culture' are much more nuanced than the sweeping denunciations made by Medved. He recognises 'some excellent work' and attributes 'savviness' to television audiences. Yet Gitlin's objections to 'glibness' and especially 'nihilism', echo Medved's attack on 'the glorification of ugliness'. Serious issues are treated glibly, particularly on chat shows and, in screen culture generally, a nihilistic view of the world is projected. The sheer volume of violence represented in crime shows, for instance, repeatedly depicts human life as expendable and meaningless, according to Gitlin.

Medved claims not to be in favour of restoring draconian censorship to the movies, in spite of his assertion that the Hays Code provided 'eminently reasonable guidelines' (1992: 91). At the very least, however, Medved's arguments have delivered ammunition to more avowedly censorious right-wingers than himself. None the less, his critique has opened up important questions of public debate. Similarly, the left-of-centre communitarian movement in the USA raises controversial issues of 'morality' and moral regulation. There is a preparedness in communitarianism to countenance and, indeed, propose unusually severe restrictions on personal liberty, such as curfews on the young to reduce juvenile delinquency, and to advocate dramatic expressions of disapprobation, such as public shaming of drunk drivers. However, communitarian values, in spite of these examples, are generally more liberal than those of the Moral Majority position represented by Medved. Amitai Etzioni, the leading spokesperson for communitarianism, does not himself advocate tough censorship measures, for instance, though the potential for censoriousness is certainly present in communitarianism.

In response to his British critics, Etzioni (1995: 25) has said, 'We cannot avoid addressing "cultural" issues and dealing head-on with the moral questions and the social arrangements that sustain a civil and ethical society.' Communitarianism is not inclined to address the economic problems that are of prime concern in most political debate. It is, instead, a movement which wages cultural and moral campaigns. Etzioni's (1993) project is to wrest discussion of 'morality' back from being the sole preserve of the authoritarian Right. This moralistic overtone has been met with a good deal of suspicion on the Left of politics yet there is, also, considerable fascination with a discourse on 'morality' in a political movement that has closer affinities with liberalism, in the American sense, and social democracy, in the European sense, than it does with conservatism. Introducing *The Spirit of Community*, Etzioni outlines the agenda for communitarian thought and practice:

> First, we discuss how we may reraise our moral voice – implant it in renewed families, cultivate it in schools, and shore it up in communities. Communities themselves need some fixing if they are to provide the social foundation for a life that is more cognizant of the values we all share. Second, we examine how we can save the moral and civil order of communities from those who would mint even more rights but who shy away from assuming responsibility. Specifically we discuss where to redraw the line between saying 'Give me' and asking what you can do for your community. Third, we look critically at the political system. That is, how did it happen that interest groups captured so much of the national and local systems of governance and what we need to do to reenergize the public interest – the one that represents the community at large.
>
> (1993: 20)

Etzioni is interested in the relations between 'private and public realms' and ' "habits of the heart": values that command our support because they are morally compelling' (p. 24). He wants to promote values that transcend the selfish individualism promoted unashamedly by the New Right in the 1980s without falling into the opposite trap of excessive collectivism: hence, the cultivation of personal and social responsibility is of key concern. Repeatedly, Etzioni denounces 'the curse of either/or', especially when it presents a straight choice between 'authoritarian' and 'libertarian' solutions to problems of culture and morality. The main target of criticism, however, is quite definitely amoral market reasoning: 'The moral patrimony of the eighties has been the proliferation of cost-benefit analysis into realms in which it has no place; it has devalued matters such as life, companionship, and integrity that ought not to be subject to such superficial quantification' (p. 27).

The strength of Etzioni's general position, much more than any of his particular proposals, is that he is willing to ask the kind of question that has been very largely outlawed in left-liberal discourse since the 1960s. For example, his suggested moratorium on creating fresh rights, albeit extremely disputable, is based on a serious argument concerning the necessary relation between rights and obligations. A favourite example of Etzioni's in this respect concerns the surveyed opinions of young Americans on the matter of jury service. If charged with an offence, they want trial by a jury of their own peers but they are reluctant to actually serve on a jury themselves. In challenging such a commonplace inconsistency, Etzioni seeks to reassert the imperative of ethical reciprocity, a principle, incidentally, which Zygmunt Bauman's (1993) 'postmodern ethics' does not allow.

Etzioni's views on the family have incensed many feminists because he seems to be calling for a restoration of 'traditional' family values, a call which can very easily be construed as having retrogressively patriarchal implications for women's roles in childcare and housework. Etzioni (1995) denies such an accusation but refuses to withdraw his indictment of 'the parenting deficit'. Like any good moralist, Etzioni is concerned with the upbringing of children, which is fundamental to social, cultural and ethical reproduction. He is an advocate of the two-parent family but, unlike Charles Murray, Etzioni does not want to punish single-parent families. His argument, rather, is that it is very difficult to bring up children by oneself: it is better if the workload is shared between equals. Etzioni also advocates the value of 'self-discipline' for the young as a principle of educational socialisation, particularly in the USA, where, in his opinion, '[e]xcessive self-control . . . is uncommon' (p. 92).

Etzioni (1993: 193) asks, 'What is the proper balance between the right to free speech and the need to sustain community?' He points out that the First Amendment to the US Constitution was qualified by the 1942 Supreme Court Judgement in *Chaplinsky* v. *New Hampshire*: it made 'fighting words' an exception to free speech. This is the American constitutional rationale for prohibiting representations that incite harmful action yet, in practice, the framing of satisfactory legislation is almost impossible. For example, in the case of child pornography, Etzioni observes, action is best conducted under the Child Protection Act since it is demonstrably abusive of children to use them to make pornography. Etzioni goes on to say, 'It is unclear, though, how the Court will draw a line between a statue of a naked child and what some may consider child pornography' (pp. 198–199).

By and large, Etzioni has greater faith in the taboos that any human community produces for itself than he does in the utility of censorious legislation: he prefers the 'nonlegal remedies' of educational and communicative action. In the case of 'political correctness' on campus, for instance, most American universities have not actually introduced speech codes, yet, according to Etzioni, racist and sexist expressions have become increasingly taboo. The argument here is broadly consistent with Curry Jansen's (1991) distinction between constitutive and regulative censorship. You can legislate for regulative censorship, in spite of the difficulties over deciding what actually to ban, but you cannot legislate for constitutive censorship, the kind of censorship which is, according to Curry Jansen, more fundamental to the operations of discursive control.

The underlying weakness of communitarianism is its core idea, the very concept of community. To say that one is in favour of 'community' is to say something both banal and extremely vague. Who could possibly be against 'community'? But what is it? One of the dangers of 'community' is its evocation of a nostalgic and place-bound signified, for instance a mythical English village shorn of bigotry. Any collectivity can be called a 'community', however internally oppressive and conflictual. The appeal of 'community' is also utopian since it invokes the desire for social transcendence, a secular heaven where selfish individualism has finally been banished. Ray Pahl (1995) has argued that communitarianism is sociologically unconvincing because it addresses ideal rather than actual community. For Pahl, actual community is spontaneous, not planned with do-gooding intentions. In this connection, he cites self-help groups amongst black single mothers in the USA, a kind of supportive community which is quite different from the white middle-class notion of community that seems to be lurking behind much communitarian rhetoric. Pahl (p. 22) believes that ethical individualism is more realistic than the ideal of moral community: 'Let us move beyond communitarianism to a diverse, tolerant and friendly society based on creative individuality.'

Ethical individualism is, similarly, at the heart of Zygmunt Bauman's (1993) restatement of existentialism in the form of 'postmodern ethics'. He says that '[t]he great issues of ethics – like human rights, social justice, balance between peaceful cooperation and personal self-assertion, synchronization of individual conduct and collective welfare – have lost nothing of their topicality' (p. 4). Yet the philosophical foundations and modernist ethical codes for dealing with such issues have simply crumbled away. 'Community' is a foundational concept and is just as disbelievable, in Bauman's estimation, as all foundational concepts. Communitarianism represents another hopeless quest for 'a *non-ambivalent, non-aporetic ethical code*' (p. 9) and is, therefore, doomed to failure since it is no longer realistic to even dream of such a reliable guide to action. If, in Lyotard's (1984) terms, postmodernity is incredulity towards grand narratives of knowledge, then, in Bauman's view, postmodern ethics is incredulity towards universalising codes of 'morality'. 'Morality' has been put in quotation marks and there it must stay. The postmodern subject is condemned to choose, to make decisions in chronic uncertainty. Following Lévinas, Bauman contends that the genuinely ethical decision cannot even be grounded by reciprocity, which is an exchange relation implying unwarranted assumptions about the Other's orientation. The ethical decision has to be made *for* the Other and not in expectation of being rewarded: ' "I am ready to die for the Other" is a moral statement; "He should be ready to die for me" is, blatantly, not' (p.51). Although Bauman represents his postmodern ethics as ethically liberating, I personally find it morally bleak. Yet, as a parent, if for no other reason, I can see what he means.

PROTECTING THE INNOCENT

Perhaps the main reason why children's media consumption is such a perennial issue of cultural policy is that it poses immense problems of judgement, responsibility and, indeed, censorship for adults. I believe it is reasonable to assume that most parents want to bring up their children well; and, I am sure, they make ethical decisions in relationship to the otherness of childhood that are not necessarily motivated by expectations of reciprocity. These matters are not exclusively 'private' but they are deeply personal, instantiating the complex dialectic between 'personal troubles of milieu' and 'public issues of social structure', in C. Wright Mills's (1970) classic terms. However, discussion of children's media consumption, especially when it comes to 'violence', rarely displays dialectical reasoning. Instead, a fierce stand-off usually occurs. On any cultural policy issue there are likely to be several ideological discourses in play yet it is remarkable just how frequently debate over children's media consumption is cast in the form of a tediously predictable binary opposition, an 'either-or' dispute. Either television is good for children or bad for them; either certain forms of media representation are harmful to children or they are not; either there should be tougher censorship measures or there should not; either children are innocents to be protected or they are not. In debates over media violence and, particularly in Britain, the debate over 'video nasties', which has raged since the early 1980s, an intellectual stalemate has been reached.

The polar positions tend, putting it schematically, to be right-wing authoritarian and left-wing libertarian, which is not to say you cannot have left-wing authoritarianism or right-wing libertarianism. The range of perspectives may, in reality, be much more varied, making actual judgement in practical situations aporetic indeed. However, the usual polarisation of debate between the extreme positions, arising from specific socio-political contradictions and historical conditions, is an important phenomenon in its own right. 'Free-market' ideology, articulated by conservative governments and influencing the policies of centrist and leftish governments as well, sets up a tension within conservatism, a tension with older traditions of authoritarianism and statism. The tension has been particularly evident in the field of culture. And while right-wing authoritarians may routinely attack liberals and socialists, they are, in a real sense, reacting to the effects of 'the free market' on the production and circulation of cultural products. It is interesting as well that, in a period of historical defeat, the Left has become increasingly preoccupied with cultural matters. This 'cultural turn', which also characterises recent developments in the social sciences (Chaney, 1994), represents an intellectual advance over earlier forms of economistic reduction in social criticism, but, simultaneously, a certain acquiescence with triumphant capitalism. Cultural theorising and debate now have much greater prominence than the critique of political economy and devising alternative economic strategy in the academy. The intellectual Left, however, still provides the most solid and reliable guardianship for the liberal freedoms of thought and practice that are perpetually under siege from the authoritarian Right.

A distinguished figure in this respect is Martin Barker, who has waged a ceaseless battle against the forces of moral rectitude and censoriousness that are targeted upon children's media consumption in Britain. In an early work, *A Haunt of Fears* (1984a), Barker showed how, during the 1950s, the British Communist Party campaigned covertly and with legislative success against horror comics, labelling them illiberally as a decadent form of 'Americanised' popular culture. Also, in the early 1980s, when the panic over 'video nasties' first broke and hasty legislation was enacted by the Conservatives, Barker organised a response to the myths and distortions that were propagated at the time, an excellent collection of critical essays, *The Video Nasties* (1984b). Barker has since then campaigned prominently against moves to further restrict video release around the Bulger case.[7] The 2-year-old James Bulger was abducted from a shopping centre and brutally killed by two 10-year-old boys in February 1993. Following the trial of these boys in the spring of 1994, the child psychologist Elizabeth Newson issued a 'report' to the press, signed by a number of her colleagues, which claimed that psychologists had suddenly seen the light: they no longer doubted the harmful behavioural effects on vulnerable children of viewing violent films on video. This was wholly disingenuous since behavioural psychology had for many years sought to provide academic 'proof' in support of the common-sensical assumption of direct and unmediated 'copycat' and other effects. The judge at the Bulger trial was merely reiterating this widespread yet erroneous belief when he mentioned 'video nasties' as the possible incitement to childish murder. Britain's most widely read tabloid paper, the *Sun*, cited *Child's Play 3* specifically as the video nasty in question. There was no evidence, in fact, that the two boys had even seen that particular movie and, as Barker has pointed out, 'the message' of *Child's Play 3* could be read much more plausibly as quite contrary in meaning to that of valorising, even in fantasy, violence amongst children.

The enormous publicity given to 'the Newson Report' in 1994 illustrated how public anxieties are whipped up periodically over children's media consumption, especially when linked to an event so disturbing and apparently inexplicable as the Bulger murder. 'Evidence of media effects' provides some easy answers and quick policy solutions to difficult questions of explanation and intractable problems of moral regulation. Newson presented no new research. Her 'report', in fact a short essay, reiterated a set of dog-eared behaviourist assumptions and research findings that are not difficult to refute since they reduce immeasurable problems of interpretation and meaning to behavioural responses that can be measured. The experimental method of psychological 'effects' research has to eliminate the semiotic complexity of media texts by reducing them to transparent 'messages', and, in consequence, fails to grasp the interpretive process, how children actually make sense of fiction and distinguish fantasy from reality.

The long history of recurrent panics over children's media consumption has had more to do with cultural elitism and successive waves of moral reaction than with any incontrovertible proof concerning predictable and harmful effects. The flawed 'findings' of positivistic social science have functioned largely, in effect, to supply ideological ballast in the form of scientific legitimation for censorious campaigns. In an article for the film magazine, *Sight and Sound*, Barker says:

> The resurgence of fears about the effects of 'the media' ought to prompt us to look again at the history of such fears, from which there are valuable lessons to be learned. From the penny dreadfuls (Britain) and dime novels (USA) of the late nineteenth century, through the street theatres and music hall of the turn of the century, early cinema, the 50s crime and horror comics, paperback novels, television video nasties, to video games the same litany of fears has been endlessly rehearsed . . . . Among the continuities such a history reveals is the willing of magic powers on the media – sometimes quite literally.
>
> (Barker, 1993: 11)

There was an interesting coda to this article. The editor of *Sight and Sound*, Barker reports, said to him, 'All this history and analysis is fine, but your readers are going to turn around and say, "yes, but what would *you* do if a child came home with a pornographic video?" ' (p. 12). Barker claims he would be able to remain consistent when presented with such an eventuality. Having repeated yet again his view that the relationship between media consumption and social action cannot be pinned down to any predictable effect, Barker goes on, however, to make an important distinction between *parental censorship* and *state censorship*: 'Of course, parents, myself included, are constantly involved in acts of control (yes, sometimes censorship) of all kinds of things, from food through videos to bedtimes. That has not one element in common with state censorship' (p. 12).

So, difficult ethical decisions do have to be made after all. Are these purely personal and private? Barker is occasionally called upon to represent his position on television round-table programmes, where he gives no quarter to the enemy. It is wrong to assume that children are adversely affected and influenced by their media consumption, Barker usually says when confronted with the dubious claims of Newson and others. Yet he does not seem to allow the same general autonomy to parents. A typical rhetorical feature of these programmes is the presentation of commissioned survey findings as a focus for discussion. Although it is wise to be sceptical of such opinion polls, nevertheless, they do typically reveal widespread parental worries about children's media consumption, especially with regard to 'violence'.[8] The answers given in these polls may often be hypocritical: expressing responsible concern to a pollster while, perhaps, actually letting children watch whatever they like. Barker tends to attribute the usual poll results, curiously, to *media influence*, panics that are generated and amplified particularly by tabloid journalism. In spite of the various qualifications and distinctions that need to be made about different kinds of media influence, it seems reasonable to ask: how is it that children are safe from 'bad' media influence whereas their parents are not?

The left-libertarian position in media and cultural studies, represented by Martin Barker, has not taken expressions of parental concern about 'violence' seriously enough. And although it displays an intellectual superiority to the positivistic social science that does address such concern, libertarian media and cultural studies effectively eliminates itself from the possibility of making really incisive contributions to the policy process in this area of public debate. As Stuart Cunningham has observed:

> Media violence is a perennial issue because it is of enduring, if regularly changing public concern. Cultural studies critics, who have tended to remain aloof from this concern, risk irrelevance in debates about the influence of the media, which, more than most debates, need perspectives alternative to those which traditionally lay claim to authoritative status in the field.

> (1992b: 97)

The academic perspectives expounded by Barker in Britain and Bob Hodge and David Tripp (1986) in Australia are indicative of a paradigm

171

shift in media analysis which has moved decisively away from positivistic social science. However, the terms of public debate have not shifted to anything like the same extent. There is, then, a missing link here between analysis and policy. Drawing upon the Australian Broadcasting Tribunal's inquiry, *TV Violence in Australia*, Cunningham recommends 'the concept of community perceptions of violence' as just such a linkage for policy-oriented research. As Cunningham notes, this concept is close to George Gerbner's notion of a 'mean world syndrome', an attitudinal structure which Gerbner claims is cultivated by the sheer volume and ubiquity of televisual representations of violence. Gerbner's perspective on television and violence is supported by longitudinal research from the Cultural Indicators project that he initiated at the Annenburg School of Communication back in 1967. Gerbner (1995: 547) has said, 'Humankind may have had more bloodthirsty eras, but none as filled with *images* of violence as the present.' Yet, in Gerbner's estimation: 'The usual question – "Does television incite real-life violence?" – is itself a symptom rather than diagnostic tool of the problem. It obscures and, despite its alarming implications and intent, trivializes the issues involved.'

Gerbner's *cultivation model* is constructed deliberately as an alternative to the *effects model* of positivistic social science. The cultivation model aims to circumvent the futile quest of positivistic psychology and sociology to measure short-term behavioural effects of exposure to particular media materials. Instead, it is concerned with much longer-term transformations in public perceptions of life and the world: in this sense, then, the cultivation model provides a framework for analysing reconfigurations of value and shifting attitudes. A major contention of Gerbner and his colleagues is that American television has, over the past thirty years, cultivated 'the feeling of living in a mean and gloomy world' (Gerbner, 1995: 553), the kind of perception that encourages a self-protecting and privatised existence, cocooned in the 'middle-class' home, safeguarded from fearful public space. This can be said to have the complex effect of a self-fulfilling prophecy: encouraging the evacuation of public space and, indeed, more abstractly, the public sphere itself, thus contributing to the creation, in actuality, of an alien and frightening terrain beyond the safe confines of domestic space. There is, in this long-term trend, a discernible correspondence to be drawn between the stories that are told and the commodities that are sold in the domestic technologies of the imagination developed by media corporations at an accelerating rate, including newer forms of televisual and computerised narratives and equipment.

In concluding this chapter, I want to mention two North American studies that have opened up a fruitful set of questions about children's media culture, censorship and moral regulation, along similar lines to Gerbner's cultivation model: Marsha Kinder's *Playing with Power in Movies, Television and Video Games* (1991) and Stephen Kline's *Out of the Garden – Toys and Children's Culture in the Age of TV Marketing* (1993). Kinder's approach is post-structuralist, applying psychoanalytic and semiotic techniques to the gender-coded and consumerist texts of children's media culture. She examines the commodification of intertextuality across film, television and video games, illustrated by the multiple circulation of the *Mutant Turtles* around 1990. Kinder (1991: 119) also analyses the oedipal attraction and cognitive value of these packages of commodity and meaning: 'because of the ideological assumptions implicit in the software and marketing of cartridges, video games not only accelerate cognitive development but at the same time encourage an early accommodation to consumerist values and masculine dominance'. The 'effects', then, according to Kinder, are subtle and contradictory, aiding cognitive development through pleasurable play while at the same time exploiting young boys' castration anxiety and teaching thoroughly disputable values.

Although Kinder touches upon the global political economy of this cultural and moral economy, she does not treat in any detail the industrial and marketing aspects of children's media culture. In a lengthy and exceptionally well-documented study, Stephen Kline (1993) seeks to produce just such an analysis, which, in the conceptual terminology discussed earlier in this chapter, can be taken to illustrate the contemporary operations of *panopticism* and *market propaganda* targeted upon the young and disseminated worldwide by the pioneering media industries of North America. Kline traces the modern history of infantile cultural consumption through the ever more sophisticated production of toys, their preferred meanings and marketing tie-ins with audio-visual products, paying particular attention to the consequences of de-regulation in US television during the 1980s, which allowed the development of the 'half-hour commercial', animation programmes that are funded as advertising vehicles by character toy manufacturers.

Although Kline himself does not use the term, his account of marketing to children is a profound illustration of panopticism. He remarks: 'The ordinary consumer has little sense of how marketing research and planning, shop layout, product design, packaging, public relations and advertising exert a constant pressure on contemporary social experience' (Kline, 1993: 29). If 'the ordinary consumer', whom one might assume to be an adult, has little sense of all this, what chance the child? Kline observes: 'The research methods commonly used with adults, such as focus groups, storyboard tests, direct observation and interviews, had to be adapted for use with children' (p. 187). Although perhaps oblivious to its aims, children are less inclined than adults to serve as the docile subjects of market research. A favourite technique, then, amongst several available forms of surveillance used for testing out 'play value' is to observe children with prototype toys from behind a one-way glass, to observe without being observed.

Kline does not view the merchandising of meaning to children as simply manipulative, worthless or measurably harmful in its effects, informed as he is by the interpretive audience research methods and reading techniques of cultural studies, methods and techniques of which marketers themselves are now, also, very well aware. Nevertheless, Kline does stress how children are given a moral education in the ways of consumption that may have impoverishing effects on the development of their imaginative capacities. The tenor of his analysis is summarised as follows:

> Though their sights are set on simply selling their products, the situation of modern merchandising demands that marketers manage their communication with children in order to increase sales. In the current context this means using television as the primary channel of communication with the children's market. As long as no 'harm' to children is proven, public policy makers have acceded to the marketers' view that television should now be governed by the principle of commercial speech and so this medium has become the marketer's primary vehicle for consolidating and amplifying children's fascination with toys and sweets. Surely nobody can feign surprise anymore that commercial television fails to educate, inform and inspire our children. Nor should we be startled when we find that children become jaded with their toys and mimic in their play what they have seen on television. Children are simply finding their place within our consumer culture. But does this constitute a harm to children or diminish or interfere with their maturation? Clearly not, for these children are simply being socialized into the way of life of our consumer culture .... What the issue of proven harm obscures is the fact that we have granted to marketers enormous powers to meddle in the key realms of children's culture – the peer group, fantasy stories and play. The key question we must pose is why the marketplace must be given so much influence within the matrix of socialization.
>
> (Kline, 1993: 349–350)

Gerbner makes a substantially similar point when he says:

> The first amendment of the US Constitution forbade the only censors its authors knew – government – from interfering with the freedom of the press. Since then large conglomerates, virtual private governments, have imposed their formulas of overkill on media they own. Therefore, raising the issue of overkill directs attention to the controls that in fact abridge creative freedom, dominate markets and constrain democratic policy.
>
> (1995: 549)

The way forward, according to Gerbner, is for citizens to join in a *cultural environment movement* aimed at challenging, however unequal the odds, the power of the conglomerates and marketing technologies that have come to rule our imaginations and our deepest sense of self and the world. This is not, by any means, a call for new forms of regulative censorship but, rather, a call for the construction or reconstruction of a public sphere in the field of culture to articulate issues that routinely affect everyone's lives on a daily basis. From the perspective of an American cultural critic, Gerbner (1995: 556) finds Western European traditions of 'public participation in making decisions about cultural investment and cultural policy' an inspiring alternative to the anti-democratic command of the unfettered market in the USA.

9

CULTURE AND THE PUBLIC SPHERE

The institutional core of the public sphere comprises communicative networks amplified by a cultural complex, a press and, later, mass media; they make it possible for a public of art-enjoying private persons to participate in the reproduction of culture, and for a public of citizens of the state to participate in the social integration mediated by public opinion.

Jürgen Habermas, 1987a: 319

The Australian agenda for 'cultural policy studies', inspired by a particular reading of Michel Foucault on governmentality (Bennett, 1992a), was questioned for its instrumentalism in the first chapter of this book. French gurus of Foucault's ilk are rarely called upon to provide intellectual authority for a mode of knowledge production that is motivated by the imperatives of administration. Foucault's authority in this respect is a dubious one, to be sure, but not entirely without warrant. Because he refused to ground his subtle and compelling analyses of power in norms of critical judgement, Foucault's work lends itself to radically dissimilar forms of interpretation and application. That the anarchist Foucault should have become, in effect, a theoretical source for a kind of management consultancy in the service of cultural administration is oddly plausible. Although Habermas once dubbed Foucault a 'young conservative',[1] hastily as he later admitted, Jürgen Habermas's (1987b) most carefully considered objection to Michel Foucault was to do with this deliberate lack of normative purpose. Habermas's objection is wholly relevant to discussion concerning the rationale for cultural policy studies, particularly since it raises a practical rather than a purely theoretical problem. The question remains to be answered, however: what kinds of practicality are most and least appropriate in cultural policy studies?

A concept of the public sphere, however much it needs to be revised and adapted under perpetually changing conditions, of necessity, invokes the normative values of rational-critical debate, which was the historical legacy bestowed upon subsequent generations by the original bourgeois version with all its well-documented faults. Throughout the course of this book I have sought to apply certain norms of social criticism and democratic egalitarianism to a number of concrete and substantive issues of cultural policy, including questions of evaluative judgement and public administration; culture, economy, geography and history; cultural identity, citizenship, censorship and morality. These studies represent no grand theoretical plan. The aim has been, instead, to identify and interrogate urgent issues of cultural policy from the point of view of an emancipatory knowledge interest, in the Habermasian sense but in a sense not at all peculiar to Habermas (1972). The intention, then, has not been to come up with a handy set of immediately practical policy proposals or even to frame the technical criteria for doing so. Cultural policy is treated here as an object of *praxis*, an object of theoretical interpretation and of public debate.

TALKING POWER

Who could doubt that the operations of power and of discursively formed knowledge are closely intertwined? That is hardly contentious. What is contentious, however, is the claim that power and discourse are identical, of the very same coin. The oft-repeated truism 'knowledge is power' is simply untrue or, at best, a partial truth. Not even Foucault actually believed it, although he is often misunderstood as doing so. We should never forget the coercive aspect of power, where brute force rules. The remainder, the other side of power, the persuasive and manipulative force, might still, however, be equated with command over discourse and knowledge. Such an assumption seems to be confirmed by much Foucauldian analysis, albeit customarily qualified by the enabling clause, the insistence that power not only subjugates but enables.

The persistent temptation to simply equate power with discourse is countered by Habermas's theory of communicative action. Habermas believes it is possible for human beings to communicate with one another without necessarily exercising coercion or manipulation. Mutual understanding can be reached and is modelled by Habermas (1979) in terms of the ideal speech situation of universal pragmatics. This is not only an ideal but, according to Habermas, a feature of ordinary conversation and a practical means of defending reason (see Habermas in Dews, 1992). At the very least, such a claim opens up the space for distinguishing between discursive interaction which is heavily power-laden and, hence, distorted, on the one hand, and communicative arrangements that are comparatively unrestrained by force, on the other hand. If Habermas is right, his theory of communicative action has immense political significance because it presents a critical measure of how democratic communication is blocked. Moreover, the critical measure, according to Habermas, is derived from a shared human interest in mutual understanding. The implications of such theorising for cultural policy are a subset of the wider politics of communicative action, informing analysis of the *conditions of culture* in both the aesthetic and anthropological definitions. The theory of communicative action is not, however, a theory of aesthetics. 'How, for instance,' Nick Stevenson (1995: 67) asks, 'could we apply the ideal speech situation to a visit to the cinema?' The short answer is: with difficulty. It would be seriously mistaken to reduce the functions of aesthetic communication to a normative procedure for achieving mutual understanding, Arguably, art is at its most interesting, in any case, when it is distorting language and representation for creative purposes. The logic of art is different from the logic of democratic politics since there is no need to terminate critical discussion of artistic culture with a rational agreement on the meaning and worth of any particular aesthetic expression. In politics, truth, rightness and sincerity are norms, however, with a reasonable claim to universal validity and applicability, which is not to say, of course, they are by any means universally valued or applied. Habermas spells out 'the internal structure of processes of reaching understanding in terms of':

> (a) the three world-relations of actors and the corresponding concepts of the objective, social, and subjective worlds; (b) the validity claims of propositional truth, normative rightness, and sincerity or authenticity; (c) the concept of a rationally motivated agreement, that is, one based on the intersubjective recognition of criticizable validity claims; and (d) the concept of reaching understanding as the cooperative understanding of common definitions of the situation.
>
> (1984: 137)

Sue Curry Jansen's (1991) advocacy of 'reflexive power-talk', in her study of censorship, is a Habermasian proposal inflected by a Foucauldian attention to power. Drawing as well upon the work of Bruce Ackerman, she identifies three rules of such discourse: rationality, consistency and reflexivity. First, Curry Jansen believes that power-holders should be called to account on the grounds of communicative rationality: they must be willing to answer questions about the legitimacy of their power and, in Curry Jansen's ideal polity, they 'would not be permitted to invoke canons of instrumental rationality to silence questioning of goals' (p. 209). Second, those who have the privilege of holding power should be further called upon to provide consistent reasons in defence of their actions. Third, for Curry Jansen, a necessary reflexivity means that '[p]ower-holders cannot assert that their conceptions of the good or plans for the future are intrinsicially superior to those of their fellow citizens' (p. 210). She goes on to say, 'Rule Three requires all power-holders to put their cards on the table and play the game fairly.' If nothing else, these three rules illustrate the mundane good sense of discourse ethics and, perhaps also, the mundanity of cynicism and quietism, that we know only too well that few power-holders actually behave like this and how sceptical we are of the likelihood that they ever will. In this sense, we are constrained not only by naked power but also by the limits of our imagination, limits that have been set in their turn by the systems of power and money that shape much of our lives. And yet, as Habermas (1990: 19) remarks, to use a quotation for the second time in this book that I am rather fond of, 'Everyday communication makes possible a kind of understanding that is based on claims to validity and thus furnishes the only real alternative to exerting influence on one another in more or less coercive ways.' To appreciate the faith and hope that Habermas places in everyday communication, it is important to grasp his distinction between 'system' and 'lifeworld'.

For Habermas (1987a), 'system' is represented by economy and bureaucracy with their respective steering mechanisms of money and power. Modern society is systemically very complex, functioning above and beyond most of our everyday understandings. These systems work according to an instrumental rationality which suspends questions of human value and meaning. Such questions are consigned, instead, to the lifeworld, where our sense of self and the situations we live in day-to-day are circumscribed. Modernisation, in effect, argues Habermas (1987a: 155), brings about an 'uncoupling of system and lifeworld'. The point is that the lifeworld, under modern conditions, continues to operate according to principles of communicative rationality whereas instrumental rationality animates systemic processes. The medium of communicative rationality is language, which facilitates the shared orientation to mutual understanding: the media of instrumental rationality are money and power, systems of reward and punishment, the carrot and the stick.

In addition to the 'uncoupling' of lifeworld and system there is also the chronic problem, identified by Habermas, of the 'colonization' of the lifeworld by system imperatives. Strange as it may seem in the postmodern world, once upon a time there was a political project dedicated to attacking these systems of domination head-on that had a certain historical credibility. It imagined the possibility of abolishing capitalism and even the 'withering away' of state bureaucracies. This has become an implausible imaginary, according to Habermas (1992: 444). The best we can hope for now, under present conditions, is to defend and extend the communicative rationality of 'the lifeworld' against the instrumentalist encroachments of 'the system'. With this diagnosis, Habermas (1987a: 392) is a keen supporter of what he calls 'the new politics', which in its various forms, including green politics and popular cultural and social movements in general, is concerned with 'the quality of life'. From the mature position of discourse ethics, Habermas (1992) remains committed to a renewal of the public sphere. The difficulty here, however, is that the public sphere was originally conceived of as an artefact of the modern nation-state and what was, in practice, a restrictive class, gender and racial culture in the context of the geo-political hegemony of imperial Europe.

179

Nicholas Garnham (1992) has made a spirited defence of a unitary notion of the public sphere. His main reason for so doing is that a democratic polity needs to be commensurate with the scope of the global economy, which has transcended the powers of the nation-state. More in line with current thinking, though, is Nancy Fraser's (1992) reconceptualisation of the public sphere as a multiplicity of forms, a position also enunciated by Kenneth Baynes (1994). Fraser's argument goes back to one of the standard criticisms of Habermas's (1962/1989) thesis, his neglect of 'competing public spheres' and what Fraser calls *subaltern counterpublics*'. The great value of Fraser's case is that it reconciles a cultural politics of difference with an updated conception of the public sphere. Her main example, however, is to do not with 'race' but, instead, with the culture of American feminism:

> Perhaps the most striking example is the late twentieth century U.S. feminist subaltern counterpublic, with its variegated array of journals, bookstores, publishing companies, film and video distribution networks, lecture series, research centers, academic programs, conferences, conventions, festivals, and local meeting places. In this public sphere, feminist women have invented new terms for describing social reality, including 'sexism', 'the double shift', 'sexual harrassment', and 'marital, date and acquaintance rape'. Armed with such language, we have recast our needs and identities, thereby reducing, although not eliminating, the extent of our disadvantage in official public spheres.
>
> (Fraser, 1992: 123)

COMMUNICATING TECHNOLOGIES

Democracy is about the rights of citizens; culture is about meaning and pleasure. What, then, are the conditions for achieving expressive citizenship? Satisfactory means of communication. Stated so baldly, the answer is simple. And simple answers are the stock-in-trade of technological optimists, especially those who put their faith in new communications media. Optimism of this kind is always met, however, with scepticism and, indeed, pessimism. Throughout the twentieth century, new media of communication have frequently been viewed by technological pessimists as harbingers of doom, not as means of political and cultural liberation but, instead, as fresh means of manipulation. Theodor Adorno and Max Horkheimer (1944/1979) held such a view of cinema and radio whereas, in the 1930s, Walter Benjamin (1936/1973a) and Bertolt Brecht (Willett, 1964) held exactly the opposite view. Benjamin saw the cinema as a means of democratising aesthetics and Brecht believed that every radio receiver should be a transmitter, thereby realising broadcasting's potential as an interactive medium of popular communication. Adorno and Horkheimer were not only protesting against the technologies as such; they were objecting to the capitalist control and use of cinema and radio. Benjamin and Brecht neglected these matters in extolling the communicative properties of cinema and radio. That recurrent tension of cultural analysis and critique, exemplified here by the German debates of the 1930s and 1940s, is not merely a fault of binary thought: it is the dialectic of a complex reality.

Take, for example, television.[2] We live in a world where television is a massively globalising industry and ubiquitous representational machinery. Television was once commanded very largely by nation-states in more or less restrictive ways. The hold of the nation-state over television has now, however, been loosened, frontiers have been opened up, and major corporations are in command of 'the medium' across the globe. A communication technology which is so important in the lifeworld, if only because we spend a great deal of our time watching it, and is controlled at the systemic level over and above the comprehension and control of most people, television appears in everyday life as somehow naturally given or, rather, sold to and bought by 'sovereign consumers' and, therefore, an uncontroversial distributor of what the market currently makes available in terms of everyday entertainment and information. Yet critics complain persistently of ideological distortion, misrepresentation and exclusion in mainstream television. Activists impelled by such criticism try, however unequally, to use television differently. The technology does indeed lend itself to differences of use. Cheap camcorders can be seen to empower disempowered people, not only to record their own private lives, but to enter the margins of the public sphere. An organisation like Undercurrents in Britain distributes video cassettes around campaigning groups to inform and aid their campaign strategies. Moreover, in the USA, Deep Dish beams such video footage onto satellite to be downloaded and circulated by community cable. In this way, Deep Dish challenged mainstream television's coverage of the 1991 Gulf War and the 1992 Los Angeles riots (see Dowmunt, 1993, for this and other examples). Annabelle Sreberny-Mohammadi has commented upon the implications of 'tactical TV' in a television documentary programme transmitted by mainstream broadcasting, albeit at the midnight hour on Channel Four in Britain:

> I think we've got contradictory forces at work. On the one hand, you've got global transnationals and an industrialised form of culture production penetrating almost all national spaces. The whole world is going to dance to the Hollywood beat . . . . At the same time, the spread of video technologies, camcorders in the hands of small groups, potentially creates an alternative globalisation, a world public sphere that actually empowers many different groups and many different communities.[3]

Writing in the mid-1990s, one can hardly fail to notice how the prime site of such political optimism has shifted to an extent away from contestation with the so-called 'mass media', despite the continuing expansion of television, in the direction of the opportunities afforded by computer-mediated communications (CMC) and an emergent and parallel 'cybersociety' (Jones, 1995). There are many players in this power game, including big government and big business, not only anarchists delighted by the virtual powers they experience on the Internet. The Clinton administration, in 1993, declared itself committed to the construction of an 'Information Superhighway' and was soon followed by the Republican Newt Gingrich's conservative populist brand of the latest wave of info-tech hype. In 1994, the European Union also attempted to kickstart 'the information society' bandwagon with its Bangemann Report (Ward, 1995). Meanwhile, Microsoft's Bill Gates and other entrepreneurs of cyberspace were busy planning to commodify and privatise the Net.

That a publicly funded American information network, which started out in 1969 as a Cold War device aimed at surviving Russian invasion, should have become the beloved object of a reawakened counter-culture is just one of the many ironies we have to live with nowadays. The absence of a central authority, the Internet's very decentredness, designed originally to facilitate guerilla tactics against communism, has served something like its intended function, for enthusiasts, but adapted to resisting capitalism. The Net has, to a degree, proven to be a cheap and convenient means for circumventing the restrictions of mainstream communications media. Moreover, the Net has a number of apparently distinctive properties of its own that are not just reducible to speeding up the post through e-mail.

Howard Rheingold (1994) has sought to theorise 'the virtual communities' that arise in cyberspace in the terms of Habermas's theory of the public sphere. According to Rheingold (1994: 5), '*virtual communities* are social aggregations that emerge from the Net when enough people carry on ... public discussions long enough, with sufficient human feeling, to form webs of personal relationships in cyberspace'. In modern societies a sense of community is elusive yet a medium like the Internet creates the conditions for strangers to meet across space and where the inhibitions of face-to-face communication are inoperative. Dialogue and creative exchange between digitalised versions of the self in Usenet bulletin boards and MUDs (multi-user domains) are comparatively undistorted by extraneous power and authority. Communication is only regulated by enabling rules of 'netiquette' (see, McLaughlin *et al.*, 1995). For Rheingold, the virtual communities of the Internet are not only of therapeutic value: they invoke new practices of citizenship. Personal capacities are extended. Novel forms of interaction and personal relationship are created. The powers of citizenship are rediscovered and enhanced. Says Rheingold (1994: 14), 'The political significance of CMC lies in its capacity to challenge the existing political hierarchy's monopoly on powerful communications media, and perhaps thus revitalize citizen-based democracy.' Rheingold, however, also writes with foreboding of how 'the electronic agora' might be strangled at birth: 'we *temporarily* [my emphasis] have access to a tool that could bring conviviality and understanding into our lives and revitalize the public sphere'.

Were it not for his deep sense of foreboding and sharp-eyed awareness of the threats to virtual community, Rheingold's advocacy of the Internet's democratic qualities would read less convincingly. By the early 1990s, media corporations and transnational conglomerates were well advanced in planning the wholesale commodification of the actual and potential services of CMC. Opportunities for cultivating and supplying 'consumer needs' through telecommunications, particularly home-based entertainment and shopping, were being seized. Rheingold also notes the processes of surveillance associated with the deployment of telecommunications in market propaganda.

Rheingold (1994) identifies three kinds of social criticism relevant to assessing the prospects for CMC: commodification, panopticism and what he calls 'hyper-realism'. On the question of commodification, Rheingold (pp. 281–289) reviews Habermas's arguments concerning how the public sphere is undermined by an unrestrained capitalist market. He also raises the issue of how the public sphere is merely simulated under such conditions, giving rise to the phenomenon of a 'phantom public sphere' in the place of democratic communications (see Robbins, 1993). The example that Rheingold uses in discussion of the panoptic qualities of CMC represents, however, a fleeting instance of public resistance. In 1991, Lotus announced the launch of a market research CD-ROM that contained information on 120 million people and was entitled 'Marketplace'. This was so heavily criticised as an invasion of privacy that the firm withdrew its product. Yet, as Rheingold points out, interactive television systems are routinely linked into computerised market research. Every choice made and every dollar spent are logged and used to ascertain taste preference and spending power. Finally, there is the 'hyper-realist' view of Jean Baudrillard (1988), which Rheingold mistakenly considers critical of how the virtual world of CMC displaces the real world.

Mark Poster's *The Second Media Age* (1995) may be taken to instantiate the 'hyper-realist' position and its comparative paucity of critical insight. For Poster, cyberspace is like an objective correlative for certain themes of both post-structuralist and postmodernist thought, an almost Hegelian realisation of the spirit of contemporary theory. So the decentredness of cyberspace is at one with the decentredness of the postmodern subject, and the fragmented particularisms of discussion groups correspond to a postmodern disaggregation of knowledge and the eclipse of universalising narratives. In Poster's account, Baudrillard's cynical assertion that meaning has imploded once and for all in the communications media is contrasted

favourably with Habermas's critical theorising of the conditions for democratic communication. Julian Stallabrass (1995: 12) holds a similar but,
unlike Poster, critical view of the communicative properties of cyberspace.
It is not somewhere that 'agreement is founded on reasoned conversation,
but something more fractured and postmodern'. He would apparently
prefer cyberspace to be the way that Rheingold tells it. There is, however,
'a fundamental problem', according to Stallabrass (1995: 14): 'the virtual
community demands a real one prior to it in order to function successfully'.
He goes on to put the most telling criticism of excessive immersion in
cyberspace, whether from a Habermasian or a Baudrillardian position.
Drawing his inspiration from Walter Benjamin, Stallabrass talks of

> the solipsism of cyberspace, which is merely a literal expression of the
> situation of the individual in contemporary society, and more specifi-
> cally of business people and their camp followers (engineers and
> intellectuals) spinning universalizing fantasies out of their desire to
> ride the next commercial wave. This wondrous but specious tech-
> nology threatens to act as another curtain between those who con-
> sume it and the condition of the world: as the poor are excluded
> from cyberspace, and will appear on it only as objects, never as
> subjects with their own voices, there is a danger that they recede
> even further from the consciousness of the comfortable. As the real
> world is left to decline, the air once again becomes full of phantoms,
> this time digital, promising at the last moment to pluck utopia from
> apocalypse.
>
> (1995: 32)

That there is a yawning gulf between the information-haves and the
information-have-nots is no fantasy, in spite of the repeated claims by
CMC enthusiasts that access to the technology is becoming increasingly
egalitarian due to mass-marketisation. It is true that we have here a commodity system with rapid built-in obsolescence and falling prices that
capture rising numbers of consumers in rich countries.[4] The poor in such
countries and, to a much greater extent, in the most deprived parts of the
world are, nevertheless, excluded from a cyberspace which may not necessarily be worth entering in any event, depending on how one sees its use
value. As Ray Thomas (1995: 95) remarks, 'For the foreseeable future most
of the world's population will not have easy access to a telephone, let
alone digital services.'

PRAXIS AND TECHNE

In his 'neo-Luddite treatise' on computer-mediated communications, *The
Cult of Information* (1994), Theodore Roszak complains of the contemporary reduction of thought to information-processing. Roszak is not so much

opposed to computing and telecommunications, however, as he is to the ideology of knowledge that is implicit in the repeatedly exaggerated claims that are made for CMC. The cult of information did not, to be sure, arrive for the first time with these twentieth-century technologies. According to Roszak, the cult of information can be traced back to the late-eighteenth-century school of utilitarian philosophy, led by Jeremy Bentham. That particular English branch of the European Enlightenment was, in comparison with the French and German branches, less concerned with systematic theorising and abstract principles of action than with empirical evidence and technical control. To quote Roszak (1994: 156–157): 'The Benthamites are one of the first distinctly modern movements in political philosophy; they are inextricably part of an industrial system. The very name they took for themselves – Utilitarianism – reflects the hard-headed practicality, the unsentimental assertion of material values that dominated the new economic order of their day.' The utilitarians sought to produce information that was of immediately practical use to capital and the state. They would aim to establish the facts, formulate the policies and evaluate the effectiveness of social control mechanisms thus set in place. Theirs was a matter-of-fact and no-nonsense approach to knowledge, the kind of approach that is today characterised at a distance by, say, market research and management systems. They were, of course, the very opposite of Romantics. Their conception of an intellectual was that of an information manager.

Some would say the utilitarian conception of an intellectual is no conception of an intellectual at all, which is the view that Edward Said stated sharply in his 1993 Reith Lectures. Although his aim was to retrieve the heroic and critical conception of the intellectual, Said (1994) quite rightly acknowledged Antonio Gramsci's (1971) thinking of the 1930s on the function of intellectuals in a modern and complex social formation. Gramsci's category of 'organic' intellectual, although usually treated as a guide to oppositional practice, in fact referred first and foremost to a growing army of administrators, managers and technocrats, very different intellectually from cloistered academics and maverick writers, the 'traditional' intellectuals. Gramsci thus anticipated later discussions of the role of knowledge workers in 'the information society'. Said's intellectual, however, is somewhat different:

> [T]he intellectual is an individual with a specific public role in society that cannot be reduced simply to being a faceless professional, a competent member of a class just going about her/his business. The central fact for me is, I think, that the intellectual is an individual endowed with a faculty for representing, embodying, articulating a message, a view, an attitude, philosophy or opinion to, as well as for a public. And, this role has an edge to it, and cannot be played

185

without a sense of being someone whose place it is publically [*sic*] to raise embarrassing questions, to confront orthodoxy and dogma (rather than to produce them), to be someone who cannot easily be co-opted by governments and corporations, and whose *raison d'être* is to represent all those people and issues that are routinely forgotten or swept under the rug. The intellectual does so on the basis of universal principles: that all human beings are entitled to expect decent standards of behaviour concerning freedom and justice from worldly powers or nations, and that deliberate or inadvertent violations of these standards need to be testified and fought against courageously.

(1994: 8–9)

Said's conception of the intellectual is a noble one: to be a tribune of the people and, when necessary, to speak out as a lone voice against injustice. Edward Said himself has performed exactly such a role, both as a cultural critic and as an activist in the Palestinian cause. He cites others of his ilk such as Noam Chomsky and Jean-Paul Sartre. But, it has to be said, not everyone employed in intellectual work can be a Chomsky, a Sartre or a Said. This leaves a rather stark separation between the information manager, on the one hand, and the critical intellectual, on the other hand.[5]

The division, in practical terms, may well be that extreme; and this has something to do with how the relationship between theory and practice is understood. It is a problem of the most general significance and, also, one of very specific relevance to a policy-oriented cultural studies. When Tony Bennett (1992a: 406) suggests that the educational purpose of 'cultural policy studies' should be to train cultural *technicians* capable of making governmental adjustments to culture, he bends the stick deliberately away from the practice of 'cultural critique as an instrument for changing consciousness'. This clearly relates, in Bennett's 'Right' Foucauldian scheme of things, to Michel Foucault's notion of a 'specific intellectual' as the only viable alternative to the hopeless pretensions of a Sartrean 'universal intellectual'. Foucault was indeed a critic of universalising modernism, yet, none the less, he remained a critic. Unlike Said, however, Foucault (1986: 74–75) did not believe in the possibility of 'speaking truth to power': 'it's not a matter of emancipating truth from every system of power (which would be a chimera, for truth is already power), but of detaching the power of truth from the forms of hegemony, social, economic, and cultural, within which it operates at the present time'.

In his reflections on theory and practice, Habermas (1974) returned to the Aristotelian distinction between *praxis* and *techne* (see Bernstein, 1995). For the privileged class in ancient Greece, politics was about theorising 'the good and just life': that constituted the object of *praxis*. Habermas

(1974: 42) observes, 'This had nothing to do with *techne*, the skilled production of artifacts and the expert mastery of objectified tasks.' Although *techne* was regarded as the lesser art, *techne* and *praxis* are not mutually exclusive: we are not obliged to choose between them. Without *techne* nothing would ever get made but without *praxis* there would be no sense to the making. The main reason for insisting upon *praxis* as a form of practicality, a form of practicality to which this book is dedicated, is that systemic forces tend relentlessly to reduce *praxis* to *techne*, theoretically informed practice to mere technical means in the utilitarian and instrumentalist way. Habermas draws the vital distinctions with precision:

> Technical questions are posed with a view to the rationally goal-directed organization of means and the rational selection of instrumental alternatives, once the goals (values and maxims) are given. Practical questions, on the other hand, are posed with a view to the acceptance or rejection of norms, especially norms for action, the claims to the validity of which we can support or oppose with reasons. Theories which in their structure can serve the clarification of practical questions are designed to enter into communicative action. Interpretations which can be gained within the framework of such theories cannot, of course, be directly effective for the orientation of action: rather, they find their legitimate value within the therapeutic context of the reflexive formation of volition.
>
> (1974: 3)

Techne, then, is instrumental rationality's mode of practicality; *praxis* is communicative rationality's mode of practicality. That this latter mode of practicality, according to Habermas, does not tell us *directly* what to do, in the sense of providing technically applicable rules of action, will always be regarded as unsatisfactory by those who prefer to act without thinking; in effect, those who want recipe knowledge but not critical thought, information but not ideas.[6] There is, however, a certain value in indirection, which is, after all, a constitutive feature of communication and culture.

In her research on the Native Americans Hall at the National Museum of Natural History in Washington, DC, Constance Perin (1992: 184) makes this point concerning 'the communicative circle' between museum professionals and visitors: 'As they construct exhibitions museum professionals assume one-way communication and an unmediated relationship between sending and receiving.' Alternatively, '[a]cknowledging the property of indirection disabuses exhibition makers of the assumption that the clarity of their intentions equals the clarity of audiences' reception' (p. 194). Which is not to deny that museum professionals, in spite of neglecting indirection, have become more concerned to find out about their visitors. Visitors may be categorised stereotypically as 'streakers', 'strollers' and 'readers'; and sophisticated market research techniques are used routinely.

These are objectifying practices, however, that display little or no sense of communicative action as an intersubjective accomplishment. Perin talked informally with visitors about the meanings they made out of the exhibition, apparently to the astonishment of museum professionals: ' "You're actually *listening* to visitors?" ' (p.198). Perin situates this local problem, to do specifically with her particular interest in anthropology and museums, within a much larger perspective on how we live now and in relation to cultural institutions in general:

> One research question for cultural studies is the extent to which museum visits (compared to other leisure activities) activate the integration and synthesis of adults' lives. People living in a society that compartmentalizes and institutionalizes lived experience – dividing it into work, family, politics, and religion, for example – depend upon cultural institutions for their opportunities to achieve coherence, growth, and an evolving sense of identity.
>
> (1992: 216)

Questions of cultural policy are too important to be left solely to cultural technicians. While it is true that nothing much would happen in any sphere of life without technical know-how and technological capability, nevertheless, without a critical practice that is at least one step removed from the immediate pragmatics of problem-solving, emancipatory purpose would be lost. That is why a policy-oriented cultural studies must not be reduced to instrumental reason. It is obliged, instead, to take the actual and potential operations of the public sphere seriously because that is the meeting place, albeit beleagured, of the lifeworld and critical reason. As Habermas (1971: 61) puts it, 'The redeeming power of reflection cannot be supplanted by the extension of technically exploitable knowledge.'

Finally, in conclusion, I want to explore this question of the politics of intellectual practice in the cultural field a little further since it points up some important issues concerning administration and critique that are germane to any understanding of the actual and potential operations of a public sphere today. Douglas Kellner (1995b) has drawn upon Jean-Paul Sartre's (1974) 'A Plea for Intellectuals', his series of lectures delivered in Japan in 1965, in order to set out an agenda for cultural politics regarding current developments in the use of information and media technologies. Before considering Kellner's own arguments, Sartre's basic position on intellectuals needs to be set out.[7]

For Sartre, the modern European intellectual, as opposed to the 'organic' intellectual of the Enlightenment, emerged during the Dreyfus affair of 1896. Emile Zola's 'J'accuse' challenged the false allegations that were made for anti-semitic reasons by the French military establishment against Captain Alfred Dreyfus. This act and the role performed by the *Dreyfusards* in general defined the intellectual as '*someone who meddles in what is not his [sic] business'* (Sartre, 1974: 230). According to Sartre, intellectuals in this precise and critical sense, are those 'technicians of practical knowledge' who have become dissatisfied with the contradictoriness of their situation. The numbers caught up in such a contradiction have grown enormously during the twentieth century with the prodigious expansion of occupations for producing and circulating information and knowledge, including the practices of applied social science, advertising, copywriting and designing. Their education typically inculcates in them a capacity for questioning and inquiry which knows no limits to its potential universality, yet their practical employment requires them to observe and apply particularistic ideologies routinely that are ultimately traceable back, in Sartre's reasoning, to the interests of the ruling class. Two options are available to intellectual workers who experience this contradiction acutely: they may become 'false' intellectuals who remain securely in position while kidding themselves and others that the universal has been realised in the present; or, alternatively, they may become 'true' intellectuals casting themselves adrift from the patronage of their bosses but not necessarily finding a place of ready acceptance amongst the subordinate groups whom they may seek, in some sense, to represent.

Kellner (1995b: 431) says he wants to 'reject the particular/universal dichotomy in favour of developing a normative concept of the *public intellectual*'. In his formulation, such an intellectual is not a privileged representative of any group but must engage, instead, in practical matters on the terms of those groups whose interests he or she may wish to advance and by deploying to this effect the most advanced technologies. To quote Kellner:

> [I]n the contemporary high-tech societies there is emerging a significant expansion and redefinition of the public sphere and ... these developments, connected primarily with media and computer technologies, require a reformulation and expansion of the concept of the critical or committed intellectual. ... My argument is that, first, broadcasting media like radio and television, and now computers, have produced new public spheres and spaces for information, debate and participation that contain both the potential to reinvigorate democracy and to increase the dissemination of critical and progressive ideas – as well as new possibilities of manipulation and social control. But participants in these new public spheres – computer bulletin boards and discussion groups, talk radio and television, and the emerging public sphere of what I call cyberspace democracy require intellectuals to gain new skills and to master new technologies.
> (1995b: 437, 438)

'Traditional intellectuals' are castigated by Kellner for their alleged hostility to technology; and if indeed they are hostile to technology *per se*,

189

then, surely, they must be castigated. The problem with Kellner's position, however, is its partiality with regard to critical intellectuality. In one sense he is merely asking those who wish to be critical to use computing for research and debate, as well as generally promoting media education as a necessary resource for everyone in a highly mediated society. These considerations do not exhaust the problems of intellectuals, particularly if one takes Sartre's category of 'technicians of practical knowledge' seriously.

Who are these 'technicians of practical knowledge'? In the main, they are not critical intellectuals in a grandly Sartrean or even in a more street-wise Kellnerian sense. Most of the readers of this book are likely to be students and their teachers who are indeed working upon Sartre's problem of the universal and the particular, or, to put it another way, exploring and trying to resolve the tension between knowledgeability and employability. Other readers, amongst whom must be included many of the students when they eventually pass out of education, are living that problem in a rather more practical and immediate fashion. It is not just that, for remunerative work, the tasks they are given might conflict with whatever critical learning they may have culled. They could well have access to all the technology they need to fulfil such tasks. The point is that the practical tasks themselves are increasingly 'theorised', most particularly by management theory. After all, nobody is going to read this book to learn the techniques of video-editing or net-surfing. But they may read this book if they are engaged in some form of communication and cultural management. Since it does not purport to provide recipe knowledge, such a reading may turn out to be a disappointment: when that happens it might be to do with the fact that the possibilities of critical knowledge in a practical context have already been closed off. That clearly relates to Douglas Kellner's question, which has been a guiding question of this book: how can critical intellectuals be practical? There is, however, another question that I am posing as well: how can practical intellectuals be critical?

NOTES

1 CULTURAL POLICY STUDIES

1 Paul Willis's 'common culture' project (1990a, 1990b and 1991) is a notable exception to cultural studies' general record of neglect concerning practical matters of cultural policy.
2 There is a voluminous literature on the American 'culture wars' and 'political correctness' in general. See, for instance, Berube (1994) and Dunant (1994).
3 See, for example, my critique of populism in cultural studies (McGuigan, 1992 and 1996).
4 According to Stuart Cunningham's (1992a) distribution of political positions, Tony Bennett and his immediate Brisbane associates, such as Ian Hunter, are on the 'Right', Tom O'Regan of Murdoch University is on the 'Left', whereas Cunningham, of Queensland University of Technology, styles himself a 'Centrist'. All these writers contributed to the collection of essays that provided a showcase for Australian cultural studies, *Nation, Culture, Text*, edited by Graeme Turner (1993).
5 During the 1980s, in his role as the leading author of the Open University's Popular Culture course, Tony Bennett (1986) advocated a Gramscian turn in cultural studies. The later shift from a Gramscian to a Foucauldian position can be observed in his article on the nineteenth-century 'exhibitionary complex' (Bennett, 1988a). Bennett's (1995) collection of essays on the history of the museum is entitled *The Birth of the Museum*, a title which echoes and pays homage to Foucault's *Birth of the Clinic*.
6 An instrumentalist version of Foucauldian thought is not peculiar to Bennett and his Australian school of cultural policy studies. It was also recommended as a more 'realistic' agenda for education in communications and culture during the Thatcherite 1980s in Britain (Tolson, 1986; Rice and Rice, 1989), the argument being that student empowerment derives from the acquisition of technical and immediately marketable skills rather than the intellectual capacity to critically analyse cultural and social arrangements.
7 The interpretive disputes over Foucault and Habermas, their differences and also their similarities, are well represented in the book edited by Michael Kelly (1994), *Critique and Power – Recasting the Foucault/Habermas Debate*.
8 On its publication in English in 1989, a conference on *The Structural Transformation of the Public Sphere* was held at the University of North Carolina that was attended by Habermas himself and for which he produced a generous response to the criticisms made of his first major work. The conference proceedings, including Habermas's response, are published in the volume *Habermas*

191

and the Public Sphere, edited by Craig Calhoun (1992). One of the critics, Michael Schudson (1992: 160), on challenging the accuracy of Habermas's historical account of the public sphere and indeed its very existence, still concluded by saying, 'the public sphere . . . is indispensable as a model of what a good society should achieve'.

9 See Habermas's contribution to Calhoun (1992). The deficiencies of a concept of the public sphere modelled upon the 'bourgeois' as opposed to the 'proletarian' experience is the main theme of Oskar Negt and Alexander Kluge's (1972/1993) *The Public Sphere and Experience*, which had considerable impact on the West German Left when originally published in 1972.

10 In spite of their considerable differences of analytical idiom and national context, there is a certain affinity between Habermas's thinking on the public sphere and Williams's thinking on democratic communications and common culture (see McGuigan, 1993 and 1995).

2 QUESTIONS OF VALUE

1 It has been said that Bourdieu's work on the politics of culture lacks a genuinely strategic focus (Wilson, 1988; Garnham, 1993a). This is perhaps unfair, especially in biographical terms, since, for instance, Bourdieu himself worked on a new educational policy for the socialist government in France during the 1980s at the invitation of President Mitterrand.

2 Bourdieu's *oeuvre* is very complex and wide-ranging, from anthropological fieldwork in North Africa during the 1950s, through his sociology of education of the 1960s and 1970s, to the more recent writings on methodology, in addition to his sociology of taste (see Jenkins, 1992, for a superb account of Bourdieu's work, and Robbins, 1991, for a comparable treatment).

3 The thesis of 'reflexive modernisation' (Giddens, 1990 and 1991; Beck, 1992; Beck, *et al.*, 1994) offers, in my opinion, a more satisfactory account of the present condition than does *post*modernisation, and makes sense of many of the changes discussed by David Harvey (1989a).

4 Justin O'Connor and Derek Wynne at Manchester Metropolitan University's Institute for Popular Culture have sought to test Bourdieu's (1984) framework for analysing petit-bourgeois culture and revise it according to their research findings on 'new cultural intermediaries' in the 'post-industrial city' (O'Connor and Wynne, 1993; Wynne and O'Connor, 1995).

5 Hare said his piece on a BBC2 *Late Show* in October 1991 and it became a focus of public debate for a few months in subsequent editions of the now defunct *Late Show* and in the 'quality' press. His trite preference for John Keats over Bob Dylan would not have been worthy of debate except for the way in which it touched upon a pervasive dissatisfaction with the excesses of what I have in a different context called 'cultural populism' (McGuigan, 1992). It was unfortunate that Hare should have articulated such dissatisfaction by calling for a return to absolute standards of aesthetic judgement, thus drawing the debate at that point down a blind alley.

3 FROM STATE TO MARKET

1 Janet Minihan's *The Nationalization of Culture* (1977) covers the main mid-nineteenth- to mid-twentieth-century developments in public arts policy. Also see Nicholas Pearson's *The State and the Visual Arts* (1982). For detailed accounts of the post-Second World War period through to the 1990s, see

Oliver Bennett (1995), who concentrates exclusively on the changing system and rationalisation crisis of public arts patronage, and Robert Hewison's extensive survey, *Culture & Consensus* (1995). Although Hewison overstates the importance of the Arts Council of Great Britain by putting it at the centre of the picture, his book also provides a very broad-based analysis of cultural change, decade by decade, since the 1940s.

2 One of the first grants from the new National Lottery, disbursed by the Arts Council in 1995, was £55 million for the renovation of the Royal Opera House in Covent Garden, thus maintaining a fifty-year-old and perenially controversial tradition of priority funding.

3 On policy developments in the 1980s related to the under-exploited profit potential of television in Britain, see Tom O'Malley's Campaign for Press and Broadcasting Freedom pamphlet *Switching Channels* (1988).

4 See Barnett and Curry (1994) for a blow-by-blow account of 'the battle for the BBC'.

5 At the Edinburgh Television Festival in 1994, the late Dennis Potter, leading British television dramatist of his day, denounced with great satirical verve the managerialist rhetoric and practice that had become normalised in the BBC. It is significant that Potter's incisive and highly publicised remarks were not met with a reasoned reply of any substance from the BBC's management.

6 A campaign was waged, however, for Lottery money to be spent on, for instance, theatrical production and not just on infrastructure. Considering that the international trend is for lotteries to gradually replace public investment in art and culture (Schuster, 1994–1995), this may have been a rash position to adopt.

4 CULTURAL INDUSTRIES

1 The launch of Microsoft's Windows 95 was an outstanding illustration of how lavish marketing campaigns typically exaggerate the innovativeness of a 'new' product. Windows 95 was no more than a further incorporation of Macintosh usability within the more cumbersome operating system of Microsoft. Still, Windows 95 was hyped as yet another major technological breakthrough by the market leader in computer software.

2 Tony Banks, Chair of the Arts and Recreation Committee, spelt out the committee's aims in an interview with the magazine *Artery* in 1982 (vol. 6, no. 4). No mention was made of the kind of cultural industries strategy that was later to be promoted by the GLC.

3 The papers by Garnham and position papers by a number of other researchers were reprinted in the 1985 GLC publication *The State of the Art or the Art of the State?* Garnham's key paper, 'Public Policy and the Cultural Industries', is included in his 1990 collection of essays.

4 Garnham quoted figures that spoke for themselves: in 1982 public cultural expenditure in Britain amounted to £673.8 million while over £13 billion was spent on cultural commodities.

5 In a recent managerial and postmodernist study of 'the culture business', Björkegren (1996) has explored the various strategies that are deployed typically in the publishing, music and film industries. He remarks, 'A prominent feature of arts-related businesses is . . . a high level of uncertainty in the market response to individual products. Because of this uncertainty, the business strategies of arts-producing organizations tend to be "emergent" rather than deliberate, an

outcome of interaction with the environment rather than the result of internally generated business plans.' (p. 43).

6 The research of the Lancaster School concerning the cultural industries is reported on in, for instance, Scott Lash and John Urry's *Economies of Signs and Space* (1994) and Celia Lury's *Cultural Rights* (1993).

5 URBAN REGENERATION

1 During the mid-1990s, Manchester and Leeds, in the once 'gloomy' North of England, sought to become 'twenty-four-hour cities', inspired at first rather implausibly by cities like Barcelona. Licensing hours were extended and the early evening link between day-time work and shopping and night-time entertainments was cultivated. In 1993, a twenty-four-hour city conference was held in Manchester that was followed by a similar one in Leeds, in 1994, at which a motley gathering of local politicians, police chiefs, publicans and nightclub owners discussed how to 'Europeanise' the English city.

2 See Castells's book with Peter Hall (1994), which examines and compares 'technopoles' across the globe.

6 NATIONAL HERITAGE

1 I am referring here to Deyan Sudjic's *Guardian* piece, 'Preserve Us from a State of Stagnation', of 14 September 1994, the source of the epigraph at the beginning of this chapter.

2 Although I believe that the theme of 'enterprise' has had greater consequence than 'heritage', this should not be taken to imply that heritage is insignificant. Its role in defining a sense of national identity is very important indeed.

3 For a critical appreciation of Will Hutton's *The State We're In*, see Colin Leys's (1995) article 'A Radical Agenda for Britain'.

4 Patrick Wright (1985) also discusses the sheer eccentricity of Deep Englandism: for instance, the elderly woman who had her Tudor house removed from Hertfordshire to Norfolk so as to escape a roundabout that was built around it without her consent.

5 In *Iron Britannia*, Anthony Barnett (1982) quite rightly disputed the commonly held view that the Falklands' victory led directly to Margaret Thatcher's first re-election in 1983. This does not, however, detract from the general point that the Conservatives did exploit the war symbolically for domestic political gain.

6 Ascherson (1987a) called heritage 'right-wing' as well as denouncing its 'vulgar English nationalism' (1987b).

7 Raphael Samuel (1981) edited a seminal collection of History Workshop papers entitled *People's History and Socialist Theory*. Moreover, his was the leading role in History Workshop, its pamphlets, journal and annual conferences, since its inception as 'an informal seminar' dedicated to the study of 'movements of popular resistance', in Samuel's own words, at Ruskin College, Oxford, in 1966.

8 Stratford, the birthplace of William Shakespeare and regional base for the Royal Shakespeare Company, understandably exploits the reputation of its most famous son by presenting itself to tourists almost entirely in terms of 'bardolatory' (Holderness, 1988).

7 IDENTITY, 'RACE' AND CITIZENSHIP

1 At the time of writing, the *Guardian* had recently run a spread entitled 'Black in Britain' (20.3.95), describing how much more at ease British citizens of Afro-Caribbean origin appeared than in the 1980s. Ironically, however, this was soon followed, in June 1995, by 'rioting' in the Manningham district of Bradford, involving British-born Asian youth, which was sparked-off by heavy-handed policing in a similar manner to the 1980s riots involving Afro-Caribbean youth.

2 The *Asian, Caribbean and African Arts Strategy*, produced by Qnun Ltd (1992), for the West Midlands Arts Board in England, is one of the best examples I have come across of a cultural policy document informed by the kind of sophisticated theorising on identity, 'race' and citizenship discussed in this chapter.

3 The term 'multiculturalism' has had a rather different meaning in Britain than in the USA. While in the USA it is closely associated with a radical 'cultural politics of difference' and 'political correctness', in Britain it still tends to denote a rather soft liberalism and was defined as such by the 'anti-racist' lobby during the 1970s and 1980s.

4 See Hiro (1992) for a detailed account of the different historical experiences and trajectories of non-white migrants to Britain.

8 CENSORSHIP AND MORAL REGULATION

1 The BBFC also classifies films distributed on video for domestic consumption, which has been the main focus of controversy in recent years, due especially to children's access to videos in the home. See Dewe Matthews (1994).

2 I personally prefer to remain agnostic on the effects of pornography. The evidence is dubious yet the issue is undoubtedly important. However, I also believe that feminist debates on pornography are a good example of what a properly argumentative public sphere should be like, except for the bitterness and recrimination.

3 The regulation of conduct exceeds the mainly communicative issues discussed in this chapter. For example, E. P. Thompson (1993) analysed how work and leisure practices were transformed by the factory system during the nineteenth century in his classic essay from the 1960s, 'Time, Work-Discipline and Industrialism Capitalism'. More recently, the Regulation School of political economy (Aglietta, 1987; Lipietz, 1987) has examined such transformations in the shift from Fordism to post-Fordism.

4 When Foucault died in 1984 the use of information technology for surveillance was, of course, already well advanced. See Poster (1990) for an approach to information technology inspired by Foucault.

5 The status of Noam Chomsky himself in the USA may be seen as further confirmation of 'the propaganda model' (see Achbor, 1994). The theorist of generative grammar is widely acknowledged as one of the most brilliant intellectuals of his time yet, in the USA, Chomsky is often calumnised for his political beliefs and his political writings are marginalised by mainstream publishing and reviewing: this, in spite of the fact that Chomsky, a libertarian socialist, was never a Soviet sympathiser.

6 Stuart Hall (1993) points out that market philosophy articulates a normative regime for which the self has to be re-engineered. He discusses this process interestingly with reference to the transformation of working practices in British public sector organisations, including the universities.

7 Martin Barker was kind enough to send me the first chapter of his forthcoming book with Guy Cumberbatch, which includes the full text of Newson's 'report' and a detailed and critical analysis of it.

8 The *Observer*/ICM poll of April 1994 (Observer, 10.4.94), commissioned at the time of the Newson 'report', presented evidence of current parental anxiety concerning children's media consumption.

9 CULTURE AND THE PUBLIC SPHERE

1 Habermas's original attack on post-structuralist and postmodernist thought was made in his *New German Critique* article of Winter 1981, 'Modernity Versus Postmodernity'.

2 When I had nearly finished this book, Peter Dahlgen's *Television and the Public Sphere* (1995) was published. His approach is rather different from mine yet, I believe, complementary since this book is not primarily about television, which, I agree with Dahlgren, is the most important medium of the public sphere.

3 The quotation is taken from the interview with Annabelle Sreberny-Moham-madi for 'Tactical TV', an episode of Channel Four's 1993 series, *Channels of Resistance*.

4 As Simon Caulkin (1995) has noted, 'Last year, the £60 billion industry toppled the motor car as the ultimate symbol of consumer capitalism, selling 60 million PCs across the globe.' He goes on to observe, 'So far, for all their market research, all the computer makers have done is toss their technology over the wall and trust buyers would find a use for it. They did: but only the well-educated, the well-heeled and mainly male consumer.'

5 This is a rather different distinction and polarity from Zygmunt Bauman's 'modern legislator' and 'postmodern interpreter', which fails to classify the growing army of information managers and, in consequence, does not address the problems of instrumentalism that concern me here.

6 I believe there is a certain affinity with the argument cast in this book in explicitly Habermasian terms and Charles Landry and Franco Bianchini's (1995) call for more 'creative' ways of thinking in cultural planning.

7 Doug Kellner's critical and constructive comments on the draft of this book made me realise the need to further clarify my criticisms of instrumental practice in cultural policy with regard to the role of intellectuals and thus prompted these observations. Kellner's recourse to Sartre, who has very much fallen out of intellectual favour in recent years, is congenial to me since I have long been influenced by Sartrean thought (see McGuigan, 1977).

REFERENCES

Achbor, M., ed. (1994) *Manufacturing Consent – Noam Chomsky and the Media*, Montreal and New York: Black Rose Books.

Adam Smith Institute (1989) *The Art of the State*, London: Adam Smith Institute.

Adorno, T. (1945) 'A Social Critique of Radio Music', *Kenyon Review*, no. 7.

—— (1991) *The Culture Industry*, London and New York: Routledge.

Adorno, T. and Horkheimer, M. (1944/1979) *Dialectic of Enlightenment*, London: New Left Books.

Aglietta, M. (1987) *A Theory of Capitalist Regulation – The US Experience*, London: Verso.

Aksoy, A. and Robins, K. (1992) 'Hollywood for the 21st Century – Global Competition for Critical Mass in Image Markets', *Cambridge Journal of Economics*, vol. 16 no. 1.

Amin, A., ed. (1994) *Post-Fordism – A Reader*, Oxford: Basil Blackwell.

Amis, K. (1980) *An Arts Policy*, London: Centre for Policy Studies.

Anderson, B. (1991) *Imagined Communities*, (2nd edn) London and New York: Verso.

Anderson, P. (1976) *Considerations on Western Marxism*, London: New Left Books.

Arnold, M. (1970) *Selected Prose*, London: Penguin.

Arthurs, J. (1994) 'Women and Television' in Hood, S., ed., *Behind the Screens – The Structure of British Television in the Nineties*, London: Lawrence and Wishart.

Arts Council (1984) *The Glory of the Garden – The Development of the Arts in England, A Strategy for a Decade*, London: Arts Council of GB.

—— (1985) *A Great British Success Story – An Invitation to the Nation to Invest in the Arts*, London: Arts Council of GB.

—— (1993) *A Creative Future – The Way Forward for the Arts, Crafts and Media in England*, London: Arts Council of GB.

Ascherson, N. (1987a) 'Why "Heritage" is Right-Wing', *Observer*, 8 November.

—— (1987b) '"Heritage" as Vulgar English Nationalism', *Observer*, 29 November.

—— (1995) 'It is Not Snobbish to say that Leylines and Astro-archaeology are Inventions', *Independent on Sunday*, 19 February.

Auty, M. and Roddick, N., eds (1985) *British Cinema Now*, London: British Film Institute.

Barker, M. (1981) *The New Racism*, London: Junction Books.

—— (1984a) *A Haunt of Fears – The Strange History of the British Horror Comic Campaign*, London: Pluto.

—— ed. (1984b) *The Video Nasties – Freedom and Censorship in the Media*, London: Pluto.

REFERENCES

—— (1993) 'Sex, Violence and Videotape', *Sight and Sound*, May.

Barker, M. and Cumberbatch, G. (forthcoming) *The Media/Violence Debate*, London: Pluto.

Barnett, A. (1982) *Iron Britannia – Why Parliament Waged its Falklands War*, London: Alison and Busby.

Barnett, S. and Curry, A. (1994) *The Battle for the BBC – A British Broadcasting Conspiracy?*, London: Aurum.

Baudrillard, J. (1988) *Selected Writings*, Cambridge: Polity.

Bauman, Z. (1987) *Legislators and Interpreters*, Cambridge: Polity.

—— (1993) *Postmodern Ethics*, Oxford and Cambridge, Mass.: Basil Blackwell.

Baynes, K. (1994) 'Communicative Ethics, the Public Sphere and Communication Media', *Critical Studies in Mass Communication*, vol. 11.

Beard, H. and Cerf, C. (1992) *The Official Politically Correct Dictionary & Handbook*, London: Grafton.

Beck, U. (1992) *Risk Society – Towards a New Modernity*, London and Newbury Park: Sage.

Beck, U., Giddens, A. and Lash, S. (1994) *Reflexive Modernization*, Cambridge: Polity.

Benjamin, W. (1936/1973a) 'The Work of Art in the Age of Mechanical Reproduction' in his *Illuminations*, London: Fontana.

—— (1973b) *Understanding Brecht*, London: New Left Books.

Bennett, O. (1995) 'Cultural Policy in the United Kingdom – Collapsing Rationales and the End of a Tradition', *European Journal of Cultural Policy*, vol. 1, no. 2.

Bennett, T. (1986) 'The Politics of the "Popular" and Popular Culture' in Bennett, T., Mercer, C. and Woollacott, J., eds, *Popular Culture and Social Relations*, Milton Keynes: Open University Press.

—— (1988a) 'The Exhibitionary Complex', *New Formations*, no. 4.

—— (1988b) 'Museums and "the People"' in Lumley, R., ed., *The Museum Time Machine*, London: Comedia.

—— (1992a) 'Putting Policy into Cultural Studies' in Grossberg, L., Nelson, C. and Treichler, P., eds, *Cultural Studies*, London and New York: Routledge.

—— (1992b) 'Useful Culture', *Cultural Studies*, vol. 6 no. 3.

—— (1995) *The Birth of the Museum*, London and New York: Routledge.

Berger, P. (1987) *The Capitalist Revolution – Fifty Propositions About Prosperity, Equality, and Liberty*, Aldershot: Wildwood House.

Bernstein, J. M. (1995) *Recovering Ethical Life – Jürgen Habermas and the Future of Critical Theory*, London and New York: Routledge.

Berube, M. (1994) *Public Access – Literary Theory and American Cultural Politics*, London and New York: Verso.

Best, S. and Kellner, D. (1991) *Postmodern Theory*, London: Macmillan.

Bianchini, F. (1987) 'GLC R.I.P. 1981–1986', *New Formations*, no. 1.

—— (1990) 'Urban Renaissance? The Arts and the Urban Regeneration Process' in MacGregor, S. and Pimlott, B., eds, *Tackling the Inner Cities*, Oxford: Clarendon Press.

Bianchini, F. and Parkinson, M., eds (1993) *Cultural Policy and Urban Regeneration – The West European Experience*, Manchester: Manchester University Press.

Bianchini, F. and Schwengel, H. (1991) 'Re-imagining the City' in Corner, J. and Harvey, S., eds, *Enterprise and Heritage – Crosscurrents of National Culture*, London and New York: Routledge.

Bianchini, F., Fisher, M., Montgomery, J. and Worpole, K. (1988) *City Centres, City Cultures – The Role of the Arts in the Revitalisation of Towns and Cities*, Manchester: Centre for Local Economic Strategies.

Björkegren, D. (1996) *The Culture Business – Management Strategies for the Arts-Related Business*, London and New York: Routledge.

Bloch, E., Lukács, G., Brecht, B., Benjamin, W. and Adorno, T. (1977) *Aesthetics and Politics*, London: New Left Books.

Blumler, J. (1978) 'Purposes of Mass Communication Research – A Transatlantic Perspective', *Journalism Quarterly*, Summer.

Bolton, R., ed. (1992) *Culture Wars – Documents from the Recent Controversies in the Arts*, New York: New Press.

Boniface, P. and Fowler, P. (1993) *Heritage and Tourism in 'the Global Village'*, London and New York: Routledge.

Bourdieu, P. (1965/1990) *Photography – A Middle-Brow Art*, Cambridge: Polity.

—— (1971) 'Intellectual Field and Creative Project' in Young, M. F. D., ed., *Knowledge and Control – New Directions for the Sociology of Education*, London: Collier Macmillan.

—— (1973) 'Cultural Reproduction and Social Reproduction' in Brown, R., ed., *Knowledge, Education and Social Change*, London: Tavistock.

—— (1984) *Distinction – A Social Critique of the Judgement of Taste*, London: Routledge.

—— (1993) *The Field of Cultural Production*, Cambridge: Polity.

Bourdieu, P. and Darbel, A. (1969/1991) *The Love of Art*, Cambridge: Polity.

Bourdieu, P. and Haacke, H. (1995) *Free Exchange*, Cambridge: Polity.

Bowden, M. (1984) *General Pitt Rivers*, Salisbury: Salisbury and Wiltshire Museum.

Braden, S. (1978) *Artists and People*, London: Routledge.

Burkitt, I. (1991) *Social Selves – Theories of the Social Formation of Personality*, London and Newbury Park: Sage.

Calhoun, C., ed. (1992) *Habermas and the Public Sphere*, Cambridge, Mass.: MIT Press.

—— (1993) 'Habitus, Field and Capital – The Question of Historical Specificity' in Calhoun, C., LiPuma, E. and Postone, M., eds, *Bourdieu – Critical Perspectives*, Cambridge: Polity.

Campbell, B. (1993) *Goliath – Britain's Dangerous Places*, London: Methuen.

Carby, H. (1992) 'The Multicultural Wars' in Dent, G., ed., *Black Popular Culture*, Seattle: Bay Press.

Castells, M. (1994) 'European Cities, the Informational Society, and the Global Economy', *New Left Review*, no. 204.

Castells, M. and Hall, P. (1994) *Technopoles of the World – The Making of 21st Century Industrial Complexes*, London and New York: Routledge.

Caulkin, S. (1995) 'The Net Draws Ever Tighter', *Observer*, 10 September.

Chaney, D. (1994) *The Cultural Turn* London and New York: Routledge.

Christopherson, S. and Storper, M. (1986) 'The City as Studio; the World as Back Lot: The Impact of Vertical Disintegration on the Location of the Motion Picture Industry', *Economy and Planning D: Society and Space*, vol. 4.

Clarke, J. and Critcher, C. (1985) *The Devil Makes Work – Leisure in Capitalist Britain*, London: Macmillan.

Clarke, J. and Newman, J. (1993) 'The Right to Manage – A Second Managerial Revolution?', *Cultural Studies*, vol. 7 no. 3.

Clifford, J. (1992) 'Traveling Cultures' in Grossberg, L., Nelson, C. and Treichler, P., eds, *Cultural Studies*, London and New York: Routledge.

Colenutt, B. (1994) 'Docklands after Canary Wharf – The Political Impact of the Regeneration of London Docklands', paper presented at the Conference on Social Justice and the City, University of Oxford, 14–15 March.

Collins, R. (1993) 'Public Service Versus the Market Ten Years On – Reflections on Critical Theory and the Debate on Broadcasting in the UK' , *Screen*, vol. 34, no. 3.

Connor, S. (1992) *Theory and Cultural Value*, Oxford: Basil Blackwell.

Corner, J. (1993) 'Debating Culture – Quality and Inequality' in Harvey, S., Stone, G. and Drummond, P., eds, *Media Studies in Transition*, London: Association for Media, Film and Television Studies in Higher Education.

Corner, J. and Harvey, S., eds (1991) *Enterprise and Heritage – Crosscurrents of National Culture*, London and New York: Routledge.

Crofts, A. (1988) 'Enhancing the Past to Secure the Future', *Marketing Week*, 11 March.

Cunningham, S. (1992a) *Framing Culture – Criticism and Policy in Australia*, Sydney: Allen & Unwin.

—— (1992b) 'TV Violence – The Challenge of Public Policy in Cultural Studies', *Cultural Studies*, vol. 6, no. 1.

—— (1993) 'Cultural Studies from the Point of View of Cultural Policy' in Turner, G., ed., *Nation, Culture, Text – Australian Cultural and Media Studies*, London and New York: Routledge.

Curran, J. (1991) 'Rethinking the Media as a Public Sphere' in Dahlgren, P. and Sparks, C., eds, *Communication and Citizenship – Journalism and the Public Sphere in the New Media Age*, London and New York: Routledge.

Curry Jansen, S. (1991) *Censorship – The Knot that Binds Power and Knowledge*, New York: Oxford University Press.

Dahlgren, P. (1995) *Television and the Public Sphere*, London and Newbury Park: Sage.

Davis, M. (1990) *City of Quartz – Excavating the Future in Los Angeles*, London and New York: Verso.

—— (1993a) 'Who Killed LA? A Political Autopsy', *New Left Review*, no. 197.

—— (1993b) 'Who Killed Los Angeles? Part Two – The Verdict is Given', *New Left Review*, no. 199.

Debord, G. (1994 – Nicholson-Smith's translation) *The Society of the Spectacle*, New York: Zone Books.

Dent, G., ed. (1992) *Black Popular Culture*, Seattle: Bay Press.

Derrida, J. (1975) '*Différance*' in Easthope, A. and McGowan, K., eds, *A Critical and Cultural Theory Reader*, (1992) Buckingham: Open University Press.

Desai, R. (1994) 'Second-Hand Dealers in Ideas – Think Tanks and Thatcherite Hegemony', *New Left Review*, no. 203.

Dewe Matthews, T. (1994) *Censored – What They Didn't Allow You to See, And Why: The Story of Film Censorship in Britain*, London: Chatto & Windus.

Dews, P., ed. (1992) *Autonomy and Solidarity – Interviews with Jürgen Habermas*, London and New York: Verso.

Dickinson, M. and Street, S. (1985) *Cinema and State – The Film Industry and the British Government 1927–84*, London: British Film Insitute.

Diggle, K. (1984) *Guide to Arts Marketing*, London: Rheingold.

Donald, J. and Rattansi, A., eds (1992) '*Race*', *Culture & Difference*, London and Newbury Park: Sage.

Dowmunt, T., ed. (1993) *Channels of Resistance – Global Television and Local Empowerment*, London: British Film Institute.

Dunant, S., ed. (1994) *The War of the Words – The Political Correctness Debate*, London: Virago Press.

Eagleton, T. (1984) *The Function of Criticism – From the Spectator to Post-structuralism*, London and New York: Verso.

—— (1990) *The Ideology of the Aesthetic*, Oxford: Basil Blackwell.

Ehrenreich, B. and Ehrenreich, J. (1979) 'The Professional-Managerial Class' in Walker, P., ed., *Between Labour and Capital*, Boston: South End Press.

Elias, N. (1994) *The Civilizing Process*, Oxford and Cambridge, Mass. Basil Blackwell.

Enzensberger, H. M. (1974) *The Consciousness Industry*, New York: Seabury Press.

Etzioni, A. (1993) *The Spirit of Community*, New York: Touchstone.

—— (1995) 'Common Values', *New Statesman & Society*, 12 May.

Featherstone, M. (1989) 'Postmodernism, Cultural Change, and Social Practice' in Kellner, D., ed., *Postmodernism/Jameson/Critique*, Washington, DC: Maisonneuve Press.

—— (1991) *Consumer Culture & Postmodernism*, London and Newbury Park: Sage.

Feist, A. and Hutchison, R. (1990) *Cultural Trends no. 5 – Funding the Arts in Seven Western Countries*, London: Policy Studies Institute.

Fekete, J., ed. (1987) *Life After Postmodernism – Essays on Value and Culture*, Montreal: New World Perspectives.

Ferguson, M. (1992) 'The Mythology about Globalization', *European Journal of Communication*, vol. 7.

Fish, S. (1994) *There's No Such Thing as Free Speech*, New York and Oxford: Oxford University Press.

Forrester, J. (1987) 'A Brief History of the Subject' in Apignanesi, L., ed., *The Real Me – Postmodernism and the Question of Identity*, London: Institute of Contemporary Arts.

Foucault, M. (1977) *Discipline and Punish – The Birth of the Prison*, London: Allen Lane.

—— (1981a) *The History of Sexuality, Volume One – An Introduction*, London: Penguin.

—— (1981b) 'The Order of Discourse' in Young, R., ed., *Untying the Text*, London: Routledge.

—— (1986) 'Truth and Power' in Rabinow, P., ed., *The Foucault Reader*, London: Penguin.

—— (1987) *The History of Sexuality, Volume Two – The Use of Pleasure*, London: Penguin.

—— (1988) *The History of Sexuality, Volume Three – The Care of the Self*, London: Penguin.

—— (1991) 'Governmentality' in Burchill, G., Gordon, C. and Miller, P., eds, *The Foucault Effect – Studies in Governmentality*, Hemel Hempstead: Harvester Wheatsheaf.

Fraser, N. (1992) 'Rethinking the Public Sphere – A Contribution to the Critique of Actually Existing Democracy', in Calhoun, C., ed., *Habermas and the Public Sphere*, Cambridge, Mass.: MIT Press.

Friedrichs, J. and Dangschat, J. (1993) 'Hamburg – Culture and Urban Competition' in Bianchini, F. and Parkinson, M., eds, *Cultural Policy and Urban Regeneration – The West European Experience*, Manchester: Manchester University Press.

Frith, S. (1983) 'The Pleasures of the Hearth – The Making of BBC Light Entertainment', in *Formations of Pleasure*, London: Routledge.

—— (1991a) 'Popular Culture', *National Arts and Media Strategy* no. 17, London: Arts Council of Great Britain.

—— (1991b) 'Knowing One's Place – The Culture of the Cultural Industries', *Cultural Studies from Birmingham*, no. 1, University of Birmingham.

—— (1993) 'Popular Music and the Local State' in Bennett, T., Frith, S., Grossberg,

L., Shepherd, J. and Turner, G., eds, *Rock and Popular Music*, London and New York: Routledge.

Frith, S. and Savage, J. (1993) 'Pearls and Swine – The Intellectuals and the Mass Media', *New Left Review*, no. 198.

Frow, J. (1995) *Cultural Studies & Cultural Value*, Oxford: Oxford University Press.

Galbraith, J. K., (1958) *The Affluent Society*, London: Hamish Hamilton.

—— (1992) *The Culture of Contentment*, London: Sinclair-Stevenson.

Gamble, A. (1994a,) *The Free Economy and the Strong State – The Politics of Thatcherism*, (2nd edn) London: Macmillan.

—— (1994b) *Britain in Decline – Economic Policy, Political Strategy and the British State*, (4th edn) London: Macmillan.

Garnham, N. (1983) 'Public Service Versus the Market', *Screen*, vol. 24, no. 1.

—— (1990) *Capitalism and Communication – Global Culture and the Economics of Information*, London and Newbury Park: Sage.

—— (1992) 'The Media and the Public Sphere', in Calhoun, C., ed., *Habermas and the Public Sphere*, Cambridge, Mass.: MIT Press.

—— (1993a) 'Bourdieu, the Cultural Arbitrary, and Television' in Calhoun, C., LiPuma, E. and Postone, M., eds, *Bourdieu – Critical Perspectives*, Cambridge: Polity.

—— (1993b) 'The Future of the BBC', *Sight and Sound*, February.

Garreau, J. (1991) *Edge City – Life on the New Frontier*, New York: Doubleday.

Gerbner, G. (1995) 'Television Violence – The Power and the Peril' in Dines, G. and Humez, J., eds, *Gender, Race and Class in the Media*, London and Newbury Park: Sage.

Giddens, A. (1990) *The Consequences of Modernity*, Cambridge: Polity.

—— (1991) *Modernity and Self-Identity – Self and Society in the Late Modern Age*, Cambridge: Polity.

Gilroy, P. (1987) *There Ain't No Black in the Union Jack*, London: Hutchinson.

—— (1993a) *The Black Atlantic – Modernity and Double Consciousness*, London and New York: Verso.

—— (1993b) *Small Acts – Thoughts on the Politics of Black Cultures*, London: Serpent's Tail.

Gitlin, T. (1993) 'Glib, Tawdry, Savvy & Standardized – Television and American Culture', *Dissent*, Summer.

Golding, P. and Murdock, G. (1986) 'The New Communications Revolution', in Curran, J., Ecclestone, Oakley, G. and Richardson, A., eds, *Bending Reality – The State of the Media*, London: Pluto.

Gordon, C., ed. (1980) *Michel Foucault – Power/Knowledge*, Brighton: Harvester.

Graff, G. (1992) *Beyond the Culture Wars – How Teaching the Conflicts Can Revitalise American Education*, London and New York: Norton.

Gramsci, A. (1971) *Selections from the Prison Notebooks*, London: Lawrence & Wishart.

Greater London Council (1985) *The State of the Art or the Art of the State?*, London.

Greenhalgh, L., Worpole, K. and Landry, C.(1995) *Libraries in a World of Cultural Change*, University College of London Press.

Habermas, J. (1962/1989) *The Structural Transformation of the Public Sphere – An Inquiry into a Category of Bourgeois Society*, Cambridge: Polity.

—— (1971) *Toward a Rational Society*, London: Heinemann.

—— (1972) *Knowledge and Human Interests*, London: Heinemann.

—— (1974) *Theory and Practice*, London: Heinemann.

—— (1976) *Legitimation Crisis*, London: Heinemann.

—— (1979) *Communication and the Evolution of Society*, London: Heinemann.

—— (1981) 'Modernity Versus Postmodernity', *New German Critique*, Winter.

—— (1984) *The Theory of Communicative Action, Volume One – Reason and the Rationalization of Society*, New York: Beacon Press (1991, Cambridge: Polity).

—— (1987a) *The Theory of Communicative Action, Volume Two – The Critique of Functionalist Reason*, Cambridge: Polity.

—— (1987b) *The Philosophical Discourse of Modernity*, Cambridge: Polity.

—— (1989) 'The New Obscurity – The Crisis of the Welfare State and the Exhaustion of Utopian Energies' in his *The New Conservatism*, Cambridge, Massachusetts: MIT Press.

—— (1990) *Moral Consciousness and Communicative Action*, Cambridge: Polity.

—— (1992) 'Further Reflections on the Public Sphere', in Calhoun, C., ed., *Habermas and the Public Sphere*, Cambridge, Mass.: MIT Press.

—— (1994a) 'Struggles for Recognition in the Democratic Constitutional State' in Gutman, A., ed., *Multiculturalism*, Princeton, NJ: Princeton University Press.

—— (1994b) 'Citizenship and National Identity' in Van Steenbergen, B., ed., *The Condition of Citizenship*, London and Newbury Park: Sage.

Hall, S. (1986) 'Popular Culture and the State', in Bennett, T., Mercer, C. and Woollacott, J., eds, *Popular Culture and Social Relations*, Milton Keynes: Open University Press.

—— (1987) 'Minimal Selves' in *The Real Me – Postmodernism and the Question of Identity*, London: Institute of Contemporary Arts – Document 6. Reprinted in Gray, A. and McGuigan, J., eds, (1993) *Studying Culture*, London: Edward Arnold.

—— (1988a) *The Hard Road to Renewal – Thatcherism and the Crisis of the Left*, London and New York: Verso.

—— (1988b) 'New Ethnicities' in *Black Film, British Cinema*, London: Institute of Contemporary Arts – Document 7. Reprinted in Donald, J. and Rattansi, A., eds (1992) '*Race*', *Culture & Difference*, London and Newbury Park: Sage.

—— (1990) 'Cultural Identity and Diaspora' in Rutherford, J., ed., *Identity – Community, Culture, Difference*, London: Lawrence & Wishart.

—— (1992) 'The Question of Cultural Identity' in Hall, S., Held, D. and McGrew, T., eds, *Modernity and its Futures*, Cambridge: Polity/Open University.

—— (1993) *Moving On . . .*, London: Democratic Left.

—— (1995) 'Negotiating Caribbean Identities', *New Left Review*, no. 209.

Harvey, D. (1989a) *The Condition of Postmodernity*, Oxford: Basil Blackwell.

—— (1989b) *The Urban Experience*, Oxford: Basil Blackwell.

—— (1993a) 'Goodbye to All That? Thoughts on the Social and Intellectual Conditions of Contemporary Britain', *Regenerating Cities*, no. 5.

—— (1993b) 'From Place to Space and Back Again – Reflections on the Condition of Postmodernity' in Bird, J., Curtis, B., Putnam, T., Robertson, G. and Tickner, L., eds, *Mapping the Futures – Local Cultures, Global Change*, London and New York: Routledge.

—— (1993c) 'A Fur Coat and No Knickers', *City Lights, City Shadows* no. 1, Radio Four, 10 October, BBC.

—— (1993d) 'The Underclass Strikes Back', *City Lights, City Shadows no. 2, Radio Four, 17 October, BBC.*

Harvey, S. (1994) 'Channel 4 Television – From Annan to Grade' in Hood, S., ed., *Behind the Screens – The Structure of British Television in the Nineties*, London: Lawrence & Wishart.

REFERENCES

Hayward, S. (1993) 'State, Culture and the Cinema – Jack Lang's Strategies for the French Film Industry 1981–93', *Screen*, vol. 34, no. 4.

Healey, P. (1989) 'Planning for the 1990s', *Department of Town and Country Planning Working Papers* no. 7, University of Newcastle Upon Tyne.

Hebdige, D. (1987) *Cut 'n' Mix – Culture, Identity and Caribbean Music*, London: Comedia.

Henry, I. (1993) *The Politics of Leisure Policy*, London: Macmillan.

Herman, E. and Chomsky, N. (1988) *Manufacturing Consent – The Political Economy of the Mass Media*, New York: Pantheon Books.

Hewison, R. (1987) *The Heritage Industry – Britain in a Climate of Decline*, London: Methuen.

—— (1994) 'Sceptred Aisles', *Sunday Times*, 13 March.

—— (1995) *Culture & Consensus – England, Art and Politics since 1940*, London: Methuen.

Himmelfarb, G. (1995) *The De-moralization of Society*, New York: Alfred Knopf.

Hiro, D. (1992) *Black British, White British – A History of Race Relations in Britain*, London: Paladin.

Hobsbawm, E. (1990) *Nations and Nationalism Since 1780 – Programme, Myth, Reality*, Cambridge University Press.

Hobsbawm, E. and Ranger, T., eds (1983) *The Invention of Tradition*, Cambridge: Cambridge University Press.

Hodge, B. and Tripp, D. (1986) *Children and Television*, Cambridge: Polity

Holderness, G., ed. (1988) *The Shakespeare Myth*, Manchester: Manchester University Press.

Holub, R. (1991) *Jürgen Habermas – Critic in the Public Sphere*, London and New York: Routledge.

Horne, D. (1984) *The Great Museum – The Re-presentation of History*, London: Pluto.

—— (1994,) *The Public Culture – An Argument with the Future*, (2nd edn) London: Pluto.

Howarth, A. (1994) *Anti-libertarianism – Markets, Philosophy and Myth*, London and New York: Routledge.

Huczynski, A. (1993) *Management Gurus – What Makes Them and How to Become One*, London and New York: Routledge.

Hughes, R. (1993) *Culture of Complaint – The Fraying of America*, New York: Oxford University Press.

Hunter, I. (1988a) *Culture and Government – The Emergence of Literary Education*, London: Macmillan.

—— (1988b) 'Setting Limits to Culture', *New Formations*, no. 4.

Hutchison, R. (1982) *The Politics of the Arts Council*, London: Sinclair Brown.

Hutton, W. (1995) *The State We're In*, London: Jonathan Cape.

Itzin, C. (1980) *Stages in the Revolution – Political Theatre in Britain Since 1968*, London: Eyre Methuen.

—— ed. (1992) *Pornography – Women, Violence and Civil Liberties*, Oxford and New York: Oxford University Press.

Jacobs, J. (1961) *The Death and Life of Great American Cities*, London: Jonathan Cape.

Jameson, F. (1984) 'Postmodernism, or, The Cultural Logic of Late Capitalism', *New Left Review*, no. 146.

—— (1990) *Late Marxism – Adorno, or, The Persistence of the Dialectic*, London and New York: Verso.

—— (1991) *Postmodernism – Or, The Cultural Logic of Late Capitalism*, London and New York: Verso.

Jenkins, R. (1992) *Pierre Bourdieu*, London and New York: Routledge.

Jones, S., ed. (1995) *Cybersociety – Computer-Mediated Communication and Community*, London and Newbury Park: Sage.

Karp, I. and Lavine, S., eds (1991) *Exhibiting Cultures – The Poetics and Politics of Museum Display*, Washington: Smithsonian Institution.

Karp, I., Kreamer, C. and Lavine, S., eds (1992) *Museums and Communities – The Politics of Public Culture*, Washington: Smithsonian Institution.

Keane, J. (1991) *The Media and Democracy*, Cambridge: Polity.

Keat, R. and Abercrombie, N., eds (1991) *Enterprise Culture*, London and New York: Routledge.

Keat, R., Whiteley, N. and Abercrombie, N., eds (1994) *The Authority of the Consumer*, London and New York: Routledge.

Kellner, D. (1995a) *Media Culture – Cultural Studies, Identity and Politics Between the Modern and the Postmodern*, London and New York: Routledge.

—— (1995b) 'Intellectuals and New Technologies', *Media, Culture & Society*, vol. 17, no. 3.

Kelly, M., ed. (1994) *Critique and Power – Recasting the Foucault/Habermas Debate*, Cambridge, Mass.: MIT Press.

Kinder, M. (1991) *Playing with Power in Movies, Television, and Video Games*, Berkeley: University of California Press.

Kline, S. (1993) *Out of the Garden – Toys and Children's Culture in the Age of TV Marketing*, London and New York: Verso.

Landry, C., Morley, D., Southwood, R. and Wright, P. (1985) *What a Way to Run a Railroad*, London: Comedia.

Landry, C. and Bianchini, F. (1995) *The Creative City*, London: Demos.

Larrain, J. (1994) *Ideology & Cultural Identity – Modernity and the Third World Presence*, Cambridge: Polity.

Lash, S. (1993a) 'Pierre Bourdieu – Cultural Economy and Social Change' in Calhoun, C., LiPuma, E. and Postone, M., eds, *Bourdieu – Critical Perspectives*, Cambridge: Polity.

—— (1993b) 'Reflexive Modernization – The Aesthetic Dimension', *Theory, Culture & Society*, vol. 10, no. 1.

Lash, S. and Urry, J. (1987) *The End of Organized Capitalism*, Cambridge: Polity.

—— (1994) *Economies of Signs and Space*, London and New York: Sage.

Lazarsfeld, P. (1941) 'Administrative and Critical Communications Research', *Studies in Philosophy and Social Science*, no. 9.

Leach, E. (1976) *Culture and Communication*, Cambridge: Cambridge University Press.

Lee, M. (1993) *Consumer Culture Reborn – The Cultural Politics of Consumption*, London and New York: Routledge.

Le Gales, P. (1993) 'Rennes – Catholic Humanism and Urban Entrepreneurialism' in Bianchini, F. and Parkinson, M., eds, *Cultural Policy and Urban Regeneration – The West European Experience*, Manchester: Manchester University Press.

Lewis, J. (1990) *Art, Culture & Enterprise – The Politics of Art and the Cultural Industries*, London and New York: Routledge.

Lewis, J, Morley, D. and Southwood, R. (1986) *Art – Who Needs It?*, London: Comedia.

Leys, C. (1995) 'A Radical Agenda for Britain', *New Left Review*, no. 212.

Lichfield, J. (1992) 'No Particular Place to Live', *Independent on Sunday*, 15 November.

Lipietz, A. (1987) *Mirages and Miracles – The Crises of Global Fordism*, London and New York: Verso.

Luce, R. (1987) 'Speech by the Arts Minister Richard Luce to CoRAA Conference, Newcastle Upon Tyne on 8 July 1987', London: Council of Regional Arts Associations.

Lumley, R., ed. (1988) *The Museum Time Machine*, London: Comedia.

Lury, C. (1993) *Cultural Rights – Technology, Legality and Personality*, London and New York: Routledge.

Lyon, D. (1994) *The Electronic Eye – The Rise of Surveillance Society*, Cambridge: Polity.

Lyotard, J.-F. (1984) *The Postmodern Condition – A Report on Knowledge*, Manchester: Manchester University Press.

McGuigan, J. (1977) 'The Literary Sociology of Sartre: in Routh, J. and Wolff, J., eds, *Sociological Review Monograph* no. 22 – *The Sociology of Literature: Theoretical Approaches*, University of Keele.

—— (1981) *Writers and the Arts Council*, London: Arts Council of GB.

—— (1992) *Cultural Populism*, London and New York: Routledge.

—— (1993) 'Reaching for Control – Raymond Williams on Mass Communication and Popular Culture' in Morgan, J. and Preston, P., eds, *Raymond Williams – Politics, Education, Letters*, London: Macmillan.

—— (1995) ' "A Slow Reach Again for Control" – Raymond Williams and the Vicissitudes of Cultural Policy', *European Journal of Cultural Policy*, vol. 2, no. 1.

—— (1996) 'Cultural Populism Revisited' in Ferguson, M. and Golding, P., eds, *Beyond Cultural Studies*, London and Newbury Park: Sage.

McLaughlin, M., Osborne, K. and Smith, C. (1995) 'Standards of Conduct on Usenet', in Jones, S., ed., *Cybersociety*, London and Newbury Park: Sage.

Marshall, T. H. (1950/1992) *Citizenship and Social Class*, London: Pluto.

Marx, K. (1843) 'On the Jewish Question', in his *Early Writings* 1975, London: Penguin.

Massey, D. (1994) *Space, Place and Gender*, Cambridge: Polity.

Mattelart, A. (1991) *Advertising International – The Privatisation of Public Space*, London and New York: Routledge.

Medved, M. (1992) *Hollywood Vs. America – Popular Culture and the War on Traditional Values*, New York: HarperCollins.

Meiksins Wood, E. (1995) *Democracy Against Capitalism – Renewing Historical Materialism*, Cambridge University Press.

Mepham, J. (1991) 'Television Fictions – Quality and Truth-Telling', *Radical Philosophy*, no. 57.

Mercer, K. (1994) *Welcome to the Jungle – New Positions in Black Cultural Studies*, London and New York: Routledge.

Merriman, N. (1989) 'Museum Visiting as a Cultural Phenomenon' in Vergo, P., ed., *The New Museology*, London: Reaktion Books.

Miège, B. (1989) *The Capitalization of Cultural Production*, New York: International General.

Mills, C. (1970) *The Sociological Imagination*, London: Penguin.

Minihan, J. (1977) *The Nationalization of Culture – The Development of State Subsidies to the Arts in Great Britain*, London: Hamish Hamilton.

Morris, L. (1994) *Dangerous Classes – The Underclass and Social Citizenship*, London and New York: Routledge.

Mort, F. (1990) 'What's It Worth Then?', *Marxism Today*, July.

Mulgan, G. (1994) *Politics in an Antipolitical Age*, Cambridge: Polity.

Mulgan, G. and Worpole, K. (1986) *Saturday Night or Sunday Morning? From Arts to Industry –New Forms of Cultural Policy*, London: Comedia.

Murdock, G. (1980) 'Class Stratification and Cultural Consumption – Some Motifs in the Work of Pierre Bourdieu' in Smith, M., ed., *Leisure and Urban Society*, Leisure Studies Association, University of Salford.

Murdock, G. and Golding, P. (1989) 'Information Poverty – Citizenship in the Age of Privatized Communications', *Journal of Communication*, vol. 39, no. 3.

Murray, R. (1989) 'Fordism and Post-Fordism' in Hall, S. and Jacques, M., eds, *New Times – The Changing Face of Politics in the 1990s*, London: Lawrence & Wishart.

Myerscough, J. (1988) *The Economic Importance of the Arts in Britain*, London: Policy Studies Institute.

Negrier, E. (1993) 'Montpellier – International Competition and Community Access' in Bianchini, F. and Parkinson, M., eds, *Cultural Policy and Urban Regeneration – The West European Experience*, Manchester: Manchester University Press.

Negt, O. and Kluge, A. (1972/1993) *The Public Sphere and Experience -Toward an Analysis of the Bourgeois and Proletarian Public Sphere*, Minneapolis: University of Minnesota Press.

O'Connor, J. and Wynne, D. (1993) 'From the Margins to the Centre – Cultural Production and Consumption in the Post-industrial City', Manchester Institute for Popular Culture Working Papers, no. 7.

O'Malley, T. (1988) *Switching Channels – The Debate over the Future of Broadcasting*, London: Campaign for Press and Broadcasting Freedom.

O'Regan, T. (1992) '(Mis)taking Cultural Policy – Notes on the Cultural Policy Debate', *Cultural Studies*, vol. 6, no. 3.

Orwell, G. (1941/1982) *The Lion and the Unicorn – Socialism and the English Genius*, London: Penguin.

Osborne, D. and Gaebler, T. (1992) *Reinventing Government – How the Entrepreneurial Spirit is Transforming the Public Sector*, Reading, Mass.:Addison-Wesley.

Owusu, K. (1986) *The Struggle for Black Arts in Britain*, London: Comedia.

Pahl, R. (1995) 'Friendly Society', *New Statesman & Society*, 10 March.

Painter, C. (1994) 'Public Service Reform – Reinventing or Abandoning Government?', *Political Quarterly* vol. 26, no. 3.

Parekh, B. (1989) 'Between Holy Text and Moral Void', *New Statesman & Society*, 24 March. Reprinted in Gray, A. and McGuigan, J., eds (1993), *Studying Culture*, London: Edward Arnold.

—— (1991) 'British Citizenship and Cultural Difference' in Andrews, G., ed., *Citizenship*, London: Lawrence & Wishart.

Parekh, B., Lynch, J., Poulter, S. and Verna G. (1990) *Britain – A Plural Society*, London: Commission for Racial Equality/Runnymede Trust.

Peacock, A. (1986) *Report of the Committee on Financing the BBC*, London: cmnd. 9824.

Pearson, N. (1982) *The State and the Visual Arts*, Milton Keynes: Open University Press.

Perin, C. (1992) 'The Communicative Circle – Museums as Communities', in Karp, I., Kreamer, C. and Lavine, S., eds, *Museums and Communities*, Washington, DC: Smithsonian Institution.

Perryman, M., ed. (1994) *Altered States – Postmodernism, Politics, Culture*, London: Lawrence & Wishart.

Peters, T. and Waterman, R. (1982) *In Search of Excellence – Lessons from America's Best-Run Companies*, New York: HarperCollins.

207

Pfeil, F. (1991) *Another Tale to Tell – Politics & Narrative in Postmodern Culture*, London and New York: Verso.

Plant, S. (1992) *The Most Radical Gesture – The Situationist International in a Postmodern Age*, London and New York: Routledge.

Poster, M. (1990) *The Mode of Information*, Cambridge: Polity Press.

—— (1995) *The Second Media Age*, Cambridge: Polity.

Qnun Ltd (1992) *Asian, Caribbean and African Arts Strategy*, Birmingham: West Midlands Arts Board.

Rattansi, A. (1992) 'Changing the Subject? Racism, Culture and Education' in Donald, J. and Rattansi, A., eds, *'Race', Culture & Difference*, London and Newbury Park: Sage.

Redhead, S. (1995) *Unpopular Cultures – The Birth of Law and Popular Culture*, Manchester: Manchester University Press.

Rees-Mogg, W. (1985) *The Political Economy of Art*, London: Arts Council of GB.

Reith, J. (1924) *Broadcast Over Britain*, London: Hodder and Stoughton.

Rheingold, H. (1994) *The Virtual Community – Surfing the Internet*, London: Martin Secker & Warburg.

Rice, J. and Rice, P. (1989) 'Future Imperfect? English and the New Vocationalism' in Brooker, P. and Humm, P., eds, *Dialogue and Difference – English Into the Nineties*, London and New York: Routledge.

Robbins, B., ed. (1993) *The Phantom Public Sphere*, Minneapolis: University of Minnesota Press.

Robbins, D. (1991) *The Work of Pierre Bourdieu*, Milton Keynes: Open University Press.

Robins, K. (1993) 'Prisoners of the City – Whatever Could a Postmodern City Be?' in Carter, E., Donald, J. and Squires, J., eds, *Space and Place – Theories of Identity and Location*, London: Lawrence & Wishart,

Rojek, C. (1993) *Ways of Escape – Modern Transformations in Leisure and Travel*, London: Macmillan.

—— (1995) *Decentring Leisure – Rethinking Leisure Theory*, London and Newbury Park: Sage.

Roszak, T. (1994) *The Cult of Information – A Neo-Luddite Treatise on High-Tech, Artificial Intelligence, and the True Art of Thinking*, (2nd edn) Berkeley and Los Angeles: University of California Press.

Rudé, G. (1980) *Ideology and Popular Protest*, London: Lawrence & Wishart.

Said, E. (1993) *Culture and Imperialism*, London: Chatto & Windus.

—— (1994) *Representations of the Intellectual – The 1993 Reith Lectures*, London: Vintage.

Samuel, R., ed. (1981) *People's History and Socialist Theory*, London: Routledge.

—— (1994) *Theatres of Memory*, London and New York: Verso.

Sartre, J.-P. (1974) 'A Plea for Intellectuals' in his *Between Existentialism and Marxism*, London: New Left Books.

Scannell, P. (1984) 'The State and Broadcasting', unit 11 of D209 *The State and Civil Society*, Milton Keynes: Open University.

—— (1989) 'Public Service Broadcasting and Modern Life', *Media, Culture & Society*, vol. 11, no. 2.

Schiller, H. (1989) *Culture Inc. – The Corporate Takeover of Public Expression*, New York: Oxford University Press.

Schudson, M. (1992) 'Was There Ever a Public Sphere? If So, When? Reflections on the American Case' in Calhoun, C., ed., *Habermas and the Public Sphere*, Cambridge, Mass.: MIT Press.

Schuster, J. M. D. (1994–1995) 'Funding the Arts and Culture Through Dedicated

State Lotteries' Parts 1 and 2, *European Journal of Cultural Policy*, vol. 1, nos 1 and 2.

Schwarz, B. (1991) 'Where Horses Shit a Hundred Sparrows Feed – Docklands and East London During the Thatcher Years' in Corner, J. and Harvey, S., eds, *Enterprise and Heritage – Crosscurrents of National Culture*, London and New York: Routledge.

Seabrook, J. (1990) *The Myth of the Market*, Bideford: Green Books.

Sennett, R. (1990) *The Conscience of the Eye – The Design and Social Life of Cities*, London: Faber & Faber.

Shaw, R. (1993) *The Spread of Sponsorship – In the Arts, Sport, Education, the Health Service & Broadcasting*, Newcastle: Bloodaxe Books.

Skovmand, M. and Schrøder, K., eds (1992) *Media Cultures – Reappraising Transnational Media*, London and New York: Routledge.

Soja, E. (1989) *Postmodern Geographies – The Reassertion of Space in Critical Social Theory*, London and New York: Verso.

Sparks, C. (1994) 'Independent Production – Unions and Casualisation' in Hood, S., ed., *Behind the Screens – The Structure of Television in the Nineties*, London: Lawrence & Wishart.

Spivak, G. (1988) 'Can the Subaltern Speak?' in Nelson, C. and Grossberg, L., eds, *Marxism and the Interpretation of Culture*, London: Macmillan.

Squires, J., ed. (1993) *Principled Positions – Postmodernism and the Rediscovery of Value*, London: Lawrence & Wishart.

Sreberny-Mohammadi, A. (1991) 'The Global and the Local in International Communications' in Curran, J. and Gurevitch, M., eds, *Mass Media and Society*, London: Edward Arnold.

Stallabrass, J. (1995) 'Empowering Technology – The Exploration of Cyberspace', *New Left Review*, no. 211.

Stevenson, N. (1995) *Understanding Media Cultures – Social Theory and Mass Communication*, London and Newbury Park: Sage.

Sudjic, D. (1993) *The 100 Mile City*, London: Flamingo.

—— (1994) 'Preserve Us from a State of Stagnation', *Guardian*, 14 September.

Sutherland, J. (1982) *Offensive Literature – Decensorship in Britain 1960–1982*, London: Junction Books.

Taylor, C. (1994) 'The Politics of Recognition' in Gutman, A., ed., *Multiculturalism*, Princeton, NJ: Princeton University Press.

Therborn, G. (1989) 'The Two-Thirds, One-Third Society' in Hall, S. and Jacques, M., eds, *New Times – The Changing Face of Politics in the 1990s*, London: Lawrence & Wisehart.

Thomas, R. (1995) 'Access and Inequality' in Heap, N., Thomas, R., Einon, G., Mason, R. and Mackay, H., eds, *Information Technology and Society*, London: Sage.

Thompson, E. P. (1963) *The Making of the English Working Class*, London: Victor Gollancz.

—— (1979) *The Poverty of Theory & Other Essays*, London: Merlin.

—— (1993) *Customs in Common*, London and New York: Penguin.

Thompson, J. B. (1993) 'The Theory of the Public Sphere', *Theory, Culture & Society*, vol. 10, no. 3.

Tolson, A. (1986) 'Popular Culture – Notes and Revisions' in MacCabe, C., ed., *High Theory/Low Culture – Analysing Popular Film and Television*, Manchester: Manchester University Press.

Townsend, P. (1979) *Poverty in the United Kingdom – A Survey of Household Resources and Standards of Living*, London: Penguin.

REFERENCES

Turner, B., ed. (1993) *Citizenship and Social Theory*, London and Newbury Park: Sage.

—— (1994) 'Postmodern Culture/Modern Citizens' in Van Steenbergen, B., ed., *The Condition of Citizenship*, London and Newbury Park: Sage.

Turner, G., ed. (1993) *Nation, Culture, Text – Australian Cultural and Media Studies*, London and New York: Routledge.

Urry, J. (1990) *The Tourist Gaze*, London and Newbury Park: Sage.

Vance, C. (1992) 'The War On Culture' in Bolton, R., ed., *Culture Wars – Documents From the Recent Controversies in the Arts*, New York: New Press.

Vergo, P., ed. (1989) *The New Museology*, London: Reaktion Books.

Wachtel, D. (1987) *Cultural Policy in Socialist France*, New York: Westwood.

Wainwright, H. (1994) *Arguments for a New Left*, Oxford: Basil Blackwell.

Walsh, K. (1992) *The Representation of the Past – Museums and Heritage in the Postmodern World*, London and New York: Routledge.

Walzer, M. (1994) 'Comment [on Taylor's "The Politics of Recognition"]' in Gutman, A., ed., *Multiculturalism*, Princeton, NJ: Princeton University Press.

Ward, D. (1995) *Rewiring Democracy – The Role of Public Information in Europe's Information Society*, London and Brussels: McLellan Ward Research.

Wasko, J. (1994) *Hollywood in the Information Age*, Cambridge: Polity.

Wellmer, A. (1991) *The Persistence of Modernity*, Cambridge: Polity.

Wernick, A. (1991) *Promotional Culture – Advertising, Ideology and Symbolic Expression*, London and Newbury Park: Sage.

West, B. (1988) 'The Making of the English Working Past – A Critical View of the Ironbridge Gorge Museum' in Lumley, R., ed., *The Museum Time Machine*, London: Comedia.

West, C. (1992) 'Nihilism in Black America' in Dent, G., ed., *Black Popular Culture*, Seattle: Bay Press.

—— (1993) 'The New Cultural Politics of Difference' in During, S., ed., *The Cultural Studies Reader*, London and New York: Routledge.

White, A. (1990) *De-Stalinization and the House of Culture – Declining State Control Over Leisure in the USSR, Poland and Hungary, 1953–89*, London and New York: Routledge.

Wilding, R. (1989) *Supporting the Arts – A Review of Arts Funding*, London: Arts Council of GB.

Willatt, H. (1980) 'How the Arts are Promoted' in Pick, J., ed., *The State and the Arts*, London; John Offord Publications.

Willett, J., ed. (1964) *Brecht on Theatre*, New York: Hill & Wang.

Williams, R. (1958) *Culture and Society 1780–1950*, London: Chatto & Windus.

—— (1961) *The Long Revolution*, London: Chatto & Windus.

—— (1962) *Communications*, London: Penguin.

—— (1974) *Television, Technology and Cultural Form*, London: Fontana.

—— (1979) 'The Arts Council', *Political Quarterly*, vol. 50, no. 2.

—— (1980) 'A Hundred Years of Culture and Anarchy' in his *Problems in Materialism and Culture*, London: Verso.

—— (1981) *Culture*, London: Fontana.

—— (1983a) 'Culture' in McLellan, D., ed., *Marx – The First 100 Years*, London: Fontana.

—— (1983b) *Towards 2000*, London: Chatto & Windus.

—— (1983c) *Keywords*, London: Flamingo.

—— (1984) 'State Culture and Beyond' in Apignanesi, L., ed., *Culture and the State*, London: Institute of Contemporary Arts.

Williams, S.A. (1992) 'Two Words on Music – Black Community' in Dent, G., ed., *Black Popular Culture*, Seattle: Bay Press.

Willis, P. (1990a) *Common Culture*, Milton Keynes: Open University Press.

—— (1990b) *Moving Culture – An Enquiry into the Cultural Activities of Young People*, London: Calouste Gulbenkian Foundation.

—— (1991) 'Towards a New Cultural Map', *National Arts and Media Strategy* no. 18, London: Arts Council of GB.

Wilson, E. (1988) 'Picasso and Pâté de Foie Gras – Pierre Bourdieu's Sociology of Culture', *Diacritics*, Summer.

Wilson, W. J. (1994) 'Citizenship and the Inner-City Ghetto Poor' in Van Steenbergen, B., ed., *The Condition of Citizenship*, London and Newbury Park: Sage.

Wolff, J. (1983/1993) *Aesthetics and the Sociology of Art*, London: Macmillan.

Worpole, K. (1991) 'Trading Places – The City Workshop' in Fisher, M. and Owen, U., eds, *Whose Cities?* London and New York: Penguin.

—— (1992) *Towns for People*, Milton Keynes: Open University Press.

Wright, E. O. (1978) *Class, Crisis and the State*, London: New Left Books.

—— (1985) *Classes*, London: Verso.

—— (1993) 'Class Analysis, History and Emancipation', *New Left Review*, no. 202.

Wright, P. (1985) *On Living in an Old Country – The National Past in Contemporary Britain*, London: Verso.

—— (1991) 'Putting Culture in the Picture', *Guardian*, 28 November.

—— (1992) *A Journey Through Ruins – The Last Days of London*, London: Paladin.

—— (1995) 'Heritage Clubs Slug it Out', *Guardian*, 4 February.

Wynne, D. and O'Connor, J. (1995) 'City Cultures and the "New Cultural Intermediaries"', paper presented to British Sociological Association Annual Conference, Leicester, April.

Yoshimoto, M. (1994) 'Images of Empire – Tokyo Disneyland and Japanese Cultural Imperialism' in Smoodin, E., ed., *Disney Discourse – Producing the Magic Kingdom*, London and New York: Routledge.

Young, R., ed. (1981) *Untying the Text*, London: Routledge.

Zukin, S. (1988) *Loft Living – Culture and Capital in Urban Change*, London: Century Hutchinson.

—— (1991) *Landscapes of Power – From Detroit to Disneyworld*, Berkeley: University of California Press.

—— (1992) 'Postmodern Urban Landscapes – Mapping Culture and Power' in Lash, S. and Friedman J., eds, *Modernity and Identity*, Oxford: Basil Blackwell.

INDEX

212